Fro... W9-BWR-018

PORTABLE

Dublin

5th Edition

by Suzanne Rowan Kelleher

Wiley Publishing, Inc.

Published by:

WILEY PUBLISHING, INC.

111 River St.
Hoboken, NJ 07030-5774

ISBN 0-7645-7788-3

Editor: Myka Carroll del Barrio, Cate Latting
Production Editor: Bethany André
Photo Editor: Richard Fox
Cartographer: Nicholas Trotter
Production by Wiley Indianapolis Composition Services

For information on our other products and services or to obtain technical support, please contact our Customer Care Department within the U.S. at 800/762-2974, outside the U.S. at 317/572-3993 or fax 317/572-4002.

Wiley also publishes its books in a variety of electronic formats. Some content that appears in print may not be available in electronic formats.

Manufactured in the United States of America

5   4   3   2   1

Contents

List of Maps

ABOUT THE AUTHOR

Suzanne Rowan Kelleher is a freelance travel writer and the former Europe Editor of *Travel Holiday* magazine. Her work has appeared in many publications, including *Cigar Aficionado, Esquire, Four Seasons,* and *Newsweek.* In addition, she is a frequent host of online chats about Ireland for MSNBC.com's travel website. She has recently repatriated to the U.S. after having lived in Ireland and traveled extensively there for years.

AN INVITATION TO THE READER

In researching this book, we discovered many wonderful places—hotels, restaurants, shops, and more. We're sure you'll find others. Please tell us about them, so we can share the information with your fellow travelers in upcoming editions. If you were disappointed with a recommendation, we'd love to know that, too. Please write to:

Frommer's Portable Dublin, 5th Edition
Wiley Publishing, Inc. • 111 River St. • Hoboken, NJ 07030-5774

AN ADDITIONAL NOTE

Please be advised that travel information is subject to change at any time—and this is especially true of prices. We therefore suggest that you write or call ahead for confirmation when making your travel plans. The authors, editors, and publisher cannot be held responsible for the experiences of readers while traveling. Your safety is important to us, however, so we encourage you to stay alert and be aware of your surroundings. Keep a close eye on cameras, purses, and wallets, all favorite targets of thieves and pickpockets.

FROMMER'S STAR RATINGS, ICONS & ABBREVIATIONS

Every hotel, restaurant, and attraction listing in this guide has been ranked for quality, value, service, amenities, and special features using a **star-rating system.** In country, state, and regional guides, we also rate towns and regions to help you narrow down your choices and budget your time accordingly. Hotels and restaurants are rated on a scale of zero (recommended) to three stars (exceptional). Attractions, shopping, nightlife, towns, and regions are rated according to the following scale: zero stars (recommended), one star (highly recommended), two stars (very highly recommended), and three stars (must-see).

In addition to the star-rating system, we also use **eight feature icons** that point you to the great deals, in-the-know advice, and unique experiences that separate travelers from tourists. Throughout the book, look for:

Finds	Special finds—those places only insiders know about
Fun Fact	Fun facts—details that make travelers more informed and their trips more fun
Kids	Best bets for kids and advice for the whole family
Moments	Special moments—those experiences that memories are made of
Overrated	Places or experiences not worth your time or money
Tips	Insider tips—great ways to save time and money
Value	Great values—where to get the best deals

The following **abbreviations** are used for credit cards:

AE	American Express	DISC	Discover	V	Visa
DC	Diners Club	MC	MasterCard		

FROMMERS.COM

Now that you have the guidebook to a great trip, visit our website at **www. frommers.com** for travel information on more than 3,000 destinations. With features updated regularly, we give you instant access to the most current trip-planning information available. At Frommers.com, you'll also find the best prices on airfares, accommodations, and car rentals—and you can even book travel online through our travel booking partners. At Frommers. com, you'll also find the following:

- Online updates to our most popular guidebooks
- Vacation sweepstakes and contest giveaways
- Newsletter highlighting the hottest travel trends
- Online travel message boards with featured travel discussions

Planning Your Trip to Dublin

It's nearly impossible for first-time visitors to appreciate just how far Dublin has come in a very short time. Native "Dubs," however, who left years ago and returned to the "Celtic Tiger" economy, can't believe their eyes. Their beloved—if slightly down-at-the-heels—hometown has metamorphosed into a bastion of trendy coffee shops and juice bars, fusion-cuisine restaurants, minimalist interiors, designer boutiques, and Mercedes-Benz and BMW dealerships. In the late 1990s, Ireland had the fastest-growing economy in the European Union and continues to thrive economically. And Dublin, as Ireland's capital, is at the epicenter of the boom.

Twenty years ago most visitors to Ireland either bypassed "dirty aul' Dublin" altogether or made a mad dash from the ferry to the train station, determined to spend their first night beyond the pale. Now Dublin certainly gets the glamour vote as one of Europe's trendiest cities. Sightings of Julianne Moore, Gwyneth Paltrow, Britney Spears, Robert De Niro, and Cate Blanchett have become so commonplace that locals barely blink an eye. (The Irish polite indifference to celebrity is a slice of nirvana for privacy-loving stars.)

Greater Dublin's population has swollen to 1.5 million; more than a third of the entire country lives here. The time has passed when aspiring Irish artists owed it to themselves to emigrate. Today they dig in. If Joyce and Beckett and Wilde could see Dublin today, they'd be back.

Chances are that you've been looking forward to this trip to Dublin for some time. You've probably set aside a significant amount of hard-earned cash, taken time off from work, school, or other commitments, and now want to make the most of your holiday. So where do you start? The aim of this chapter is to provide you with the information you need to make sound decisions when planning your trip. You'll find all the necessary resources, along with addresses, phone numbers, and websites here.

1 Visitor Information

To get your planning under way, contact the following offices of the Irish Tourist Board. They are eager to answer your questions and have bags of genuinely helpful information, mostly free of charge.

After you've perused the brochures, surf the Web to scoop up even more information.

IN THE UNITED STATES

Irish Tourist Board, 345 Park Ave., New York, NY 10154 (© **800/223-6470** in the U.S. or 212/418-0800; fax 212/371-9052; www.tourismireland.com)

IN CANADA

Irish Tourist Board, 2 Bloor St. W., Suite 1501, Toronto, ON M4W 3E2 (© **800/223-6470;** fax 416/929-6783; www.tourismireland.com)

IN THE UNITED KINGDOM

Irish Tourist Board, 150 New Bond St., London W1Y 0AQ (© **020/7493-3201;** fax 020/7493-9065; www.tourismireland.com)

IN AUSTRALIA

All Ireland Tourism, 36 Carrington St., 5th Level, Sydney, NSW 2000 (© **02/9299-6177;** fax 02/9299-6323; www.tourismireland.com)

IN NEW ZEALAND

Irish Tourist Board, Dingwall Building, 2nd Floor, 87 Queen St., Auckland (© **0064-9/379-8720;** fax 0064-9/302-2420; www.tourismireland.com)

IN IRELAND

Irish Tourist Board/Bord Fáilte, Baggot Street Bridge, Dublin 2 (© **1850-230330;** fax 01/602-4100; www.ireland.travel.ie)

2 Entry Requirements & Customs

ENTRY REQUIREMENTS

For citizens of the United States, Canada, Australia, and New Zealand entering the Republic of Ireland for a stay of up to 3 months, no visa is necessary, but a valid passport is required.

Citizens of the United Kingdom, when traveling on flights origi-
nating in Britain, do not need to show passports to enter Ireland
(though they do need some form of identification). Nationals of the
United Kingdom and colonies who were not born in Great Britain
or Northern Ireland must have a valid passport or national identity
document.

CUSTOMS
WHAT YOU CAN BRING TO IRELAND
Like all the European Union (E.U.) member states, Ireland is
mainly concerned with two categories of goods: (1) items bought
duty-paid and value-added-tax-paid (VAT-paid) in other E.U. countries and (2) goods bought under duty-free and VAT-free allowances
at duty-free shops.

The first case normally applies to Irish citizens, visitors from
Britain, and travelers from other E.U. countries. If the goods are for
personal use, you won't need to pay additional duty or VAT. The
limits for goods in this category are 800 cigarettes, 10 liters of spirits, 45 liters of wine, and 55 liters of beer.

The second category pertains primarily to overseas visitors, such
as U.S. and Canadian citizens. The limit on duty-free and VAT-free
items that may be brought into the E.U. for personal use: 200 cigarettes, 1 liter of liquor, 2 liters of wine, and other goods (including
beer) not exceeding the value of €150 ($181) per adult. There are
no restrictions on bringing currency into Ireland.

If you're coming from the United States or another non-E.U.
country, use the Green Channel if you don't exceed the duty-free
allowances and the Red Channel if you have extra goods to declare.
If you are like most visitors, bringing in only your own clothes
and personal effects, use the Green Channel. The Blue Channel is
exclusively for use by passengers entering Ireland from other E.U.
countries.

In addition to your luggage, you may bring in sports equipment
for your own recreational use or electronic equipment for your own
business or professional use while in Ireland. Prohibited goods
include firearms, ammunition, and explosives; narcotics; meat,
poultry, plants, and their byproducts; and domestic animals from
outside the United Kingdom.

WHAT YOU CAN BRING HOME
Onboard the flight back to the United States, you'll be given a Customs declaration to fill out. Be sure to pack the goods you'll declare

separately and have your sales receipts handy. Returning **U.S. citizens** who have been away for 48 hours or more are allowed to bring back, once every 30 days, $800 worth of merchandise duty-free, as long as you bring it with you as accompanied baggage. You'll be charged a flat rate of duty on the next $1,000 worth of purchases. On gifts, the duty-free limit is $200. You cannot bring fresh food-stuffs into the United States; tinned foods are allowed. For specifics on what you can bring back, download the invaluable free pamphlet *Know Before You Go* online at **www.cbp.gov**. Or contact the **U.S. Customs & Border Protection (CBP),** 1300 Pennsylvania Ave. NW, Washington, DC 20229 (② **877/287-8667**) and request the pamphlet.

Citizens of the United Kingdom who are returning from a European Community (EC) country will go through a separate Customs Exit (called the "Blue Exit") especially for E.U. travelers. In essence, there is no limit on what you can bring back from a E.U. country, as long as the items are for personal use (this includes gifts), and you have already paid the necessary duty and tax. However, customs law sets out guidance levels. If you bring in more than these levels, you may be asked to prove that the goods are for your own use. Guidance levels on goods bought in the E.U. for your own use are 3,200 cigarettes, 200 cigars, 400 cigarillos, 3 kilograms of smoking tobacco, 10 liters of spirits, 90 liters of wine, 20 liters of fortified wine (such as port or sherry), and 110 liters of beer. For more information, contact HM Customs & Excise at ② **0845/010-9000** (from outside the U.K., 020/8929-0152), or consult their website at www.hmce.gov.uk.

For a clear summary of **Canadian** rules, write for the booklet *I Declare,* issued by the **Canada Border Servies Agency** (② **800/ 461-9999** in Canada or 204/983-3500; www.cbsa-asfc.gc.ca).

Australians can obtain a helpful brochure, *Know Before You Go,* available from Australian consulates or Customs offices. For more information, call the **Australian Customs Service** at ② **1300/363-263,** or log on to www.customs.gov.au.

New Zealand citizens should obtain a free pamphlet available at New Zealand consulates and Customs offices: *New Zealand Customs Guide for Travelers,* Notice no. 4. For more information, contact **New Zealand Customs,** The Customhouse, 17–21 Whitmore St., Box 2218, Wellington (② **04/473-6099** or 0800/428-786; www.customs.govt.nz).

3 Money

CURRENCY

The Republic of Ireland has adopted the single European currency known as the **euro.** In this volume, the € sign symbolizes the euro. In converting prices to U.S. dollars, we used the rate €1 = $1.20.

Euro notes come in denominations of €5, €10, €20, €50, €100, €200, and €500. The euro is divided into 100 cents; coins come in denominations of €2, €1, 50¢, 20¢, 10¢, 5¢, 2¢, and 1¢. It may seem awkward, particularly for Americans, but the terms "euro" and "cent" are never pluralized. That is, €50.25 is spoken as "50 euro, 25 cent."

Note: The value of the euro fluctuates daily, so it is best to begin checking exchange rates well in advance of your visit to gain a sense of their recent range.

CREDIT CARDS

Leading international credit cards such as Visa, MasterCard (also known as Access or Eurocard), American Express, and Diners Club are readily accepted throughout all 32 counties. Most establishments display on their windows the logos of the credit cards they accept. Note that MasterCard and Visa are far more widely accepted than American Express, and Diners Club is accepted at only very upscale restaurants and hotels.

However handy it is to make purchases with credit, note that many banks add a "currency conversion fee" (sometimes as high as 3%) to all transactions made in a foreign currency; check with your card's issuer before you leave to avoid a nasty surprise when you get your bill.

ATMs

Repeat this until it sticks: The best way to get cash is with your bank card in an automated teller machine (ATM). Any town large enough to have a bank branch (all but the smallest villages) will have an ATM linked to a network that includes your home bank. **Cirrus** (© 800/424-7787; www.mastercard.com) and **PLUS** (© 800/843-7587 in the U.S. or 1800/558002 toll-free in Ireland; www.visa.com) are the two most popular networks. Using ATMs gets you the best possible exchange rate because Cirrus and PLUS let you take advantage of their high-volume wholesale exchange rate, which leaves all other players—traveler's checks, exchange bureaus, and credit cards—in the dust. Use the toll-free numbers to locate ATMs in your destination.

Tips **Avoiding Bank Fees**

Remember that each time you withdraw cash from an ATM, your bank will likely slap you with a fee of between $4 and $8 (check how much your bank charges before leaving home). Rather than taking out small denominations again and again, it makes sense to take out larger amounts every 2 to 3 days. Not only will this keep you from racking up fees, but you won't waste time in lines waiting for a free machine.

Most ATMs accept PINs of four to six digits. One hiccup, however, is that they often don't have alphanumeric keypads. So to withdraw cash using your bank card, your PIN must be made up of just numbers. If your PIN features letters (STAN37), use a telephone dial to figure out the numeric equivalents (or better yet, memorize it before you get to Ireland).

TRAVELER'S CHECKS

Traveler's checks are something of an anachronism from the days before the ATM made cash accessible at any time, but some travelers still like the perceived security of the tried-and-true. You can get them at almost any bank for a small service charge. American Express traveler's checks are also available over the phone by calling ℃ **800/221-7282** or 800/721-9768, or you can purchase checks online at **www.americanexpress.com**. In Ireland, American Express has an office at 61–63 S. William St. in Dublin (℃ **01/617-5555**). Amex gold or platinum cardholders can avoid paying the fee by ordering over the telephone; platinum cardholders can also purchase checks fee-free in person at Amex Travel Service locations. American Automobile Association members can obtain checks with no fee at most AAA offices.

4 When to Go

CLIMATE

To get a feel for just how hilarious Irish weather is, just tune into one of the TV or radio weather forecasts. Nowhere else will you hear the phrase, "Today we can expect showers, followed by periods of rain." Categorizing rain is an art form in Ireland. First you have "soft rain," which is like being spritzed by a spray bottle. Then you have "spitting," just a few random drops that don't even leave the ground wet. Next come "showers," brief intervals of rain that last only a few minutes—often while the sun is shining. The Irish don't consider it to be true rain unless it's steady and ongoing enough to warrant an umbrella. In a downpour, you may hear someone complain that it's "lashing," "bucketing," or "pelting."

The only thing consistent about Irish weather is its changeability, with the best of times and the worst of times often only hours, or minutes, apart. There's a saying that in Ireland you get "all four seasons in one day," which means you could start your day in heavenly, summery sunshine, get caught in a brief springlike downpour by lunchtime, go through an autumnal, dry but windy spell in midafternoon, and need a sweater as a wintry evening chill sets in. In other words, when packing, think *layers* for any time of year.

In Ireland the thermometers, gratefully, are a lot less busy than the barometers. Temperatures are mild and fluctuate within what any New Englander would call "spring." The generally coldest months, January and February, bring frosts but seldom snow, and the warmest months, July and August, rarely become truly hot. Remember, the Irish consider any temperature over 68°F (20°C) to be "roasting," and below 34°F (1°C) as truly "freezing." Both are unusual, but funny things happen. On occasion, summer days can get positively scorching, and last winter Ireland got hit with several harsh cold snaps that brought not only snow but gale-force winds of 113kmph (70 mph). Think of it this way: The Irish climate is responsible for those 40 shades of green you'll encounter on your travels.

For a complete online guide to Irish weather, including year-round averages, daily updates, and a weather cam of Dublin's city center, consult www.ireland.com/weather.

Average Monthly Temperatures in Dublin

	Jan	Feb	Mar	Apr	May	June	July	Aug	Sept	Oct	Nov	Dec
Temp (°F)	36–46	37–48	37–49	38–52	42–57	46–62	51–66	50–65	48–62	44–56	39–49	38–47
Temp (°C)	2–8	3–9	3–9	3–11	6–14	8–17	11–19	10–18	9–17	7–13	4–9	3–8

HIGH & LOW SEASONS

Apart from climatic considerations, there's the matter of cost and crowds. Dublin gets tourists year-round and doesn't really have a low season. It's always fairly crowded, and hotel prices never truly plummet. A few generalizations, however, might be helpful.

In summer, transatlantic airfares, car-rental rates, and hotel prices are at their highest and crowds at their most intense. But the days are brilliantly long (6am sunrises and 10pm sunsets), the weather is warmest, and every sightseeing attraction and B&B is open.

In winter you can get rock-bottom prices on airfare, especially if you book a package through a good travel agent or Aer Lingus (see "Getting There," later in this chapter). Because your destination is Dublin, the weather will not likely be a defining factor, since so much of Dublin's lure dwells indoors.

All things considered, best of all are the hedge months—April, May, and mid-September through October—when you're most likely to get simultaneously lucky with weather, crowds, and prices.

HOLIDAYS

The Republic observes the following national holidays: New Year's Day (Jan 1), St. Patrick's Day (Mar 17), Easter Monday (variable), May Day (May 1), first Mondays in June and August (Summer Bank Holidays), last Monday in October (Autumn Bank Holiday), Christmas (Dec 25), and St. Stephen's Day (Dec 26). Good Friday (the Fri before Easter) is mostly observed, but not statutory. Holidays that fall on weekends are celebrated the following Monday.

DUBLIN CALENDAR OF EVENTS

This sampling of events is drawn from 2004 schedules. Be sure to consult the calendars available from the tourist board of Ireland for 2005; they're usually released in January. The most up-to-date listings of events can be found at **www.eventguide.ie** and **www.visitdublin.com**.

January

Funderland. Royal Dublin Society, Ballsbridge, Dublin 4. An annual indoor funfair, complete with white-knuckle rides, carnival stalls, and family entertainment (© **061/419988;** www.fun fair.ie). December 26 to January 13.

January Sales. The best blowout sale in Ireland lasts all month long, with deep savings of up to 70% at practically every department store, shop, and boutique in Ireland.

February

Six Nations Rugby Tournament. Lansdowne Road, Ballsbridge, County Dublin. This annual international tourney features Ireland, England, Scotland, Wales, France, and Italy. It's a brilliant atmosphere, be it at Lansdowne Road or a neighborhood pub. Contact Irish Rugby Football Union, 62 Lansdowne Rd., Dublin 4 (© **01/668-4601;** fax 01/660-5640). Alternate Saturdays, early February to April.

Antiques and Collectibles Fair. Newman House, 85 St. Stephen's Green, Dublin 2. About 60 dealers sell small pieces and collectors' items (②/fax **01/670-8295**; antiquesfairsireland@esatclear.ie). Four consecutive Sundays in February.

March

St. Patrick's Dublin Festival. It's a massive 4-day fest that's open, free, and accessible to everyone. Street theater, carnival acts, sports, music, fireworks, and other festivities culminate in Ireland's grandest parade, with marching bands, drill teams, floats, and delegations from around the world (② **01/676-3205;** fax 01/676-3208; www.stpatricksday.ie). March 15 to March 18.

April

Dublin Film Festival. Irish Film Centre, Temple Bar, Dublin 2, and various cinemas in Dublin. More than 100 films are featured, with screenings of the best in Irish and world cinema, plus seminars and lectures on filmmaking (② **01/679-2937;** fax 01/679-2939). April 18 to 27.

June

Diversions Temple Bar. Dublin 2. This is an all-free, all-outdoor, all-ages cultural program, featuring a combination of day and night performances in dance, film, theater, music, and visual arts. Beginning in May, the Diversions program includes live music, open-air films, and a circus (② **01/677-2255;** fax 01/677-2525; www.temple-bar.ie). June to August.

AIB Music Festival in Great Irish Houses. Various venues throughout counties Dublin, Wicklow, and Kildare. This 10-day festival of classical music performed by leading Irish and world-renowned international artists is intimately set in the receiving rooms of stately buildings and mansions (② **01/278-1528;** fax 01/278-1529). June 5 to 15.

Bloomsday Festival. Various venues in Dublin. This unique day of festivity commemorates 24 hours in the life of Leopold Bloom, the central character of James Joyce's *Ulysses*. Every aspect of the city, including the menus at restaurants and pubs, seeks to duplicate the aromas, sights, sounds, and tastes of Dublin on June 16, 1904. Special ceremonies are held at the James Joyce Tower and Museum, and there are guided walks of Joycean sights. Contact the James Joyce Centre, 35 N. Great George's St., Dublin 1 (② **01/878-8547;** fax 01/878-8488; www.jamesjoyce.ie). June 12 to 16.

August

Kerrygold Horse Show. RDS Showgrounds, Ballsbridge, Dublin 4. This is the most important equestrian and social event on the Irish national calendar. Aside from the dressage and jumping competitions each day, highlights include a fashionable ladies' day (don't forget your hat!), formal hunt balls each evening, and the awarding of the Aga Khan Trophy and the Nation's Cup (© **01/668-0866;** fax 01/660-4014; www.rds.ie). August 6 to 10.

September

National Heritage Week. More than 400 events are held throughout the country—walks, lectures, exhibitions, music recitals, and more (© **01/647-2455;** www.heritageireland.ie). September 7 to 14.

All-Ireland Hurling and Gaelic Football Finals. Croke Park, Dublin 3. The finals of Ireland's most beloved sports, hurling and Gaelic football, are Ireland's equivalent of the Super Bowl. If you can't be at Croke Park, experience this in the full bonhomie of a pub. Tickets can be obtained through Ticketmaster at www.ticket master.ie (© **01/836-3222;** fax 01/836-6420). Hurling Final September 5; Gaelic Football Final September 19.

Irish Antique Dealers' Fair. RDS Showgrounds, Ballsbridge, Dublin 4. Ireland's premier annual antiques fair, with hundreds of dealers from all over the island (© **01/285-9294**). September 22 to 26.

October

Dublin Theatre Festival. Theaters throughout Dublin. Europe's largest theater-dedicated event showcases new plays by every major Irish company (including the Abbey and the Gate) and presents a range of productions from abroad (© **01/677-8439;** fax 01/679-7709; www.iftn.ie/diary/index.htm). September 30 to October 27.

Dublin City Marathon. On the last Monday in October, more than 5,000 runners from both sides of the Atlantic and the Irish Sea participate in this popular run through the streets of the capital (© **01/626-3746;** www.dublincitymarathon.ie). October 25.

December

Leopardstown National Hunt Festival. Leopardstown Racecourse, Foxrock, Dublin 18. This festival offers 3 days of winter racing for thoroughbreds (© **01/289-2888;** fax 01/289-2634; www.leopardstown.com). December 26 to 29.

5 Health & Insurance

STAYING HEALTHY

As a rule, no health documents or vaccinations are required to enter Ireland from the United States, Canada, the United Kingdom, Australia, New Zealand, or most other countries. If, however, you have visited areas in the previous 14 days where a contagious disease is prevalent, proof of immunization may be required.

If you have a condition that could require emergency care but might not be readily recognizable, consider joining **MedicAlert** (© 800/432-5378; www.medicalert.org). It provides ID tags, cards, and a 24-hour emergency information hot line. If you are diabetic, the **American Diabetes Association** (© 800/342-2383; www.diabetes.org) offers plenty of good advice for traveling with diabetes.

If you require the services of a physician, dentist, or other health professional during your stay in Dublin, your accommodations host may be in the best position to recommend someone local. Otherwise, contact the **consulate** of your home country (see "Fast Facts: Dublin" in chapter 2) or the **Irish Medical Council,** Lynn House, Portabello Court, Lower Rathmines Road, Dublin 6 (© **01/496-5588**), for a referral.

INSURANCE
TRAVEL INSURANCE AT A GLANCE

Check your existing insurance policies before you buy travel insurance to cover trip cancellation, lost luggage, medical expenses, or car-rental insurance. You're likely to have partial or complete coverage. But if you need some, ask your travel agent about a comprehensive package. The cost of travel insurance varies widely, depending on the cost and length of your trip, your age and overall health, and the type of trip you're taking.

Keep in mind that in the aftermath of the September 11, 2001, terrorist attacks, a number of airlines, cruise lines, and tour operators are no longer covered by insurers. *The bottom line:* Always, always check the fine print before you sign on; more and more policies have built-in exclusions and restrictions that may leave you out in the cold if something does go awry.

For information, contact one of the following popular insurers:

- **Access America** (© **866/807-3982;** www.accessamerica.com)
- **Travel Guard International** (© **800/826-4919;** www.travelguard.com)

- **Travel Insured International** (𝒞 800/243-3174; www.travel insured.com)
- **Travelex Insurance Services** (𝒞 888/457-4602; www. travelex-insurance.com)

TRIP-CANCELLATION INSURANCE (TCI)

There are three major types of trip-cancellation insurance—one, in the event that you prepay a cruise or tour that gets canceled and you can't get your money back; a second when you or someone in your family gets sick or dies and you can't travel (but beware that you may not be covered for a preexisting condition); and a third, when bad weather makes travel impossible. Some insurers provide coverage for events like jury duty; natural disasters close to home, like floods or fire; even the loss of a job. A few have added provisions for cancellations due to terrorist activities. Always check the fine print before signing on, and don't buy trip-cancellation insurance from the tour operator that may be responsible for the cancellation; buy it only from a reputable travel insurance agency. Don't overbuy. You won't be reimbursed for more than the cost of your trip.

MEDICAL INSURANCE

Most health insurance policies cover you if you get sick away from home—but check, particularly if you're insured by an HMO. For travel overseas, most health plans (including Medicare and Medicaid) do not provide coverage, and the ones that do often require you to pay for services upfront and reimburse you only after you return home. Even if your plan does cover overseas treatment, most out-of-country hospitals make you pay your bills upfront, and send you a refund only after you've returned home and filed the necessary paperwork with your insurance company.

Some credit cards (American Express and certain gold and platinum Visa and MasterCards, for example) offer automatic flight insurance against death or dismemberment in case of an airplane crash if you charged the cost of your ticket.

If you require additional medical insurance, try **MEDEX Assistance** (𝒞 410/453-6300; www.medexassist.com) or **Travel Assistance International** (𝒞 800/821-2828; www.travelassistance.com; for general information on services, call the company's Worldwide Assistance Services, Inc., at 𝒞 800/777-8710).

The cost of travel medical insurance varies widely. Check your existing policies before you buy additional coverage. Also, check to see if your medical insurance covers you for emergency medical evacuation: If you have to buy a one-way same-day ticket home and forfeit your nonrefundable round-trip ticket, you may be out big bucks.

6 Specialized Travel Resources

FOR TRAVELERS WITH DISABILITIES

One of the best Irish-based online resources is **www.disability.ie**. Click on the "holidays" button for good advice on traveling in Ireland with a disability, and companies that specialize in helping travelers with disabilities.

You can join the **Society for Accessible Travel and Hospitality** (**SATH;** ✆ 212/447-7284; www.sath.org) to gain access to their vast network of connections in the travel industry. Membership requires a tax-deductible contribution of $45 annually for adults, $30 for seniors and students.

Finding accessible lodging can be tricky in Ireland. Unfortunately, many of the older hotels, small guesthouses, and landmark buildings still have steps both outside and within. The **National Rehabilitation Board of Ireland,** 24–25 Clyde Rd., Ballsbridge, Dublin 4 (✆ 01/608-0400), publishes several guides, the best of which is *Guide to Accessible Accommodations in Ireland.* Also, **O'Mara Travel** (disability@omara-travel.com), in association with the Disability.ie website (see above), often offers special deals on accommodations to travelers with disabilities.

Travelers with vision impairments should contact the **American Foundation for the Blind** (✆ 800/232-5463) for information on traveling with Seeing Eye dogs.

The **Irish Wheelchair Association,** 24 Blackheath Dr., Clontarf, Dublin 3 (✆ 01/833-8241; www.iwa.ie), loans free wheelchairs to travelers in Ireland. A donation is appreciated. If you plan to travel by train in Ireland, be sure to check out Iarnrod Eireann's website (**www.irishrail.ie**), which includes services for travelers with disabilities. A Mobility Impaired Liaison Officer (✆ 01/703-2634) can arrange assistance for travelers with disabilities if given 24-hour notice prior to the departure time.

FOR SENIORS

One of the benefits of age is that travel often costs less. Always bring a photo ID, especially if you've kept your youthful glow. Also mention the fact that you're a senior when you first make your travel reservations, since many airlines and hotels offer discount programs for senior travelers.

Members of **AARP** (formerly known as the American Association of Retired Persons), 601 E St. NW, Washington, DC 20049 (© **888/687-2277**; www.aarp.org), get discounts on hotels, airfares, and car rentals. AARP offers members a wide range of benefits, including *AARP: The Magazine* and a monthly newsletter. Anyone over 50 can join.

Seniors, known in Ireland as OAPs (old age pensioners), enjoy a variety of discounts and privileges. Native OAPs ride the public transport system free of charge, but the privilege does not extend to tourists. Visiting seniors can avail themselves of other discounts, however, particularly on admission to attractions and theaters. Always ask about a senior discount if special rates are not posted.

The Irish Tourist Board publishes a list of reduced-rate hotel packages for seniors, *Golden Holidays/For the Over 55s.* These packages are usually available during the hedge months, from March to June and September to November.

Some tour operators in the United States give notable senior discounts. **CIE Tours International** (© **800/243-8687** or 973/292-3438; www.cietours.com), which specializes in Ireland, gives a $55 discount to travelers age 55 and up who book early on selected departures of regular tour programs. In addition, **SAGA Tours** (© **800/343-0273** or 617/262-2262) operates tours to Ireland specifically geared to seniors or anyone over 50. **Elderhostel** (© **877/426-8056;** www.elderhostel.org) offers a range of educational travel programs for seniors.

FOR STUDENTS, TEACHERS & YOUTHS

With almost half its population under age 25, Ireland is geared to students, whether you're planning to study or are just passing through.

An excellent source book that will help you explore the opportunities for study in Ireland is *The Transitions Abroad Alternative Travel Directory,* published by Transitions Abroad (**www.transitions abroad.com**) and available in bookstores.

Ireland in general is extremely student-friendly. A range of travel discounts are available to students, teachers (at any grade level, kindergarten through university), and youths (ages 12–25). Most attractions have a reduced student-rate admission charge, with the presentation of a valid student ID card.

Two popular student ID cards are the ISE Card (International Student Exchange Card) and the ISIC (International Student

Identity Card). For a look at the various travel benefits that come with membership, go to www.isecard.com and www.isiccard.com. The ISIC card is available for $22 from **STA Travel** (© 800/781-4040 in North America; www.sta.com), the biggest student travel agency in the world. If you're no longer a student but are still under 26, you can get a **International Youth Travel Card (IYTC)** for the same price from the same people, which entitles you to some discounts (but not on museum admissions). **Travel CUTS** (© 800/667-2887 or 416/614-2887; www.travelcuts.com) offers similar services for both Canadians and U.S. residents.

In Ireland, STA Travel's affiliate is **USIT, the Irish Student Travel Service,** 19 Aston Quay, Dublin 2 (© **01/679-8833;** www.usitnow.ie). In the United States, USIT is at 891 Amsterdam Ave., New York, NY 10025 (© **212/663-5435**).

U.S. firms offering educational travel programs to Ireland include **Academic Travel Abroad** (© **800/556-7896** or 202/785-9000; www.academic-travel.com), **North American Institute for Study Abroad** (© **570/275-5099** or 570/275-1644; www.naisa.com), and **Irish American Cultural Institute** (© **800/232-3746** or 973/605-1991; www.irishaci.org).

FOR FAMILIES

So you're bringing the kids to Dublin. You'll all have a fantastic time, especially if you realize that traveling with kids—like doing anything with kids—requires a bit of extra planning. And the best way to raise your kids' enthusiasm is to involve them in the decision-making process. So pore over brochures and maps together. Perhaps each family member can choose one or two "must" destinations or activities.

Use the time leading up to the trip to rent some movies set in Ireland—for younger kids and preteens, *Into the West, Waking Ned Devine,* and *The Secret of Roan Inish* are delightful and packed with picture-postcard views. Encourage your kids to read books set in Ireland. Favorites include *O'Sullivan Stew,* by Hudson Talbott (for 4–8-year-olds); and *A Wizard Abroad,* by Diane Duane (for 9–12-year-olds).

Also for over 9s: If your kids like Harry Potter, they'll likely love the excellent, bestselling, chilling, thrilling Artemis Fowl books by Irish author Eoin (pronounced *Owen*) Colfer. The first book in the series was shortlisted on the Whitbread Children's Book of the Year several years ago and film rights have been sold.

Teenagers can discover a classic by James Joyce, Brendan Behan, or Sean O'Casey, or try out the king of contemporary Irish writing, Roddy Doyle.

Your first goal will be to find truly child-friendly places to stay. Hotels that *say* they welcome small children and hotels that really provide for them are, sadly, not always the same. To sort the wheat from the chaff, the most helpful website is **www.irelandhotels.com**. Under "Find Accommodation," click "detailed search" to choose the options that are important to you: Kids' meals? Pool? Outdoor playground? Babysitting service? Supervised playroom? The site churns out a list of hotels and guesthouses that have exactly what you need.

If your kids are under the age of 6, consider staying a few days to a week in one place with an Irish Tourist Board–approved farm stay (www.irishfarmholidays.com) or a self-catered vacation home (www. selfcatering-ireland.com). It's a lot more relaxing to have a home base and make day trips from there than to have to pack and unpack daily to stick to an on-the-go itinerary. Another plus is that your children may have the opportunity to meet and make friends with local kids.

If given 24-hour advance notice, most airlines can arrange for a special children's menu. If you're renting a car, be sure to reserve car seats if your kids are small—don't assume that the car-rental companies will have extras on hand. Throughout the island, entrance fees and tickets on public transportation are often reduced for children under 12. Family rates for parents with children are also commonplace. In this guide, a "family" rate, unless otherwise stated, is for two adults with two children. Additional increments are often charged for larger families. Aside from all-too-familiar fast-food fare, many hotels and restaurants offer children's menus. Some hotels, guesthouses, and B&Bs provide babysitting, and others can arrange it. Let hotels know in advance if you'll need a baby crib or any other equipment.

FOR GAY & LESBIAN TRAVELERS

Gay Ireland has rapidly come out of the closet since homosexuality became legal in the North in 1982 and in the Republic in July 1993. Although the gay and lesbian community has received increasing support over the past several years, some of (mainly rural) Ireland continues to discourage its gay population. In cities such as Dublin, Cork, and Galway, however, gay and lesbian visitors can find enthusiastic support.

The most essential publication is *Gay Community News,* a monthly free newspaper of comprehensive Irish gay-related information, available in gay venues and bookshops. *In Dublin,* the city's leading event listings guide, dedicates several pages to gay events, current club information, AIDS and health information resources, accommodations options, and helpful organizations.

The most comprehensive websites for gay organizations, events, issues, and information are **Gay Ireland Online** (www.gay-ireland. com) and **Outhouse** (www.outhouse.ie).

The following organizations and help lines are staffed by knowledgeable and friendly people:

- **Outhouse Community & Resource Centre,** 105 Capel St., Dublin 1 (© **01/873-4932;** fax 01/873-4933; www.outhouse. ie), available Monday to Friday 10am to 5pm.
- **National Lesbian and Gay Federation (NLGF),** 2 Scarlet Row, Dublin 2 (© **01/671-0939;** fax 01/671-3549; nlgf@ tinet.ie), available Monday to Friday noon to 6pm.
- **Gay Switchboard Dublin,** Carmichael House, North Brunswick Street, Dublin 7 (© **01/872-1055;** fax 01/873-5737; www.gayswitchboard.ie), Monday to Friday 8 to 10pm and Saturday 3:30 to 6pm.
- **Lesbian Line Dublin,** Carmichael House, North Brunswick Street (© **01/872-9911**), Thursday 7 to 9pm.
- **LOT** (Lesbians Organizing Together), the umbrella group of the lesbian community, 5 Capel St., Dublin 1 (©/fax **01/872-7770**), accommodates drop-ins Monday to Thursday 10am to 6pm and Friday 10am to 4pm. LOT also sponsors LEA/ Lesbian Education Awareness (©/fax **01/872-0460;** leanow@ indigo.ie).
- **AIDS Helpline Dublin** (© **01/872-4277**), run Monday to Friday 9am to 7pm and Saturday 3 to 5pm, offers assistance with HIV/AIDS prevention, testing, and treatment.

Gay and lesbian travelers seeking information and assistance on travel abroad might want to consult the **International Gay and Lesbian Travel Association (IGLTA),** 52 W. Oakland Park Blvd. #237, Wilton Manors, FL 33311 (© **800/448-8550** or 954/776-2626; fax 954/776-3303; www.iglta.org).

Many agencies offer tours and travel itineraries specifically for gay and lesbian travelers. **Above and Beyond Tours** (© **800/397-2681;** www.abovebeyondtours.com) is the exclusive gay and lesbian tour operator for United Airlines. **Now, Voyager** (© 800/255-6951; www.nowvoyager.com) is a well-known San Francisco–based gay-owned and operated travel service.

7 Getting There

BY PLANE

About half of all visitors from North America arrive in Dublin on direct transatlantic flights to Dublin Airport. The other half fly first into Britain or Europe, then "backtrack" into Ireland by air or sea. In the Republic, there are seven smaller regional airports, all of which (except Knock) offer service to Dublin and several of which receive some European traffic. They are Cork, Donegal, Galway, Kerry, Knock, Sligo, and Waterford. Services and schedules are always subject to change, so be sure to consult your preferred airline or travel agent as soon as you begin to sketch your itinerary. The routes and carriers listed below are provided to suggest the range of possibilities for air travel to Ireland.

FROM THE UNITED STATES

The Irish national carrier, **Aer Lingus** (© 800/474-7424; www.aerlingus.com) is the traditional leader in providing transatlantic flights to Ireland, with scheduled, nonstop flights from New York (JFK), Boston, Chicago, Los Angeles, and Baltimore to Dublin. From there, you can connect to Ireland's regional airports. *Note:* Aer Lingus offers a wide range of excellent-value packages that bundle your flight with a rental car and/or accommodations. These aren't tours—you still travel independently once you get to Ireland—but by booking all the elements at once rather than separately, your savings can be significant. As you'd expect, the discounts are deepest in the winter months.

   American Airlines (© 800/433-7300; www.aa.com) flies directly from New York (JFK) and Chicago to Dublin. **Delta Airlines** (© 800/241-4141; www.delta.com) flies directly from Atlanta to Dublin. **Continental Airlines** (© 800/231-0856; www.continental.com) offers nonstop service to Dublin from its Newark hub.

   It's possible to save big by booking your air tickets through a consolidator (aka bucket shop) who works with the airlines to sell off their unsold air tickets at a cut price. But note that the savings generally range from miniscule in the high season to substantial in the off season. **Ireland Consolidated** (© 888/577-2900; www.irelandconsolidated.com) sells tickets to Ireland on regular Delta, British Airways, and Continental flights.

Tips **Backtracking to Ireland**

Your favorite airline doesn't fly to Ireland? Many travelers opt to fly to Britain and backtrack into Ireland (see "From Britain," below). Carriers serving Britain from the United States include **American Airlines** (© 800/433-7300; www.aa.com), **British Airways** (© 800/247-9297; www.ba.com), **Continental Airlines** (© 800/231-0856; www.continental.com), **Delta Airlines** (© 800/241-4141; www.delta.com), **Northwest Airlines** (© 800/447-4747; www.nwa.com), **United** (© 800/241-6522; www.united.com), and **Virgin Atlantic Airways** (© 800/862-8621; www.virgin-atlantic.com).

FROM BRITAIN

The London-Dublin route is one of the busiest flight paths in Europe, and competition is stiff—which means that you can often get a fantastic deal.

The following carriers offer direct flights from London: **Aer Lingus** (© **800/474-7424** in the U.S. or 020/8899-4747 in Britain); **Lufthansa** (© **800/581-6400** in the U.S.; www.lufthansa.co.uk), and **bmi baby** (© **800/788-0555** in the U.S. or 0870/607-0555 in Britain; www.iflybritishmidland.com). Two low-cost airlines making the London-Dublin hop are **CityJet** (© **0345/445588** in Britain) and **Ryanair** (© **0541/569569** in Britain; www.ryanair.com).

FROM THE CONTINENT

Major direct flights into Dublin from the Continent include service from Amsterdam on **KLM** (© **800/374-7747** in the U.S.; www.klm.com); Madrid and Barcelona on **Iberia** (© **800/772-4642** in the U.S.; www.iberia.com); Brussels on **Ryanair** (www.ryanair.com); Copenhagen on **Aer Lingus** and **SAS** (© **800/221-2350** in the U.S.; www.scandinavian.net); Frankfurt on **Aer Lingus** and **Lufthansa** (© **800/645-3880** in the U.S.; www.lufthansa.com); Paris on **Aer Lingus** and **Air France** (© **800/237-2747** in the U.S.; www.airfrance.com); Prague on **CSA Czech Airlines** (© **212/765-6588** in the U.S.; www.csa.cz); and Rome on **Aer Lingus.**

FLY FOR LESS: TIPS FOR GETTING THE BEST AIRFARES

- **Book early.** Booking your ticket at least 14 days in advance will almost always get you a lower fare. Be sure you understand cancellation and refund policies before you buy.

- **Travel midweek.** Flying Tuesday to Thursday is cheaper than flying on weekends. An added bonus: Midweek transatlantic flights are sometimes half empty, allowing you to stretch out across extra seats. Ahhhh, nice.
- **Stay over Saturday.** To exclude business travelers from the cheapest fares, most airlines offer lower rates for trips that include at least 1 Saturday night. So don't book a 6-night trip where you arrive on Sunday and depart for home the following Saturday, or you'll pay more than you have to.
- **Use a consolidator.** Also known as a bucket shop, a consolidator is a gold mine for low fares, often below the airlines' discounted rates. There's nothing shady about them—basically, they're just wholesalers that buy in bulk and pass some of the savings on to you. Some of the most reliable consolidators include **Cheap Tickets** (© 800/377-1000; www.cheaptickets.com), **STA Travel** (© 800/781-4040; www.statravel.com), **Lowestfare.com** (© 888/278-8830; www.lowestfare.com), **Cheap Seats** (© 800/451-7200; www.cheapseatstravel.com), and **1-800-FLY-CHEAP** (www.flycheap.com).
- **Surf the Internet.** This is the hot way to buy air tickets, though it's still best to compare your findings with the research of a dedicated travel agent. See "Planning Your Trip Online," below.
- **Make a bid.** You can also bid for seats on your desired flight with travel auctioneers such as **Priceline** (www.priceline.com). In some cases—though very rarely—winning bids are as low as $5.
- Consider a **charter flight.** They're often dirt cheap, but the downsides are that they offer fewer frills, offer fewer flights per week, and their tickets are ordinarily nonrefundable. From the United States, **Sceptre Charters** (© 800/221-0924 or 516/255-9800) operates the largest and most reliable charter program to Ireland. It sells tickets on America Trans Air flights to Shannon from Boston, Philadelphia, Chicago, and Los Angeles. Several companies in Canada operate charter flights from Toronto to Ireland, including **Signature Vacations** (© 800/268-7063 in Canada or 800/268-1105 in the U.S.), **Air Transat Holidays** (© 800/587-2672 in Canada or 514/987-1550), and **Regent Holidays** (© 800/387-4860 in Canada or 905/673-3343).

BY FERRY

If you're traveling to Ireland from Britain or the Continent, especially if you're behind the wheel of a car, ferries can get you there.

The Irish Sea has a reputation for making seafarers woozy, however, so it's always a good idea to consider an over-the-counter pill or patch to guard against seasickness. (Be sure to take any pills *before* you set out; once you're under way, it's generally too late.)

Several car and passenger ferries offer reasonably comfortable furnishings, cabin berths (for longer crossings), restaurants, duty-free shopping, and lounges.

Prices fluctuate seasonally and depend on your route, your time of travel, and whether you are on foot or in a car. It's best to check with your travel agent for up-to-date details, but just to give you an idea, the lowest one-way adult fare in high season on the cruise ferry from Holyhead to Dublin is €30 ($36). Add your car, and the grand total will be €190 ($229). The websites given below have regularly updated schedules and prices.

FROM BRITAIN

Irish Ferries operates from Holyhead, Wales, to Dublin. For reservations, call **Scots-American Travel** (© **561/563-2856** in the U.S.; info@scotsamerican.com) or **Irish Ferries** (© **0870/517-1717** in the U.K. or 01/638-3333 in Ireland; www.irishferries.com). **Stena Line** (© **888/274-8724** in the U.S. or 0870/570-7070 in Britain; www.stenaline.com) sails from Holyhead to Dun Laoghaire, 13km (8 miles) south of Dublin. **Brittany Ferries** (© **021/427-7801** in Cork; www.brittany-ferries.com) operates from Holyhead to Dublin. **P&O Irish Sea Ferries** operates from Liverpool to Dublin; for reservations, call Scots-American Travel (© **561/563-2856** in the U.S., 0870/242-4777 in Britain, or 01/638-3333 in Ireland; www.poirishsea.com). **Isle of Man Steam Packet Company/Sea Cat** ((© **01624/661661** in Britain or 01/874-1231 in Ireland; www.steam-packet.com) operates ferries from Liverpool to Dublin.

8 Planning Your Trip Online

SURFING FOR AIRFARES

The "big three" online travel agencies, **Expedia.com, Travelocity,** and **Orbitz** sell most of the air tickets bought on the Internet. (Canadian travelers should try expedia.ca and Travelocity.ca; U.K. residents can go for expedia.co.uk and opodo.co.uk.) Each has different business deals with the airlines and may offer different fares on the same flights, so it's wise to shop around. Expedia and Travelocity will also send you **e-mail notification** when a cheap fare becomes available to your favorite destination. Of the smaller travel agency websites, **SideStep** (www.sidestep.com) has gotten the best reviews from Frommer's authors. It's a browser add-on that purports to "search 140 sites at once," but in reality only beats competitors' fares as often as other sites do.

Also remember to check **airline websites,** especially those for low-fare carriers, whose fares are often misreported or simply missing from travel agency websites. Even with major airlines, you can often shave a few bucks from a fare by booking directly through the airline and avoiding a travel agency's transaction fee. But you'll get these discounts only by **booking online:** Most airlines now offer online-only fares that even their phone agents know nothing about. For the websites of airlines that fly to and from your destination, see "Getting There," above.

Great **last-minute deals** are available through free weekly e-mail services provided directly by the airlines. Most of these are announced on Tuesday or Wednesday and must be purchased online. Most are only valid for travel that weekend, but some (such as Southwest's) can be booked weeks or months in advance. Sign up for weekly e-mail alerts at airline websites or check mega-sites that compile comprehensive lists of last-minute specials, such as **Smarter Living** (smarterliving.com). For last-minute trips, **site59.com** and **lastminutetravel.com** in the U.S. and **lastminute.com** in Europe often have better air-and-hotel package deals than the major-label sites. A website listing numerous bargain sites and airlines around the world is **www.itravelnet.com**.

If you're willing to give up some control over your flight details, use what is called an **"opaque" fare service** like **Priceline** (www.priceline.com; www.priceline.co.uk for Europeans) or its smaller competitor **Hotwire** (www.hotwire.com). Both offer rock-bottom prices in exchange for travel on a "mystery airline" at a mysterious time of day, often with a mysterious change of planes en route. The mystery airlines are all major, well-known carriers, and the airlines' routing computers have gotten a lot better than they used to be. But your chances of getting a 6am or 11pm flight are pretty high. Hotwire tells you flight prices before you buy; Priceline usually has better deals than Hotwire, but you have to play their "name our price" game. If you're new at this, the helpful folks at **BiddingFor-Travel** (www.biddingfortravel.com) do a good job of demystifying Priceline's prices and strategies. Priceline and Hotwire are great for flights within North America and between the U.S. and Europe. But for flights to other parts of the world, consolidators will almost always beat their fares. *Note:* Priceline has added non-opaque service to its roster. You now have the option to pick exact flights, times, and airlines from a list of offers—or opt to bid on opaque fares as before.

SURFING FOR HOTELS

Shopping online for hotels is generally done one of two ways: by booking through the hotel's own website or through an independent booking agency (or a fare-service agency like Priceline; see above). These Internet hotel agencies have multiplied in mind-boggling numbers of late, competing for the business of millions of consumers surfing for accommodations around the world. This competitiveness can be a boon to consumers who have the patience and time to shop and compare the online sites for good deals—but shop they must, for prices can vary considerably from site to site. And keep in mind that hotels at the top of a site's listing may be there for no other reason than that they paid money to get the placement.

Of the "big three" sites, **Expedia.com** offers a long list of special deals and "virtual tours" or photos of available rooms so you can see

Frommers.com: The Complete Travel Resource

For an excellent travel-planning resource, we highly recommend **Frommers.com** (www.frommers.com), voted Best Travel Site by *PC Magazine*. We're a little biased, of course, but we guarantee that you'll find the travel tips, reviews, monthly vacation giveaways, bookstore, and online-booking capabilities thoroughly indispensable. Among the special features are our popular **Destinations** section, where you'll get expert travel tips, hotel and dining recommendations, and advice on the sights to see for more than 3,500 destinations around the globe; the **Frommers.com Newsletter,** with the latest deals, travel trends, and money-saving secrets; our **Community** area featuring **Message Boards,** where Frommer's readers post queries and share advice (sometimes even our authors show up to answer questions); and our **Photo Center,** where you can post and share vacation tips. When your research is done, the **Online Reservations System** (www.frommers.com/book_a_trip) takes you to Frommer's preferred online partners for booking your vacation at affordable prices.

what you're paying for (a feature that helps counter the claims that the best rooms are often held back from bargain-booking websites). **Travelocity** posts unvarnished customer reviews and ranks its properties according to the AAA rating system. Also reliable are **Hotels.com** and **Quikbook.com**. An excellent free program, **Travel-Axe** (www.travelaxe.net), can help you search multiple hotel sites at once, even ones you may never have heard of—and conveniently lists the total price of the room, including the taxes and service charges. Another booking site, **Travelweb** (www.travelweb.com), is partly owned by the hotels it represents (including the Hilton, Hyatt, and Starwood chains) and is therefore plugged directly into the hotels' reservations systems—unlike independent online agencies, which have to fax or e-mail reservation requests to the hotel, a good portion of which get misplaced in the shuffle. More than once, travelers have arrived at the hotel, only to be told that they have no reservation. To be fair, many of the major sites are undergoing improvements in service and ease of use, and Expedia will soon be able to plug directly into the reservations systems of many hotel chains—none of which can be bad news for consumers. In the meantime, it's a good idea to **get a confirmation number** and **make a printout** of any online booking transaction.

ONLINE TRAVELER'S TOOLBOX

Veteran travelers usually carry some essential items to make their trips easier. Following is a selection of online tools to bookmark and use:

- **Airplane Seating and Food**. Find out which seats to reserve and which to avoid (and more) on all major domestic airlines at www.seatguru.com. And check out the type of meal (with photos) you'll likely be served on airlines around the world at www.airlinemeals.com.
- **Mapquest** (www.mapquest.com). This best of the mapping sites lets you choose a specific address or destination, and in seconds, it will return a map and detailed directions.
- **Travel Warnings** (http://travel.state.gov/travel_warnings.html, www.fco.gov.uk/travel, www.voyage.gc.ca, www.dfat.gov.au/consular/advice). These sites report on places where health concerns or unrest might threaten American, British, Canadian, and Australian travelers. Generally, U.S. warnings are the most paranoid; Australian warnings are the most relaxed.
- **Universal Currency Converter** (www.xe.com/ucc). See what your dollar or pound is worth in more than 100 other countries.

- **Visa ATM Locator** (www.visa.com), for locations of PLUS ATMs worldwide, or **MasterCard ATM Locator** (www.mastercard.com), for locations of Cirrus ATMs worldwide.

9 Tips on Accommodations & Dining

BOTTOM LINE ON BEDS

RATES Room charges quoted in this guide include 13.5% government tax (VAT) in the Republic of Ireland. They do not (unless otherwise noted) include service charges, which are usually between 10% and 15%. Most hotels and guesthouses automatically add the service charge onto your final bill, although in recent years many family-run or limited-service places have begun the practice of not charging for service, leaving it as an option for the guest. Home-style B&Bs do not ordinarily charge for service.

The price categories used throughout this guide indicate the cost of a double room for two per night, including tax but not service charges:

Very Expensive: €250 ($301) and up

Expensive: €200 to €250 ($240–$301)

Moderate: €100 to €200 ($120–$240)

Inexpensive: Under €100 ($120)

Note: Many accommodations span more than one of these categories, and in those cases, we've done our best to assign each to the category that best represents its characteristic rates in high season.

Ordinarily, the Irish cite the per-person price of a double room—a policy not followed in this guide, which for the sake of uniform comparison assumes double occupancy. Most accommodations make adjustments for children. Children staying in their parent's room are usually charged at 20% to 50% of the adult rate. If you're traveling on your own, there is most often a supplemental charge for single occupancy of a double room.

FIVE WAYS TO SAVE

- **Spend more than 1 night.** Most Irish hotels, and many B&Bs, offer midweek and weekend breaks. A 2-day break typically includes both nights bed and breakfast plus one dinner; a 3-day break typically includes 3 nights bed and breakfast plus two dinners. The savings can be 25% to 30% off the rack rate, and you get a free evening meal or two to boot. You do the math.
- **Book from home.** If your desired hotel has a toll-free number in the United States, get a quote and compare it to what the

hotel's front desk offers. Nine times out of 10, the toll-free number's rate will be substantially lower than that offered at the door.

- **Book online.** Increasingly, hotels are offering unsold rooms at deep discounts, particularly if you're booking last minute. Nine times out of 10, the online rate will be lower than the toll-free rate. This is a particularly good way to land a luxury hotel room for less.

- **Haggle.** If you have a talent for haggling, room prices in hotels—especially privately owned hotels in the off season— are often negotiable. Your best bet is to politely ask, "Is that your best rate?" or, "Can you do a little bit better?"

- **Use a consolidator.** Just like with airfares, you can often save money on hotel accommodations if you go through a middle-man. On the Web, try **www.hotelsireland.net** for savings of up to 50% on rack rates (published rates) for two- to five-star hotels across Ireland.

TERMINOLOGY   The Irish use the phrase "en suite" to indicate a room with private bathroom. A "double" has a double bed, and a "twin" has two single beds. An "orthopedic" bed has an extra-firm mattress. Queen- and king-size beds are not common except in large, deluxe hotels.

RESERVATIONS   It usually pays to book in advance before you leave home. Many hotels can be booked through toll-free numbers in the United States, and the quoted prices offered can be appreciably (as much as 40%) lower than those offered at the door. For properties that do not have a U.S. reservation number, the fastest way to reserve is to contact the hotel directly by telephone, fax, or e-mail. Fax and e-mail are advisable, because they give you a written confirmation. You can then follow up by sending a deposit check (usually the equivalent of 1 night's room rate) or by giving your credit card number.

If you arrive in Ireland without a reservation, the staff members at the tourist offices throughout the Republic will gladly find you a room using a computerized reservation service known as **Gulliver.** In Ireland, you can also call the Gulliver line directly (② **00800/ 668-668-66**). This is a nationwide and cross-border "free-phone" facility for credit card bookings, operated daily 8am to 11pm. Gulliver is also accessible from the United States (② **011-800/668-668-66**) and on the Web at **www.gulliver.ie**.

RESTAURANTS

RESERVATIONS Except for self-service eateries, informal cafes, and some popular seafood spots, most restaurants encourage reservations. The more expensive restaurants absolutely require reservations because there is little turnover—once a table is booked, it is yours for the whole lunch period or for the evening until closing. In the most popular eateries, seatings for Friday and Saturday nights (and Sun lunch) are often booked a week or more in advance, so have a few options in mind if you're booking at the last minute and want to try out the hot spots in town.

Here's a tip for those who don't mind dining early: If you stop into or phone a restaurant and find that it is booked from 8 or 8:30pm onward, ask if you can dine early (at 6:30 or 7pm), with a promise to leave by 8pm. You will sometimes get a table. Quite a few restaurants are experimenting with lower-priced early-bird and pretheater menus to attract people for early evening seating.

TABLE D'HOTE OR A LA CARTE It's a growing trend for restaurants to offer two menus: table d'hôte, a fixed-price three- or four-course lunch or dinner with a variety of choices; and a la carte, a menu offering a wide choice of individually priced appetizers (starters), soups, main courses, salads or vegetables, and desserts (sweets).

With the former, you pay the set price whether you take each course or not. If you do take each course, the total price offers very good value. With the latter, you choose what you want and pay accordingly. If you are a salad-and-entree person, then a la carte will probably work out to be less expensive; if you want all the courses and the trimmings, stick with the table d'hôte.

PRICES Meal prices at restaurants include a 13.5% VAT in the Republic of Ireland, but the service charge is extra. In perhaps half of all restaurants, a set service charge is added automatically; it can range from 10% to 15%. In the remaining restaurants, it is now the custom not to add any service charge, leaving the tip to your discretion. This can be confusing for a visitor, but each restaurant normally prints its policy on the menu. If it is not clear, ask.

When no service charge is added, tip up to 15% depending on the quality of the service. If 10% to 12.5% has already been added to your bill, leave an appropriate amount that will total 15% if service has been satisfactory.

(Value) Dining Bargains

Restaurant prices in Ireland have gone up dramatically—in many cases by 20% to 25%—in recent years. Nobody is more aware of this than the Irish themselves, who are furious. Some people blame the price hikes on the changeover from the punt to the euro, some blame general inflation, and still others cite bold-faced greed on the part of restaurateurs. But there are some strategies you can use to keep your meal costs down:

If you want to try a top-rated restaurant but can't afford dinner, have your main meal there in the middle of the day by trying the table d'hôte set-lunch menu. You'll experience the same great cuisine at half the price of a nighttime meal.

Some restaurants offer a fixed-price three-course tourist menu during certain hours and days. These menus offer limited choices but are usually lower in price than the restaurant's regular table d'hôte menu. Look for a tourist menu with a green Irish chef symbol in the window, listing the choices and the hours when the prices are in effect.

As a final suggestion, try an inexpensive lunch of pub grub. Pub grub is usually a lot better than its name suggests; the menu usually includes sandwiches, stews, quiches, and salads. In recent years, many pubs have converted or expanded into restaurants, serving excellent, unpretentious meals at prices to which you can lift a pint.

The price categories used in this book are based on the price of a complete dinner (or lunch, if dinner is not served) for one person, including tax and tip, but not wine or alcoholic beverages:

Very Expensive: €50 ($60) and up

Expensive: €35 to €50 ($42–$60)

Moderate: €17 to €34 ($21–$41)

Inexpensive: Under €17 ($21)

DINING TIPS   Don't be surprised if you are not ushered to your table as soon as you arrive at a restaurant. This is not a delaying tactic—many of the better dining rooms carry on the old custom of seating you in a lounge or bar area while you sip an aperitif and peruse the menu. Your waiter then comes to discuss the choices and to take your order. You are not called to the table until the first course is about to be served.

Happily, for those fond of a beer with a meal, Ireland recently relaxed its liquor laws. Restaurants are now permitted to serve beer with meals (previously they could only serve wine).

Getting to Know Dublin

Dublin, like most ancient cities, lies sprawled along a river. The Liffey has divided Dublin into north and south for more than 1,000 years. Neither as romantic as the Seine nor as mighty as the Mississippi, the Liffey is just there, old and polluted, with walls to sit on or lean against when your legs give out. Still, it always has been the center of things here, and it does make for a pretty picture on a good day. The Liffey continues to divide the town as it once divided Viking from Celt and Norman from Norse.

As long as anyone can remember, the buzzing, prosperous hub of Dublin has lay mostly south of the Liffey. The area containing most of the best hotels, restaurants, shops, and sights is a small, well-defined compound that can be easily walked in an hour. It comprises a large part of Dublin 2 (the postal code for each neighborhood is listed in "The Neighborhoods in Brief," later in this chapter), beginning with the Georgian elegance of St. Stephen's Green, moving toward the river via bustling Grafton Street, heading farther north and west through the trendy cafe scene of Temple Bar.

That said, a visit confined to this small pocket of Dublin is not a true visit to Dublin. An hour's walk from the top of Grafton Street, across the Liffey, up O'Connell Street, and farther into north Dublin is a walk through time and, simultaneously, a glimpse of some of the pieces that must eventually fit together. Explore, get a haircut (in a barbershop, not a salon), get lost and ask directions, and you may uncover a time capsule from the Dublin of a century ago—or was it only a generation?

1 Orientation

Dublin is 222km (138 miles) NE of Shannon Airport, 258km (160 miles) NE of Cork, 167km (104 miles) S of Belfast, 309km (192 miles) NE of Killarney, 219km (136 miles) E of Galway, 237km (147 miles) SE of Derry, and 142km (88 miles) N of Wexford

ARRIVING

BY PLANE **Aer Lingus,** Ireland's national airline, operates regularly scheduled flights into Dublin International Airport from Chicago,

Boston, Los Angeles, Baltimore, and New York's JFK. **Delta Airlines** flies to Dublin from Atlanta and New York, and **Continental Airlines** flies to Dublin from Newark. Charters also operate from a number of U.S. and Canadian cities. You can also fly from the United States to London or other European cities and backtrack to Dublin (see "Getting There" in chapter 1).

Dublin International Airport (ℂ **01/814-1111;** www.dublin-airport.com) is 11km (7 miles) north of the city center. A Travel Information Desk located in the Arrivals Concourse provides information on public bus and rail services throughout the country.

An excellent airport-to-city bus service called **AirCoach** operates 24 hours a day, making runs at 15-minute intervals. AirCoach runs direct from the airport to Dublin's city center and south side, servicing O'Connell Street, St. Stephen's Green, Fitzwilliam Square, Merrion Square, Ballsbridge, and Donnybrook—that is, all the key hotel and business districts. The fare is €7 ($8.45) one-way or €12 ($14) round-trip; you buy your ticket from the driver. Although AirCoach is slightly more expensive than the Dublin Bus (see below), it is faster because it makes fewer intermediary stops and it brings you right into the hotel districts. To confirm AirCoach departures and arrivals, call ℂ **01/844-7118** or find it on the Web at **www.aircoach.ie**.

If you need to connect with the Irish bus or rail service, the **Airlink Express Coach** (ℂ 01/873-4222) provides express coach service from the airport into the city's central bus station, **Busaras,** on Store Street, and on to the two main rail stations, **Connolly** and **Heuston.** Service runs daily from 7am until 11pm (Sun 7:30am–8:30pm), with departures every 20 to 30 minutes. One-way fare is €5 ($6) for adults and €2 ($2.40) for children under age 12.

Finally, **Dublin Bus** (ℂ 01/872-0000; www.dublinbus.ie) service runs between the airport and the city center between 6am and 11:30pm. The one-way trip takes about 30 minutes, and the fare is €5 ($6). Nos. 16a, 33, 41, 41a, 41b, 41c, 46x, 58x, 746, 747, and 748 all serve the city center from Dublin Airport. Consult the Travel Information Desk located in the Arrivals Concourse to figure out which bus will bring you closest to your hotel.

For speed and ease—especially if you have a lot of luggage—a **taxi** is the best way to get directly to your hotel or guesthouse. Depending on your destination in Dublin, fares average between €18 and €25 ($22–$30). Surcharges include €.50 (60¢) for each additional passenger and for each piece of luggage. Depending on traffic, a cab should take between 20 and 45 minutes to get into the

Dublin Orientation

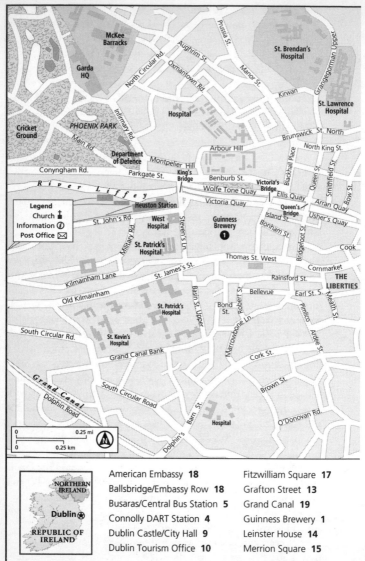

Legend
🏛 Church
ℹ Information
✉ Post Office

American Embassy **18**	Fitzwilliam Square **17**
Ballsbridge/Embassy Row **18**	Grafton Street **13**
Busaras/Central Bus Station **5**	Grand Canal **19**
Connolly DART Station **4**	Guinness Brewery **1**
Dublin Castle/City Hall **9**	Leinster House **14**
Dublin Tourism Office **10**	Merrion Square **15**

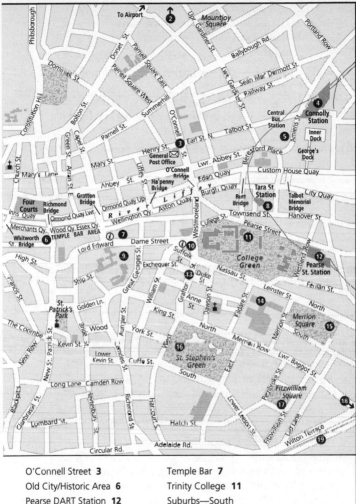

city center. A 10% tip is standard. Taxis are lined up at a first-come, first-served taxi stand outside the arrivals terminal.

Major international and local car-rental companies operate desks at Dublin Airport. For a list of companies, see "Getting Around," below.

BY FERRY   Passenger and car ferries from Britain arrive at the **Dublin Ferryport** (© 01/855-2222), on the eastern end of the North Docks, and at the **Dun Laoghaire Ferryport.** Call **Irish Ferries** (© 01/661-0511; www.irishferries.ie) for bookings and information. There is bus and taxi service from both ports.

BY TRAIN   Irish Rail (© 01/836-6222; www.irishrail.ie) operates daily train service to Dublin from Belfast, Northern Ireland, and all major cities in the Irish Republic, including Cork, Galway, Limerick, Killarney, Sligo, Wexford, and Waterford. Trains from the south, west, and southwest arrive at **Heuston Station,** Kingsbridge, off St. John's Road; from the north and northwest at **Connolly Station,** Amiens Street; and from the southeast at **Pearse Station,** Westland Row, Tara Street.

BY BUS   Bus Eireann (© 01/836-6111; www.buseireann.ie) operates daily express coach and local bus service from all major cities and towns in Ireland into Dublin's central bus station, **Busaras,** Store Street.

BY CAR   If you are arriving by car from other parts of Ireland or on a car ferry from Britain, all main roads lead into the heart of Dublin and are well signposted to An Lar (City Centre). To bypass the city center, the East Link (toll bridge €1.50/$1.80) and West Link are signposted, and M50 circuits the city on three sides.

Finds The Bird's-Eye View

To start out with the big picture and to get your bearings once and for all, make your way to **The Old Jameson Distillery** (see chapter 5) and ascend, via glass elevator, to the observation chamber atop "The Chimney Viewing Tower." In a city without skyscrapers, this is your best 360-degree vantage point on Greater (and smaller) Dublin. The trip to the top costs €5 ($6) for adults, €3.50 ($4.20) for children, and €15 ($18) for a family. Open Monday to Saturday 10am to 5:30pm, Sunday 11am to 5:30pm. Call © **01/817-3800** for more information.

VISITOR INFORMATION

Dublin Tourism operates six walk-in visitor centers in greater Dublin that are open every day except Christmas. The principal center is on Suffolk Street, Dublin 2, open from June to August Monday to Saturday from 9am to 8:30pm, Sunday and bank holidays 10:30am to 3pm, and the rest of the year Monday to Saturday 9am to 5:30pm, Sunday and bank holidays 10:30am to 3pm. The Suffolk Street office includes a currency exchange counter, a car-rental counter, an accommodations-reservations service, bus and rail information desks, a gift shop, and a cafe. For accommodations reservations throughout Ireland by credit card, contact Dublin Tourism at © **01/605-7700;** www.visitdublin.com.

The five other centers are in the **Arrivals Hall** of Dublin Airport; **Exclusively Irish,** O'Connell Street, Dublin 1; **Baggot Street Bridge,** Baggot Street, Dublin 2; **The Square Towncentre,** Tallaght, Dublin 24; and the ferry terminal at **Dun Laoghaire Harbor** (all telephone inquiries should be directed to the number listed above). All centers are open year-round with at least the following hours: Monday to Friday 9am to 5:30pm and Saturday 9am to 5pm.

For information on Ireland outside of Dublin, call **Bord Fáilte** (© **1850/230330** in Ireland; www.travel.ireland.ie).

At any of these centers you can pick up the free *Tourism News;* or the free *Event Guide,* a biweekly entertainment guide, online at **www.eventguide.ie**. *In Dublin,* a biweekly arts-and-entertainment magazine selling for €3 ($4.20), is available at most newsstands.

CITY LAYOUT

Compared to other European capitals, Dublin is a relatively small metropolis and easily traversed. The city center—identified in Irish on bus destination signs as AN LAR—is bisected by the River Liffey flowing west to east into Dublin Bay. Canals ring the city center: The Royal Canal forms a skirt through the north half, and the Grand Canal the south half. True Dubliners, it is said, live between the two canals.

Northside suburbs include Drumcondra, Glasnevin, Howth, Clontarf, and Malahide. Southside suburbs include Ballsbridge, Blackrock, Dun Laoghaire, Dalkey, Killiney, Rathgar, and Rathmines.

MAIN ARTERIES, STREETS & SQUARES   The focal point of Dublin is the **River Liffey,** with 16 bridges connecting its north and south banks. The most famous of these, **O'Connell Bridge,** was originally made of rope and could only carry one man and a donkey

Fun Fact **A Toll Tale**

Built in 1816 as one of the earliest cast-iron bridges in Britain and Ireland, the graceful pedestrians-only Ha'penny Bridge (pronounced *Hay*-penny) is the most beloved of Dublin bridges. Though officially named the Liffey Bridge, it's far better known by the toll that was initially charged to cross it: half a penny. The turnstiles were removed in 1919, when passage was declared free to the public.

at a time. It was replaced with a wooden structure in 1801. The current concrete bridge was built in 1863 and is the only traffic-carrying bridge in Europe that is wider than it is long. The newest bridge, the **Millennium Bridge,** is a footbridge erected in 1999, linking Temple Bar with the Northside.

On the north side of the river, the main thoroughfare is **O'Connell Street,** a wide, two-way avenue that starts at the riverside quays and runs north to **Parnell Square.** Enhanced by statues, trees, and a modern fountain, the O'Connell Street of earlier days was the glamorous shopping drag of the city. It is still important today, although neither as fashionable nor as safe as it used to be. Work is under way, however, to give the north side of the Liffey a mighty makeover and make it once again a focus of attention.

On the south side of the Liffey, **Grafton Street** is Dublin's main shopping street. It is home to Ireland's most exclusive department store, Brown Thomas, and has clearly bent over backward in recent years to attract and please tourists—though cynics point out, quite rightly, that much of its "Irishness" has been displaced in recent years by British chain shops. Narrow and restricted to pedestrians, Grafton Street is the center of Dublin's commercial district, surrounded by a maze of small streets and lanes that boast a terrific variety of shops, restaurants, and hotels. At the south end of Grafton Street is **St. Stephen's Green,** the city's most beloved park and an urban oasis ringed by rows of historic Georgian town houses, fine hotels, and restaurants.

At the north end of Grafton Street, **Nassau Street** rims the south side of **Trinity College.** The street is noted for its fine shops and because it leads to **Merrion Square,** another fashionable Georgian park surrounded by historic brick-front town houses. Merrion Square is also adjacent to Leinster House, the Irish House of Parliament, the National Gallery, and the National Museum.

In the older section of the city, **High Street** is the gateway to medieval and Viking Dublin, from the city's two medieval cathedrals to the old city walls and nearby Dublin Castle. The other noteworthy street in the older part of the city is **Francis Street,** Dublin's antiques row.

THE NEIGHBORHOODS IN BRIEF

Trinity College Area On the south side of the River Liffey, the Trinity College complex is a 16.8-hectare (42-acre) center of academia in the heart of the city, surrounded by fine bookstores and shops. This area lies in the Dublin 2 postal code.

Temple Bar Wedged between Trinity College and the Old City, this section took off in the 1990s and was transformed into the city's cultural and entertainment hub. As Dublin's self-proclaimed Left Bank, Temple Bar offers a vibrant array of cafes, unique shops, art galleries, recording studios, theaters, trendy restaurants, and atmospheric pubs. This is largely the stomping ground of young tourists (it's a huge stag-night destination on weekends), and it's easy to feel over the hill if you're over 25. Still, it's fun and buzzy. This area lies in the Dublin 2 and Dublin 8 postal codes.

Old City Dating from Viking and medieval times, the cobblestone enclave of the historic Old City includes Dublin Castle, the remnants of the city's original walls, and the city's two main cathedrals, Christ Church and St. Patrick's. In the past few years, Old City has rocketed on to the map as a hip shopping destination, particularly for fashion (designer boutiques, eyewear) and stylish, craft-based housewares. The area encompasses the Dublin 8 and 2 zones.

Liberties The adjacent Liberties district, just west of High Street, takes its name from the fact that the people who lived here long ago were exempt from the local jurisdiction within the city walls. Although it prospered in its early days, Liberties fell on hard times in the 17th and 18th centuries and is only now feeling a touch of urban renewal. Highlights range from the Guinness Brewery and Royal Hospital to the original Cornmarket area. Most of this area lies in the Dublin 8 zone.

St. Stephen's Green/Grafton Street Area A magnet for visitors, this district is home to some of the city's finest hotels, restaurants, and shops. There are some stunning residential town houses near the Green, but this is primarily a business and shopping neighborhood. It is part of the Dublin 2 zone.

Fitzwilliam & Merrion Square These two little square parks are surrounded by fashionable brick-faced Georgian town houses, each with a distinctive and colorful doorway. Some of Dublin's most famous citizens once resided here; today many of the houses are offices for doctors, lawyers, government offices, and other professionals. This area is part of the Dublin 2 zone.

Ballsbridge/Embassy Row Immediately south of the Grand Canal, this is Dublin's most prestigious suburb, yet it is within walking distance of downtown. Although primarily a residential area, it is also the home of some leading hotels, restaurants, and embassies, including that of the United States. There are plenty of upscale hotels in this part of town, as well as very good B&Bs. This area is part of the Dublin 4 zone.

O'Connell Street (North of the Liffey) Once a fashionable and historic focal point, this area has lost much of its charm and importance in recent years but could be poised to rebound with the arrival of the Northside's first designer hotel, the Morrison. Shops, fast-food restaurants, and movie theaters rim the wide, sweeping thoroughfare, where you'll find a few great landmarks like the General Post Office and the Gresham Hotel. Within walking distance of O'Connell Street are four theaters, plus the Catholic Pro-Cathedral, the Moore Street open markets, the Henry Street pedestrian shopping area, the new Financial Services Centre, the ILAC Centre, the Jervis Shopping Centre, and the Central Bus Station. Most of this area lies in the Dublin 1 postal code.

2 Getting Around

Getting around Dublin is not at all daunting. Public transportation is good and getting better, taxis are plentiful and reasonably priced, and there are always your own two feet. Central Dublin is quite walkable. In fact, with its current traffic and parking problems, it's a city where the foot is mightier than the wheel. If you can avoid it, don't rent a car while you're in the city.

BY BUS Dublin Bus operates a fleet of green double-decker buses, single-deck buses, and minibuses (called "imps") throughout the city and its suburbs. Most buses originate on or near O'Connell Street, Abbey Street, and Eden Quay on the north side, and at Aston Quay, College Street, and Fleet Street on the south side. Bus stops are located every 2 or 3 blocks. Destinations and bus numbers are posted above the front windows; buses destined for the city center are marked with the Irish Gaelic words AN LAR.

Dublin Area Rapid Transit (DART) Routes

Bus service runs daily throughout the city, starting at 6am (10am on Sun), with the last bus at 11:30pm. On Thursday, Friday, and Saturday nights, Nitelink service runs from the city center to the suburbs from midnight to 3am. Buses operate every 10 to 15 minutes for most runs; schedules are posted on revolving notice boards at each bus stop.

Inner-city fares are calculated based on distances traveled. The minimum fare is €.80 (95¢); the maximum fare is €2 ($2.40). The Nitelink fare is a flat €4 ($4.80). Buy your tickets from the driver as you enter the bus; exact change is required, so have your loose change available. Notes of €5 or higher may not be accepted. Discounted 1-day, 3-day, 5-day, and 7-day passes are available. The 1-day bus-only pass costs €5 ($6); the 3-day pass costs €10 ($12); the 5-day pass goes for €15 ($18); and the 7-day pass costs €18 ($22). For more information, contact **Dublin Bus,** 59 Upper O'Connell St., Dublin 1 (© **01/872-0000;** www.dublinbus.ie).

BY DART   While Dublin has no subway in the strict sense, there is an electric rapid-transit train, known as the **DART** (Dublin Area Rapid Transit). It travels mostly at ground level or on elevated tracks, linking the city-center stations at **Connolly Station, Tara Street,** and **Pearse Street** with suburbs and seaside communities as far as Malahide to the north and Greystones to the south. Service operates roughly every 10 to 20 minutes Monday to Saturday from 7am to midnight and Sunday from 9:30am to 11pm. The minimum fare is €1 ($1.20). One-day and 10-journey passes, as well as student and family tickets, are available at reduced rates. For further information, contact **DART,** Pearse Station, Dublin 2 (© **1850/ 366222** in Ireland or 01/836-6222; www.irishrail.ie).

BY TRAM   The newest addition to Dublin's public transportation network is set to be the sleek light-rail tram known as **LUAS,** which opened in the summer of 2004. Traveling at a maximum speed of 70kmph (45 mph) and departing every 5 minutes in peak hours, LUAS has already appeased Dublin's congestion problems and brought the city's transportation into the 21st century. Three lines will eventually link the city center at **Connolly Station** and **St. Stephen's Green** with the suburbs of Tallaght in the southwest and Dundrum and Sandyford to the south. For visitors, one of the handiest reasons to use the LUAS is to get between Connolly and Heuston stations. The one-way fare within the city center is €1 ($1.20); 1-day and multiple-day passes are also available. For further information, contact **LUAS** (© **01/703-2029;** www.luas.ie).

ON FOOT   Small and compact, Dublin is ideal for walking, as long as you remember to look right and then left (in the direction opposite your instincts) for oncoming traffic before crossing the street, and to obey traffic signals. Each traffic light has timed "walk–don't walk" signals for pedestrians. Pedestrians have the right of way at specially marked, zebra-striped crossings; as a warning, there are usually two flashing lights at these intersections. For some walking-tour suggestions, see chapter 5.

BY TAXI   It's very difficult to hail a taxi on the street; instead, they line up at ranks. Ranks are located outside all of the leading hotels, at bus and train stations, and on prime thoroughfares such as Upper O'Connell Street, College Green, and the north side of St. Stephen's Green near the Shelbourne hotel.

You can also phone for a taxi. Some of the companies that operate a 24-hour radio-call service are **Co-Op** (© **01/676-6666**), **Shamrock Radio Cabs** (© **01/855-5444**), and **VIP Taxis** (© **01/478-3333**). If you need a wake-up call, VIP offers that service, along with especially courteous dependability.

Taxi rates are fixed by law and posted in each vehicle. The following are typical travel costs in the city center: A 3.3km (2-mile) journey costs €8 ($9.60) by day and €10 ($12) at night; an 8km (5-mile) journey runs €10 ($12) by day and €12 ($14) at night; and a 16km (10-mile) journey costs €20 ($24) by day and €22 ($26) at night. There's an additional charge of €.50 (60¢) for each extra passenger and for each suitcase. And it costs an extra €1.50 ($1.80) for a dispatched pickup. *Be warned:* Some hotel staff members will tack on as much as €4 ($4.80) for calling you a cab, although this practice violates city taxi regulations.

BY CAR   Unless you plan to do a lot of driving from Dublin to neighboring counties, it's not practical or affordable to rent a car. In fact, getting around the city and its environs is much easier without a car.

If you must drive in Dublin, remember to keep to the *left-hand side of the road,* and don't drive in bus lanes. The speed limit within the city is 46kmph (30 mph), and seat belts must be worn at all times by driver and passengers.

Most major international **car-rental firms** are represented in Dublin, as are many Irish-based companies. They have desks at the airport, full-service offices downtown, or both. The rates vary greatly according to company, season, type of car, and duration of rental. In high season, the average weekly cost of a car, from subcompact standard to full-size automatic, ranges from €200 to €1,525 ($240–$1,830); you'll be much better off if you've made your car-rental arrangements well in advance from home. (Also see "By Car" under "Orientation" earlier in this chapter.)

International firms represented in Dublin include **Avis,** 1 Hanover St. E., Dublin 1, and at Dublin Airport (© **01/605-7500;** www. avis.ie); **Budget,** 151 Lower Drumcondra Rd., Dublin 9 (© **01/ 837-9611;** www.budget.ie), and at Dublin Airport (© **01/844-5150**); **Hertz,** 149 Upper Leeson St., Dublin 4 (© **01/660-2255;** www. hertz.ie), and at Dublin Airport (© **01/844-5466**); and **Murray's Europcar,** Baggot Street Bridge, Dublin 4 (toll-free © **1850/403803;** www.europcar.ie), and at Dublin Airport (© **01/812-0410**).

During normal business hours, free parking on Dublin streets is nonexistent. Never park in bus lanes or along a curb with double yellow lines. City officials will either clamp or tow errant vehicles. To get your car declamped, the fee is €85 ($102); if your car is towed away, it costs €165 ($198) to reclaim it.

Throughout Dublin, you'll find multibay meters and "pay and display" **disc parking.** In Dublin, a five-pack of discs costs €6.35 ($7.60). Each ticket is good for a maximum of 3 hours. The most reliable and safest places to park are surface parking lots and multi-story car parks in central locations such as Kildare Street, Lower Abbey Street, Marlborough Street, and St. Stephen's Green West. Expect to pay €1.90 ($2.30) per hour and €19 ($23) for 24 hours. Night rates run €6.35 to €9 ($7.65–$11) per hour. The bottom line here is that you're better off without a car in Dublin. The city is aggressively discouraging cars for commuters, much less for tourists.

BY BICYCLE   The steady flow of Dublin traffic rushing down one-way streets may be a little intimidating for most cyclists, but there are many opportunities for more relaxed pedaling in residential areas and suburbs, along the seafront, and around Phoenix Park. The Dublin Tourism office can supply you with bicycle touring information and suggested routes.

Bicycle rental averages €20 ($24) per day, €80 ($96) per week, with a €65 ($78) deposit. The one-way rental fee is €100 ($120). In the downtown area, bicycles can be rented from **Raleigh Ireland,** Kylemore Road, Dublin 10 (© **01/626-1333**).

FAST FACTS: Dublin

American Express **American Express International,** 41 Nassau St., Dublin 2 (toll-free *©* **1890/205511**), is a full-service travel agency that also offers currency exchange, traveler's checks, and (for members) mail-holding. It is opposite Trinity College, just off College Green, and is open Monday to Saturday 9am to 5pm. American Express also has a desk at the **Dublin Tourism Office** on Suffolk Street (*©* **01/605-7709**). In an emergency, traveler's checks can be reported lost or stolen by dialing toll-free in Ireland *©* **1890/706706.**

Banks Nearly all banks are open Monday to Friday 10am to 4pm (to 5pm Thurs) and have ATMs that accept Cirrus network cards as well as MasterCard and Visa. Convenient locations include the **Bank of Ireland,** at 1 Ormond Quay, Dublin 7, and 34 College Green, Dublin 2, and the **Allied Irish Bank,** at 64 Grafton St., Dublin 2, and 37 O'Connell St., Dublin 1.

Business Hours Banks are open 10am to 4pm Monday to Wednesday and Friday, and 10am to 5pm Thursday. **Post Offices** (known as **An Post**) are open from 9am to 12:30pm and 2 to 5:30pm Monday to Friday and from 9am to 1:30pm Saturday. The GPO on O'Connell Street is open 8am to 8pm Monday to Saturday, and 10:30am to 6:30pm Sunday (for stamps only). **Museums and Sights** are generally open 10am to 5pm Tuesday to Saturday, and 2 to 5pm Sunday. Shops generally open 9am to 6pm Monday to Friday, with late opening on Thursday until 7 or 8pm. In the city center most department stores and many shops are open noon to 6pm on Sunday.

Currency Exchange Currency-exchange services, signposted as BUREAU DE CHANGE, are in all banks and at many branches of the Irish post office system, known as **An Post.** A bureau de change operates daily during flight arrival and departure times at Dublin airport; a foreign currency note-exchanger machine is also available on a 24-hour basis in the main arrivals hall. Some hotels and travel agencies offer bureau de change services, although the best rate of exchange is usually when you use your bank card at an ATM.

Dentists For dental emergencies, contact the Eastern Health Board Headquarters, Dr. Steevens Hospital, Dublin 8 (*©* **01/679-0700**), or try **Molesworth Clinic,** 2 Molesworth Place,

Dublin 2 (℡ **01/661-5544**). See also "Dental Surgeons" in the Golden Pages (Yellow Pages) of the telephone book. The American Embassy (see "Embassies & Consulates," below) can provide a list of dentists in the city and surrounding areas. Expect to be charged upfront for services.

Doctors If you need to see a physician, most hotels and guesthouses will contact a house doctor for you. The **American Embassy** (see "Embassies & Consulates," below) can provide a list of doctors in the city and surrounding areas and you should contact them first. Otherwise, you can call either the **Eastern Health Board Headquarters,** Dr. Steevens Hospital, Dublin 8 (℡ **01/679-0700**), or the **Irish Medical Organization,** 10 Fitzwilliam Place, Dublin 2 (℡ **01/676-7273**). As with dentists, expect to pay for treatment upfront and when you return home, contact your insurance company to see if you are eligible for reimbursement.

Electricity The Irish electric system operates on 220 volts with a plug bearing three rectangular prongs. To use standard American 110-volt appliances, you'll need both a transformer and a plug adapter. Most new laptops have built-in transformers, but some do not, so beware. Attempting to use only a plug adapter is a sure way to fry your appliance or, worse, cause a fire.

Embassies & Consulates The **American Embassy** is at 42 Elgin Rd., Ballsbridge, Dublin 4 (℡ **01/668-8777**); the **Canadian Embassy** at 65–68 St. Stephen's Green, Dublin 2 (℡ **01/417-4100**); the **British Embassy** at 31 Merrion Rd., Dublin 2 (℡ **01/205-3700**); and the **Australian Embassy** at Fitzwilton House, Wilton Terrace, Dublin 2 (℡ **01/664-5300**). In addition, there is an **American Consulate** at 14 Queen St., Belfast BT1 6EQ (℡ **028/9032-8239**).

Emergencies For police, fire, or other emergencies, dial ℡ **999.**

Gay & Lesbian Resources Contact the **Gay Switchboard Dublin,** Carmichael House, North Brunswick Street, Dublin 7 (℡ **01/872-1055;** fax 01/873-5737); the **National Lesbian and Gay Federation (NLGF),** 6 S. William St., Dublin 2 (℡ **01/671-0939;** fax 01/679-1603); or the **LOT** (Lesbians Organizing Together), 5 Capel St., Dublin 1 (℡ **01/872-7770**). For fuller listings, see "Specialized Travel Resources" in chapter 1.

Hospitals For emergency care, two of the most modern are **St. Vincent's University Hospital**, Elm Park (📞 **01/269-4533**), on the south side of the city, and **Beaumont Hospital**, Beaumont (📞 **01/837-7755**), on the north side.

Hot Lines In Ireland, hot lines are called "helplines." For **emergencies, police, or fire,** dial 📞 **999**; **Aids Helpline** (📞 **01/872-4277**), Monday to Friday from 7am to 9pm and Saturday from 3 to 5pm; **Alcoholics Anonymous** (📞 **01/453-8998** and after hours 01/679-5967); **Asthma Line** (📞 **1850/445-464**); **Narcotics Anonymous** (📞 **01/672-8000**); **Rape Crisis Centre** (📞 **01/661-4911**) and **FreeFone** (📞 **1800/778-888**), after 5:30pm and weekends (📞 **01/661-4564**), and **Samaritans** (📞 **01/872-7700** and 1850/609-090).

Information For directory assistance, dial 📞 **11811**. For visitor information offices, see "Orientation," earlier in this chapter.

Internet Access In cybersavvy Dublin, public access terminals are no longer hard to find, appearing in shopping malls, hotels, and hostels throughout the city center. Like all of Dublin's public libraries, the **Central Library**, in the ILAC Centre, off Henry Street, Dublin 1 (📞 **01/873-4333**), has a bank of PCs with free Internet access. Three centrally located cybercafes are the **Central Cybercafe**, 6 Grafton St., Dublin 2 (📞 **01/677-8298**), **Planet Cyber Café**, 13 St. Andrews St., Dublin 2 (📞 **01/670-5182**), and **The Connect Point**, 33 Dorset St. Lower, Dublin 1 (📞 **01/834-9821**). A half-hour online averages €3.50 ($4.20).

Liquor Laws Individuals must be age 18 or over to be served alcoholic beverages in Ireland. Restaurants with liquor licenses are permitted to serve alcohol during the hours when meals are served. Hotels and guesthouses with licenses can serve during normal hours to the public; overnight guests, referred to as "residents," can be served after closing hours. Alcoholic beverages by the bottle can be purchased at liquor stores, at pubs displaying OFF-LICENSE signs, and at most supermarkets.

Ireland has very severe laws and penalties regarding driving while intoxicated, so don't even think about it.

Magazines The leading magazines for upcoming events and happenings are *In Dublin* (€3/$3.60), published every 2 weeks, and the free biweekly *Event Guide* (www.eventguide.ie). The *Event Guide*, which contains up-to-date listings of events throughout Ireland with a focus on Dublin, is widely available. *Where: Dublin,* published bimonthly, is aimed specifically at tourists and visitors and is a useful one-stop source for shopping, dining, and entertainment. It's free at the more exclusive hotels.

Mail In Ireland, mailboxes are painted green with the word POST on top. An airmail letter or postcard to the United States or Canada, not exceeding 25 grams, costs €.65 (78¢) and takes 5 to 7 days to arrive. Prestamped aerogrammes or air letters are also €.65.

Pharmacies Centrally located drugstores, known locally as pharmacies or chemist shops, include **Dame Street Pharmacy,** 16 Dame St., Dublin 2 (© **01/670-4523**). A late-night chemist shop is **Hamilton Long & Co.,** 5 Lower O'Connell St. (© **01/874-8456**), and its sister branch at 4 Merrion Rd., Dublin 4 (© **01/668-3287**). Both branches close at 9pm on weeknights and 6pm on Saturday.

Police Dial © **999** in an emergency. The metropolitan headquarters for the **Dublin Garda Siochana (Police)** is in Phoenix Park, Dublin 8 (© **01/666-0000**).

Post Office The Irish post office is best known by its Gaelic name, **An Post.** The **General Post Office (GPO)** is located on O'Connell Street, Dublin 1 (© **01/705-7000;** www.anpost.ie). Hours are Monday to Saturday 8am to 8pm, Sunday and holidays 10:30am to 6:30pm. Branch offices, identified by the sign OIFIG AN POST/POST OFFICE, are open Monday to Saturday only, 9am to 5pm.

Restrooms Public restrooms are usually simply called "toilets" or are marked with international symbols. In the Republic of Ireland, some of the older ones still carry the Gaelic words *Fir* (Men) and *Mna* (Women). Among the newest and best-kept restrooms are those found at shopping malls and at multistory parking lots. Free restrooms are available to customers of sightseeing attractions, museums, hotels, restaurants, pubs, shops, theaters, and department stores.

Safety The Republic of Ireland has enjoyed a traditionally low crime rate, particularly when it comes to violent crime. Those days do regrettably seem to be passing, especially in the cities. By U.S. standards, Ireland is still very safe but not safe enough to warrant carelessness. In recent years, the larger cities have been prey to pickpockets, purse-snatchers, car thieves, and drug traffickers. Dublin's busiest thoroughfares by day have been the scene of brutal, mindless beatings at night. Travelers should take normal precautions to protect their belongings from theft and themselves from harm. Be alert and aware of your surroundings, and do not wander in lonely areas alone at night. And take special care if you'll be out in Dublin when the pubs and nightclubs close for the night. Ask at your hotel about which areas are safe and which are not, and when. Take a taxi back to your hotel if you're out after midnight.

Taxes As in many European countries, sales tax is called VAT (value-added tax) and is often already included in the price quoted to you or shown on price tags. In the Republic, VAT rates vary—for hotels, restaurants, and car rentals, it is 13.5%; for souvenirs and gifts, it is 21%. For full details on VAT refunds for purchases, see "VAT Refunds" in chapter 6.

Telephone In the Republic, the telephone system is known as Eircom. Phone numbers in Ireland are currently in flux, as digits are added to accommodate expanded service. Every effort has been made to ensure that the numbers and information in this guide are accurate at the time of writing. If you have difficulty reaching a party, the Irish toll-free number for directory assistance is © **11811.** From the United States, the (toll) number to call is © **00353-91-770220.**

Local calls from a phone booth require a Callcard, a prepaid computerized card that you insert into the phone instead of coins. They can be purchased in a range of denominations at phone company offices, post offices, and many retail outlets (such as newsstands). There's a local and international phone center at the General Post Office on O'Connell Street.

Overseas calls from Ireland can be quite costly, whether you use a Callcard or your own calling card. If you think you will want to call home regularly while in Dublin, you may want to open an account with **Vartec Telecom Ireland** in Ireland © **1800/300067;** www.vartec.ie). Its rates represent a considerable savings, not only from Ireland to the United States but vice versa (handy for planning your trip as well as keeping in touch afterward). **International WORLDLINK** (© **800/864-8000** in the U.S. or 1800/551514 in Ireland) offers an array of additional services for overseas travelers—such as toll-free voice-mail boxes, fax mail, and news services—which can be crucial for keeping in touch when you don't know where or when you can be reached.

To place a call from your home country to Dublin, dial the international access code (011 in the U.S., 0011 in Australia, 0170 in New Zealand, 00 in the U.K.), plus the country code (**353** for the Republic), and finally the number, remembering to omit the initial 0, which is for use only within Ireland.

To place a direct international call from Ireland, dial the international access code (**00**) plus the country code (U.S. and Canada 1, the U.K. 44, Australia 61, New Zealand 64), the area or city code, and the number. The toll-free international access code for **AT&T** is Ⓒ 800/550-000; for **Sprint** it's Ⓒ 800/552-001; and for **MCI** it's Ⓒ 800/55-1001.

Time Ireland follows Greenwich Mean Time (1 hr. earlier than Central European Time) from November to March, and British Standard Time (the same as Central European Time) from April to October. Ireland is 5 hours ahead of the eastern United States (when it's noon in New York, it's 5pm in Ireland).

Ireland's latitude makes for longer days and shorter nights in the summer, and the reverse in the winter. In June there is bright sun until 11pm, but in December, it is truly dark at 4pm.

Tipping Most hotels and guesthouses add a service charge to the bill, usually 12.5% to 15%, although some smaller places add only 10% or nothing at all. Always check to see what amount, if any, has been added to your bill. If a smaller amount has been added or if staff members have provided exceptional service, it is appropriate to give additional cash gratuities. For porters or bellhops, tip €1 ($1.20) per piece of luggage. For taxi drivers, hairdressers, and other providers of service, tip as you would at home, an average of 10% to 15%.

For restaurants, the policy is usually printed on the menu— either a gratuity of 10% to 15% is automatically added to your bill or it's left up to you. Always ask if you are in doubt. As a rule, bartenders do not expect a tip, except when table service is provided.

Weather Phone Ⓒ **1550/122112,** or check the Web at **www.ireland.com/weather**.

Yellow Pages The classified section of the telephone book is called the Golden Pages (**www.goldenpages.ie**).

3

Where to Stay

From legendary old-world landmarks to sleek high-rises, Dublin offers a great diversity of places to stay. The good news is that we've noticed prices starting to actually come down, especially in the luxury category. So travelers on a moderate budget should be able to more easily find comfortable, attractive accommodations.

The Irish Tourist Board implements a grading system consistent with those of other European countries and international standards, ranking hotels with one to five stars. While this system is helpful as a guideline of the comfort level you can expect, it is based strictly on facilities and amenities and fails to take into consideration atmosphere, decor, charm, friendly owners, or an especially appealing breakfast. Moreover, some hotels are ungraded—usually because they are brand-new or they simply choose to remain out of the system. For example, The Clarence hotel, owned by members of the band U2, is ungraded (presumably out of preference) but certainly falls into the luxury category.

In this guide, we give each hotel zero to three stars, based on overall value for money. As a result, a fine but expensive hotel may get one star, while an excellent budget choice may get two.

In general, rates for Dublin hotels do not vary as greatly with the seasons as they do in the countryside. Some hotels charge slightly higher prices during special events, such as the Dublin Horse Show. For the best deals, try to reserve a room over a weekend, and ask if there is a reduction or a weekend package in effect. Some Dublin hotels cut their rates by as much as 50% on Friday and Saturday nights, when business traffic is low. Just to complicate matters, other hotels, especially in the off season, offer midweek specials.

It usually pays to book hotels well in advance. Many hotels can be booked through toll-free numbers in the United States, and the quoted prices offered can be appreciably (as much as 40%) lower than those offered at the door. Even better, book online. We've noticed that many hotels frequently offer the deepest discounts to travelers who book through their websites.

Dublin Accommodations

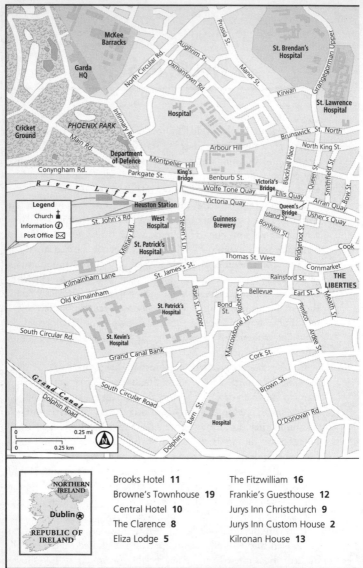

Brooks Hotel **11**
Browne's Townhouse **19**
Central Hotel **10**
The Clarence **8**
Eliza Lodge **5**

The Fitzwilliam **16**
Frankie's Guesthouse **12**
Jurys Inn Christchurch **9**
Jurys Inn Custom House **2**
Kilronan House **13**

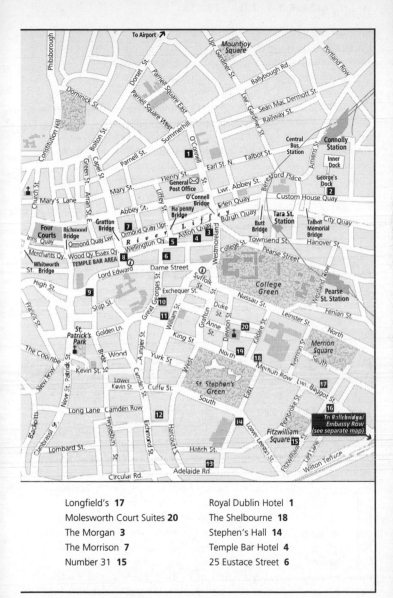

Longfield's **17**

Molesworth Court Suites **20**

The Morgan **3**

The Morrison **7**

Number 31 **15**

Royal Dublin Hotel **1**

The Shelbourne **18**

Stephen's Hall **14**

Temple Bar Hotel **4**

25 Eustace Street **6**

If you arrive in Ireland without a reservation, don't worry. One of the best sources of last-minute rooms (usually at a big discount) is **www.visitdublin.com**. The website has a handy icon that lets you view hotels and guesthouses with immediate availability.

Another option is to arrive in person at the nearest tourist office. Staff members throughout the Republic and Northern Ireland will gladly find you a room using a computerized reservation service known as **Gulliver.** In Ireland or Northern Ireland, you can also call the Gulliver line directly (© **00800/668-668-66**). This is a nationwide and cross-border "free-phone" facility for credit card bookings, operated daily 8am to 11pm. Gulliver is also accessible from the United States (© **011-800/668-668-66**) and on the Web at **www. gulliver.ie**.

A reminder: Unless otherwise noted, room rates don't include service charges (usually 10%–15% of your bill).

1 Historic Old City & Temple Bar/Trinity College Area

Temple Bar is the youngest, most vibrant niche in a young, vibrant town. Stay here and you'll be on the doorstep of practically anywhere you'd want to go. That said, it can get woefully noisy at night, so request a room on a top floor if you want some shut-eye.

If you've got more dash than cash, head just west of Temple Bar to Old City. You'll be in one of the up-and-coming pockets of town, but hoteliers haven't yet started jacking up their rates to reflect the area's newfound popularity.

VERY EXPENSIVE

The Clarence 𝒜𝒜𝒜 So what if the place is partly owned by members of the rock band U2? Don't dismiss it as a glitzy, see-and-be-seen haunt for celebrities (Robert DeNiro, Gwyneth Paltrow, and Mick Jagger are fans)—The Clarence is one of the finest and truly stylish hotels in Dublin. Situated beside the Liffey in Temple Bar, this mid-19th-century, Regency-style hotel was totally overhauled in 1996 to offer larger rooms and luxurious suites. In the process it traded antique charm for contemporary elegance. Each room features a rich color—crimson, royal blue, eggplant, chocolate, or gold—against cream walls and light Shaker-style oak furniture, including exceptionally firm beds. Twin rooms are available but most doubles feature king-size beds. Suites and deluxe rooms have balconies, some overlooking the Liffey. The Clarence's elegant Tea Room restaurant (p. 71), in what was once the ballroom, is one of the best places in town to dine on contemporary Irish cuisine. For

> ### *Tips* A Parking Note
>
> The majority of Dublin hotels do not offer parking; if you have a car, you'll have to find (and pay for) street parking. In this chapter, we've provided parking information only for the few hotels that do offer parking arrangements or discounts for guests.

drinks and lighter fare, there's the hip Octagon Bar or the Study, which has the feel of a gentlemen's club and is a relaxing hangout for guests. This hotel is at the cutting edge of gadgetry, offering an interactive TV/DVD/broadband Internet system in every room.

6–8 Wellington Quay, Dublin 2. ℂ 01/670-9000. Fax 01/407-0820. www.theclarence. ie. 50 units. €315 ($380) double; €640 ($771) 1-bedroom suite; €780 ($940) 2-bedroom suite. Full Irish breakfast €28 ($33). AE, DC, MC, V. Valet parking/service. Bus: 51B, 51C, 68, 69, or 79. **Amenities:** Restaurant (eclectic Continental); bar; concierge; salon; 24-hr. room service; babysitting; laundry/dry cleaning; nonsmoking rooms; foreign-currency exchange; study. *In room:* A/C, Interactive TV/DVD/broadband system, minibar, hair dryer, safe.

MODERATE

Eliza Lodge ✦ This hotel opened a few years ago right beside the Liffey and embodies all the exuberance and zest of Temple Bar. Rooms are very attractive, done up in neutral creams and blond woods, with big floor-to-ceiling windows—the better to take in the riverside vistas. At the top end, executive rooms have Jacuzzi tubs and mod, round bay windows perched over the quay. But a better-value splurge are the smaller penthouse doubles, which have balconies overlooking the river for €190 ($229).

23 Wellington Quay, Dublin 2. ℂ 01/671-0044. Fax 01/671-8362. www.dublinlodge. com. 18 units. €130–€152 ($157–$183) double. AE, MC, V. Bus: 51B, 51C, 68, 69, or 79. **Amenities:** Restaurant; bar; nonsmoking rooms. *In room:* A/C, TV, tea/coffeemaker, hair dryer, iron.

Jurys Inn Christchurch ✦ *Value* A good location in Old City, facing Christ Church cathedral, makes this a solid choice in the budget category. Totally refurbished in 1998, the rooms are larger than you'd expect and bright, though the decor has the same floral bedspreads and framed watercolors as every other chain hotel you've ever visited. Make your reservations early and request a fifth-floor room facing west for a memorable view of Christ Church. *Tip:* Room nos. 501, 507, and 419 are especially spacious.

Christ Church Place, Dublin 8. ℂ **800/44-UTELL** in the U.S. or 01/454-0000. Fax 01/454-0012. www.jurys.com. 182 units. €108–€117 ($130–$141) double. Service charge included. Breakfast €9.50 ($12). AE, MC, V. Discounted parking available at adjacent lot. Bus: 21A, 50, 50A, 78, 78A, or 78B. **Amenities:** Restaurant (Continental); pub; babysitting; laundry/dry cleaning; nonsmoking rooms. *In room:* A/C, TV, coffeemaker, hair dryer.

The Morgan 🏵🏵   If you love Temple Bar but can't afford to stay at The Clarence, this is a fabulous second choice. In just a few short years, this stylized little boutique hotel has developed a cult following among folks in fashion and music. Rooms are airy and minimalist, featuring light beechwood furnishings and crisp, white bedspreads against creamy neutral tones, with a smattering of modern artworks adding visual punch. The overall effect is understated elegance, with a modern, luxurious twist. But the attraction here goes beyond mere good looks. Every detail—from the classy cutlery to the way the staff is unobtrusively attentive—hits just the right note. Though it sounds like a contradiction in terms, this place manages to be both trendy and a classic at the same time.

10 Fleet St., Dublin 2. ℂ **01/679-3939.** Fax 01/679-3946. www.themorgan.com. 66 units. €126–€209 ($152–$252) double. AE, DC, MC, V. Bus: 78A or 78B. **Amenities:** Cafe; bar; fitness center; room service; aromatherapy/masseuse; babysitting; laundry/dry cleaning; video/CD library. *In room:* TV/VCR, dataport, tea/coffeemaker, iron, safe, CD player, garment press, voice mail.

Temple Bar Hotel 🏵   It's twice as big and half as stylish as The Morgan but still a solid pick if The Morgan is sold out. The five-story hotel was developed from a former bank building with great care taken to preserve the brick facade and Victorian mansard roof. The Art Deco lobby features a cast-iron fireplace and plenty of greenery. Guest rooms feature traditional mahogany furnishings and an autumnal russet-and-green color palette, with a very comfortable level of amenities. The double-size orthopedic beds are blissfully firm, though they make the rooms fairly cramped. The hotel has a sky-lit, garden-style Terrace Restaurant serving light fare (sandwiches and pasta) and an Old Dublin–theme pub called Buskers.

Fleet St., Temple Bar, Dublin 2. ℂ **800/44-UTELL** in the U.S. or 01/677-3333. Fax 01/677-3088. www.towerhotelgroup.ie. 129 units. €99–€195 ($120–$235) double. Rates include full Irish breakfast. AE, DC, MC, V. DART: Tara St. Bus: 78A or 78B.

Fun Fact **What's in a Name?**

The "bar" in Temple Bar has nothing to do with a pub or the law. It is the old Irish word for a riverside path.

Amenities: Restaurant (light fare); bar; access to a nearby health club; concierge; room service; foreign-currency exchange. *In room:* TV, tea/coffeemaker, hair dryer, garment press.

SELF-CATERING

25 Eustace Street *(Finds)* This wonderfully restored Georgian town house, dating from 1720, has an enviable location smack in the heart of Temple Bar. It is a showcase property for the Irish Landmark Trust, whose mission is to rescue neglected historic buildings and restore them. And that it does with aplomb. 25 Eustace Street is the only property that the ILT lets out for fewer than 3 nights, and it is truly a privilege to stay here for even 1 night. The house has been faithfully reinstated to the gracious, slightly sober atmosphere of a house of its period, with a superb timber-paneled staircase, fireplaces in every room, mainly mahogany furniture, and brass beds. You have the run of three entire floors of the house, including a huge drawing room with a baby grand piano, dining room, equipped galley kitchen, and three bedrooms (a double, a twin, and a triple). There are two bathrooms, one of which is enormous with an extra-roomy cast-iron claw-foot tub placed dead center. Bookshelves and deep windowsills have been thoughtfully stocked with classics by Irish novelists. Like all ILT properties, there is no TV. (To have it any other way would seem a callous intrusion.) All this, and Temple Bar at your doorstep.

25 Eustace St., Dublin 2. Contact the Irish Landmark Trust © 01/670-4733. Fax 01/670 4887. landmark@iol.ie. 1 apt. €205 ($343) per night or €1,340 ($1,615) per week. Payable by AE, MC, V at booking. **Amenities:** Full kitchen. *In room:* No phone.

2 St. Stephen's Green/Grafton Street Area

Location, location, location: The area around St. Stephen's Green is the epicenter of the city's shopping and sightseeing. So what's not to love? Prepare to pay more for less here.

VERY EXPENSIVE

The Fitzwilliam Hotel *(★★★)* Take an unbeatable location with stunning views over the Green, a two-Michelin-starred restaurant, and an ultracool, contemporary design by Terence Conran, and you have the makings of The Fitzwilliam. Conran has a knack for easygoing sophistication, using clean lines and only a few neutral colors (white, beige, gray) throughout the public rooms and guest rooms. Every detail echoes the theme of understated luxury—even the staff uniforms are custom-made by Irish designers Marc O'Neill and

Cuan Hanly. Rooms are beautifully appointed and very relaxing. One of Dublin's best restaurants, the two-Michelin-starred Thornton's, is downstairs, and you can also have a meal at the more casual restaurant, Citron, or in the traditional Inn on the Green bar. If staying somewhere designerish and trendy is important to you, this gets the nod over The Shelbourne.

109 St. Stephen's Green, Dublin 2. ℭ **01/478-7000.** Fax 01/478-7878. www. fitzwilliamhotel.com. 130 units. €340 ($410) double. Breakfast €20 ($24). AE, DC, MC, V. DART: Pearse. Bus: 10, 11A, 11B, 13, or 20B. **Amenities:** 2 restaurants (French, International); bar; concierge; room service; babysitting; laundry/dry cleaning; nonsmoking rooms; foreign-currency exchange; roof garden. *In room:* A/C, TV/VCR, fax, dataport, minibar, tea/coffeemaker, hair dryer, CD player, garment press, voice mail.

EXPENSIVE

Brooks Hotel ℛ   If you love the neighborhood but can't quite afford The Shelbourne (see below) or The Fitzwilliam (see above), this 6-year-old hotel offers excellent services and doesn't scrimp on the in-room creature comforts. Every room has a king-size orthopedic bed, handmade oak furniture from Galway, and a bold but tasteful color scheme. The bathrooms have blissfully powerful showers. Superior and executive rooms (still cheaper than a standard double at The Shelbourne or Fitzwilliam) are extra-spacious and have VCRs and antique radios. The oak-paneled drawing room is a restful oasis for tea or sherry while you peruse the *Irish Times.*

59–62 Drury St., Dublin 2. ℭ **01/670-4000.** Fax 01/670-4455. www.sinnotthotels. com/brooks. 98 units. €180–€265 ($217–$319) double. AE, DC, MC, V. Discounted overnight parking at adjacent car park. DART: Tara St. or Pearse. Bus: 10, 11A, 11B, 13, 14, 15, 15A, 15B, 20B, or 46A. **Amenities:** Restaurant (international); bar; minigym; concierge; secretarial services; room service; babysitting; laundry/dry cleaning; nonsmoking floors; foreign-currency exchange; video library. *In room:* A/C, TV, VCR (in superior rooms and up), fax, dataport, minibar, hair dryer, iron, safe, garment press.

Browne's Townhouse ℛℛ   If you love luxury but hate big chain hotels, look no further than this sumptuously restored Georgian town house with an unbeatable location on St. Stephen's Green. Originally a gentleman's club, it was converted in 2000 into one of the city's best boutique hotels and has been chalking up awards and accolades ever since. Downstairs is all Georgian splendor: comfy wingback chairs, rich upholsteries, ornate ceiling plasterwork. The 11 guest rooms come in all shapes and sizes, but all are sumptuously decorated with period furnishings, four-poster king-size beds (some of them 2.5m/8 ft. wide!), marble bathrooms, and unique architectural details. When you book, voice your decor preferences; rooms vary drastically according to masculine, feminine, classic, or elaborate tastes. If you splurge on the Thomas Leighton suite, you'll sleep on a magnificent king-size mahogany Murphy bed that once belonged to Marilyn Monroe. Downstairs, the elegant brasserie serves up excellent traditional French fare.

22 St. Stephen's Green, Dublin 2. ⓒ **01/638-3939.** Fax 01/638-3900. www.brownes dublin.com. 11 units. €210–€240 ($253–$289) double. Breakfast €10–€17 ($12–$21). MC, V. DART: Pearse. Bus: 10, 11A, 11B, 13, or 20B. **Amenities:** Restaurant (French). *In room:* A/C, TV, fax, dataport, tea/coffeemaker, hair dryer.

The Shelbourne 𝑅𝑅𝑅   While The Fitzwilliam is all about cutting-edge style, The Shelbourne is all about tradition. This is Dublin's answer to the Grand Hotel, and nothing—not even getting swallowed up by the Meridien Group—has changed its status. Founded in 1824, it has played a significant role in Irish history—the constitution was drafted here in 1922, in room no. 112. The Shelbourne often plays host to international leaders, movie stars, and literary giants. Guest rooms vary in size, but all offer up-to-date comforts and are beautifully appointed with antiques and period pieces. Ask for one that overlooks bucolic St. Stephen's Green. The public areas, replete with glowing fireplaces, Waterford chandeliers, and original artworks, are popular rendezvous spots for Dublin's movers and shakers. (Indeed, the Horseshoe Bar remains the preferred watering hole for sealing deals over a pint of Guinness.) The fitness center is state-of-the-art, and service is impeccable. Needless to say, you don't stay here just for the beds but for a slice of Irish heritage. *Note:* The Shelbourne is undergoing extensive renovations throughout 2005, with only half of the rooms available for guest stays.

27 St. Stephen's Green, Dublin 2. ⓒ **800/225-5843** in the U.S. or 01/663-4500. Fax 01/661-6006. www.shelbourne.ie. 190 units. €185–€200 ($223–$240) double. Breakfast €20–€26 ($24–$31). AE, DC, MC, V. Limited free parking. DART: Pearse. Bus: 10, 11A, 11B, 13, or 20B. **Amenities:** 2 restaurants (Continental, modern Irish); 2 bars; fitness center; concierge; room service; babysitting; laundry/dry cleaning; barber shop; beauty and spa treatments; foreign-currency exchange; safe-deposit boxes; tearoom; video library. *In room:* A/C, TV, dataport, minibar, radio.

Stephen's Hall 𝑅 *Value*   How suite it is. Wonderfully situated on the southeast corner of St. Stephen's Green in a handsome Georgian town house, this Clarion all-suite hotel offers great value for families, visitors who plan an extended stay, or folks who want to entertain or do their own cooking. Each suite is tastefully decorated and contains a sitting room, dining area, fully equipped kitchenette, bathroom, and bedroom. The luxury penthouse suites, on the upper floors, offer great views of the city. Ground-level town-house suites have private entrances.

14–18 Lower Leeson St., Dublin 2. ℭ **877/424-6423** in the U.S. or 01/638-1111. Fax 01/638-1122. www.stephens-hall.com. 33 units. €160–€230 ($193–$277) 1-bedroom suite. Rates include full breakfast. AE, DC, MC, V. Free parking. DART: Pearse. Bus: 11, 11A, 11B, 13, 13A, or 13B. **Amenities:** Restaurant (Continental); bar; access to nearby health club; concierge; babysitting; nonsmoking floor; safe-deposit boxes; video library. *In room:* TV, fax, dataport, CD player.

MODERATE

Central Hotel ❀ Between Grafton Street and Dublin Castle, this century-old five-story hotel is now part of the Best Western chain. The public areas retain a Victorian atmosphere, enhanced by an impressive collection of contemporary Irish art. Guest rooms are high-ceilinged, with cheerful and colorful fabrics, and sturdy, Irish-made furnishings. The tucked-away Library Bar is a cozy haven for a drink and a moment's calm.

1–5 Exchequer St. (at the corner of Great Georges St.), Dublin 2. ℭ **800/780-1234** in the U.S. or 01/679-7302. Fax 01/679-7303. www.centralhotel.ie. 70 units. €135–€175 ($163–$211) double. Rates include service charge and full Irish breakfast. AE, DC, MC, V. Discounted parking in nearby public lot. Bus: 22A. **Amenities:** Restaurant (Irish/Continental); lounge; bar; room service; nonsmoking rooms. *In room:* TV, mini-bar, tea/coffeemaker, hair dryer, iron, garment press, voice mail.

Molesworth Court Suites ❀ Hate hotels? Then consider an apartment. Tucked away behind Mansion House, Molesworth Courts is no more than 5 minutes on foot to Stephen's Green and yet is country quiet. These tastefully decorated, comfortable apartments offer everything you need to set up your own base in Dublin, whether for a night or a month. They all have small balconies, and the bi-level penthouses have spacious verandas. The staff here goes the extra mile to be helpful, and there's daily maid service. The internal phone system provides you with a private extension and your own voice mail. If, despite the fact that you have your own kitchen, you want to let others do your cooking, you can order out from any of the roughly 25 local restaurants listed in the *Restaurant Express* menu booklet lying only an arm's reach from the couch.

Schoolhouse Lane (off Molesworth St.), Dublin 2. ℭ **01/676-4799.** Fax 01/676-4982. www.molesworthcourt.ie. 12 units. €160 ($193) 1-bedroom apt; €200 ($240) 2-bedroom apt. Nonrefundable booking deposit of €100 ($120) due 4 weeks before arrival. AE, MC, V. DART: Pearse. Bus: 10, 11A, 11B, 13, or 20B. **Amenities:** Laundry. *In room:* TV.

Number 31 ❀❀ A discreet plaque at an elegant gated entrance in the heart of Georgian Dublin is your only clue that what lies beyond is an award-winning town-house B&B. The house is actually two beautifully renovated architectural show houses—it's the former home of Sam Stephenson, Ireland's best-known modern architect—featuring a fabulous sunken fireside seating area with mosaic tiles in the main lounge. In the main house, rooms vary from grand, high-ceilinged affairs to cozier nests. The smaller coach house has lower ceilings, but some rooms have their own patios. All the rooms are a triumph of quiet, good taste, decorated with fine fabrics against a cream backdrop. Breakfast is truly magnificent—think mushroom frittatas, cranberry bread, and scrumptious little potato cakes.

31 Leeson Close, Lower Leeson St., Dublin 2. ℂ **01/676-5011.** Fax 01/676-2929. www.number31.ie. 20 units, all with bathroom. €175–€199 ($211–$239) double. Rates include breakfast. AE, MC, V. Free parking. Bus: 11, 11A, 11B, 13, 13A, or 13B. **Amenities:** Bar; lounge. *In room:* TV, hair dryer.

INEXPENSIVE

Frankie's Guesthouse 🏵   Billed as Dublin's only guesthouse exclusively for lesbians and gays, Frankie's is a charming, mews-style building with a wonderful address in the heart of Georgian Dublin. Set on a quiet back street, the house has a Mediterranean feel, with fresh whitewashed rooms and simple furnishings. Book well in advance, especially for a weekend stay.

8 Camden Place, Dublin 2. ℂ/fax **01/478-3087.** www.frankiesguesthouse.com. 12 units, 5 with private bathroom. €100 ($120) double with private bathroom; €82 ($99) double with shared bathroom. Rates include breakfast. AE, MC, V. Bus: 16, 16A, 16C, 19A, 22, or 22A. **Amenities:** TV lounge; sauna; roof terrace. *In room:* TV, tea/coffeemaker.

3 Fitzwilliam Square/Merrion Square Area

This Georgian neighborhood feels a lot like the nearby St. Stephen's Green area, but its streets are less busy and commercialized. Fitzwilliam Square and Merrion Square are each little square parks surrounded by Georgian town houses with colorful doors. Some of Dublin's most famous citizens once resided here; today many of the houses are offices for doctors, lawyers, government officials, and other professionals. This area is only a few minutes on foot from St. Stephen's Green and Grafton Street, but accommodations tend to be considerably less pricey.

EXPENSIVE

Longfield's 🏵🏵   Created from two 18th-century Georgian town houses, this award-winning hotel is a small, elegant alternative to the large upscale hotels in this area. The hotel is named after Richard Longfield (also known as Viscount Longueville), who originally owned this site and was a member of the Irish Parliament 2 centuries ago. Totally restored and recently refurbished, it combines Georgian decor and reproduction-period furnishings of dark woods and brass trim. The standard-size rooms are on the small side; the best doubles feature four-poster beds. Like the eye of a storm, Longfield's is centrally located yet remarkably quiet, an elegant yet unpretentious getaway 5 minutes' walk from St. Stephen's Green. The restaurant, simply known as Number 10, is beloved by foodies.

10 Lower Fitzwilliam St., Dublin 2. © **01/676-1367.** Fax 01/676-1542. www. longfields.ie. 26 units. €180–€215 ($217–$259) double. Rates include full breakfast. AE, DC, MC, V. DART: Pearse. Bus: 10. **Amenities:** Restaurant (international); concierge; room service; babysitting; laundry/dry cleaning. *In room:* TV, hair dryer, clock radio.

MODERATE

Kilronan House 🏠🏠   This extremely comfortable B&B is set on a peaceful, leafy road just 5 minutes' walk from St. Stephen's Green. Much of the Georgian character remains, such as the ceiling cornicing, hardwood parquet floors, and the fine staircase. The sitting room on the ground floor is particularly intimate, with a fire glowing through the cold months of the year. The rooms are brightly inviting in white and yellow, and those facing the front have commodious bay windows. There's no elevator, so consider requesting a room on a lower floor. The front rooms, facing Adelaide Street, are also preferable to those in back, which face onto office buildings and a parking lot. Breakfast here is especially good, featuring homemade breads.

70 Adelaide Rd., Dublin 2. © **01/475-5266.** Fax 01/478-2841. www.dublinn.com. 15 units, 13 with private bathroom (shower only). €90–€152 ($108–$183) double. Rates include full breakfast. AE, MC, V. Free private parking. Bus: 14, 15, 19, 20, or 46A. *In room:* TV, tea/coffeemaker, hair dryer.

4 Ballsbridge/Embassy Row Area

Visitors want to stay here for the same reason Dubliners want to live here: quality of life. It's the most prestigious part of town, known for its embassies, tree-lined streets, and historic buildings. If you're coming to Dublin specifically for a conference at the RDS show grounds or a match at the Lansdowne Rugby Ground, this neighborhood will put you right in the thick of things. The downside is that it's a good 20- to 30-minute walk to get into the city's best sightseeing and shopping areas.

VERY EXPENSIVE

Four Seasons 🏠🏠🏠 *(Kids)*   If money is no object, the Four Seasons blows Dublin's other luxury hotels out of the water in terms of services

Ballsbridge/Embassy Row Area Accommodations

Anglesea Town House **7**

Berkeley Court **3**

Bewley's Hotel **6**

Butlers Town House **4**

Four Seasons **5**

Hibernian Hotel **2**

Waterloo House **1**

and leisure facilities. The health club is state-of-the-art, and the spa treatments top-flight (some, like massage, are available in your room). The indoor pool and whirlpool complex overlooks a sunken garden—just one small example of how beauty is worked into the overall design of the hotel. The public rooms and guest rooms share a smart and very plush look, thanks to liberal use of natural elements and fine fabrics. This is an absolutely fabulous place for families. Not only are there complimentary cribs, child-proof bedrooms, and a babysitting service, but there is also a menu of children's activities to keep the kids occupied while you have a romantic meal, grab a massage, or just kick back for some quiet meditation (the better to prepare yourself for the bill). Always check the website's rates before booking; online discounts can be fantastic.

Simmonscourt Rd., Ballsbridge, Dublin 4. (C) **800/819-5053** in the U.S. or 01/665-4000. Fax 01/665-4099. www.fourseasons.com. 259 units. €395–€795 ($476–$958) double. Breakfast €25 ($30). AE, DC, MC, V. Valet parking. DART: Sandymount (5-min. walk). Bus: 7, 7A, 7X, 8, or 45. **Amenities:** 2 restaurants (modern Continental, cafe); lobby lounge; bar; indoor pool; health club/spa; whirlpool; children's programs; concierge; room service; babysitting; laundry/dry cleaning; nonsmoking rooms. *In room:* TV/VCR, dataport, minibar, hair dryer, safe, CD player available, radio, voice mail.

EXPENSIVE

Berkeley Court ⑂   The first Irish member of Leading Hotels of the World, the Berkeley Court (pronounced *Bark*-lay) has a distinguished address near the American embassy. A favorite haunt of diplomats and international business leaders, the hotel is known for its posh gold-and-blue lobby decorated with fine antiques, original paintings, mirrored columns, and Irish-made carpets and furnishings. The guest rooms aim to convey an air of elegance, but some visitors might find them overly busy and fussy—think patterned wallpaper, patterned bedspreads, and still more patterns on the carpet. Nevertheless, they are decked out in designer fabrics, firm half-canopy beds, dark woods, and bathrooms fitted with marble accouterments. The well-tended grounds were once part of the Botanic Gardens of University College.

Lansdowne Rd., Ballsbridge, Dublin 4. (C) **800/44-UTELL** in the U.S. or 01/660-1711. Fax 01/661-7238. www.jurysdoyle.com. 188 units. €159–€700 ($192–$843) double. Breakfast €20–€26 ($24–$31). AE, DC, MC, V. Free valet parking. DART: Lansdowne Rd. Bus: 7, 8, or 45. **Amenities:** 2 restaurants (Continental, bistro); lounge; bar; concierge; salon; room service; laundry service; nonsmoking rooms; foreign-currency exchange. *In room:* TV, dataport, minibar, hair dryer, safe, garment press, radio, voice mail.

The Hibernian Hotel ⭐⭐ This grand, restored Victorian hotel manages to exude both the elegance of a graceful town house and the warmth of a fine country inn. The prestigious Small Luxury Hotels of the World named it Hotel of the Year in 1997. Antiques, graceful pillars, and floral arrangements fill the public areas. The guest rooms, of varying size and layout, are individually decorated in keeping with the Victorian period, with quality furnishings, rich fabrics, and specially commissioned paintings of Dublin and wildlife scenes. Unlike some converted 19th-century buildings, it has an elevator.

Eastmoreland Place, Ballsbridge, Dublin 4. ℂ **800/525-4800** in the U.S. or 01/668-7666. Fax 01/660-2655. www.hibernianhotel.com. 41 units. €220 ($265) double; €250 ($301) suite. AE, DC, MC, V. Free valet parking. Bus: 10. **Amenities:** Restaurant (Irish/Continental); bar; access to nearby health club (extra fee); concierge; room service; babysitting; laundry/dry cleaning; nonsmoking floor. *In room:* TV, tea/coffeemaker, hair dryer, garment press.

MODERATE

Anglesea Town House ⭐ Everyone who stays at this 1903 Edwardian-style B&B raves on and on about the same thing: the extraordinary breakfasts served by Helen Kirrane. Start with freshly squeezed orange juice. Then perhaps have a bit of homemade fruit compote or fresh yogurt and baked fruit. Next it's Helen's wonderful homemade baked cereals or porridge ("homemade" is a big thing with Helen), then tuck into your main meal: Perhaps bacon, eggs, and sausages? Or how about a smoked salmon omelet? And naturally there's always a dessert (the profiteroles are divine) and gallons of brewed coffee. The place is full of old-world comforts—rocking chairs, settees, a sun deck, and lots of flowering plants—and guest rooms are pretty and very comfortable. But it's the breakfasts that you'll remember long after you leave Dublin.

63 Anglesea Rd., Ballsbridge, Dublin 4. ℂ **01/668-3877.** Fax 01/668-3461. 7 units. €130 ($157) double. Rates include full breakfast. AE, MC, V. DART: Lansdowne Rd. Bus: 10, 46A, 46B, 63, or 84. **Amenities:** Babysitting. *In room:* TV, hair dryer.

Butlers Town House ⭐⭐ *Value* This beautifully restored and expanded Victorian town-house B&B feels like a gracious family home into which you are lucky enough to be welcomed. The atmosphere is semiformal yet invitingly elegant, class without the starched collar. Rooms are richly furnished with four-poster or half-tester beds, using top-quality fabrics and an eye for blending rich colors. It's hard to elude comfort here—the sheets are of two-fold Egyptian cotton, the shower's water pressure is heavenly, and the staff is especially solicitous. The gem here, in our opinion, is the Glendalough Room, with its lovely bay window and small library; it requires early booking. The hotel offers free tea and coffee all day. Breakfast, afternoon tea, and high tea are served in the atrium dining room.

44 Lansdowne Rd., Ballsbridge, Dublin 4. ⓒ **800/44-UTELL** in the U.S. or 01/667-4022. Fax 01/667-3960. www.butlers-hotel.com. 20 units. €150–€190 ($181–$229) double. Rates include full breakfast. AE, DC, MC, V. Closed Dec 23–Jan 10. DART: Lansdowne Rd. Bus: 7, 7A, 8, or 45. **Amenities:** Breakfast room; room service; babysitting; laundry/dry cleaning. *In room:* A/C, TV, dataport, hair dryer.

Waterloo House ⓖ Waterloo House (actually not one but two Georgian town houses) is one of the most popular B&Bs in Dublin. Perhaps it's because Evelyn Corcoran and her staff take such good care of you, in a friendly but unobtrusive way. The place is charming in an old-world kind of way, with classical music wafting through the lobby, and the elegant, high-ceilinged drawing room looking like a parlor out of an Agatha Christie novel. Guest rooms are comfortable and large (some have two double beds), but it's hard to decide whether the decor, featuring red-patterned carpet and box-pleated bedspreads, is a look that's reassuringly traditional or merely dated. The varied breakfast menu is a high point. This is a non-smoking house.

8–10 Waterloo Rd., Ballsbridge, Dublin 4. ⓒ **01/660-1888.** Fax 01/667-1955. www.waterloohouse.ie. 17 units. €78–€175 ($94–$211) double. Rates include full breakfast. MC, V. Free car parking. Closed Christmas week. DART: Lansdowne Rd. Bus: 5, 7, or 8. **Amenities:** Breakfast room. *In room:* TV, tea/coffeemaker, hair dryer, garment press.

INEXPENSIVE

Bewley's Hotel ⓖⓖ ⓥalue Kudos to Bewley's for managing to keep its rates stagnant for several years running. The hotel occupies what was once a 19th-century brick Masonic school building adjacent to the RDS show grounds and next to the British Embassy. A new wing harmonizes well with the old structure, and is indistinguishable on the interior. Public lounges and reception areas are spacious and appointed with mahogany wainscoting, marble paneling, and polished bronze. Rooms, too, are spacious and well furnished—each has a writing desk, an armchair, and either one king-size bed or a double and a twin bed. The studios have a bedroom with a double bed, plus an additional room with a foldout couch, a table (seats six), a pull-out kitchenette/bar hidden in a cabinet, and an additional bathroom (shower only). The basement restaurant (O'Connell's) is run by the Allen family of Ballymaloe fame, and offers very good food at reasonable prices; there's also an informal Bewley's tearoom. The hotel is an excellent value for families and groups; the big downside is its location outside the city center.

Merrion Rd., Ballsbridge, Dublin 4. ⓒ **01/668-1111.** Fax 01/668-1999. www.bewleys hotels.com. 304 units. €99 ($119) double. Rates include service charge and taxes. AE, DC, MC, V. DART: Sandymount (5-min. walk). Bus: 7, 7A, 7X, 8, or 45. **Amenities:** Restaurant (Irish/Continental); tearoom. *In room:* TV, dataport, kitchenette, tea/coffeemaker, hair dryer, safe, garment press.

5 O'Connell Street Area/North of the Liffey

While not generally as chic or salubrious as the South of the Liffey, the Northside is going through a spurt of rejuvenation, most visible through the arrival of The Morrison hotel (see below) several years ago. The big upside to staying here is that, while it's very central and within walking distance of all the major sights and shops, hotel rates tend to be lower than they are just across the bridge.

VERY EXPENSIVE

The Morrison ✸✸✸ Just when it seemed that everything chic and hip happened south of the Liffey, the Hong Kong–born, Irish designer John Rocha opened The Morrison and suddenly the central Northside doesn't look so shabby after all. This stunning, contemporary hotel is located a 5-minute walk from O'Connell Street and directly across the river from Temple Bar. Rocha's design uses clean lines and quality, natural elements to evoke a very sensuous, luxurious feeling of space and relaxation. Guest rooms are minimalist but don't feel cold the way minimalism can, undoubtedly because Rocha has used a palette of neutral colors such as cream, chocolate, and black. Halo, the atrium-style main restaurant, is one of the most talked-about, exciting eateries in town. The upshot: The Morrison is every bit as stylish as The Clarence (Temple Bar) and The Fitzwilliam (St. Stephen's Green), with the sky-high rates to prove it.

Lower Ormond Quay, Dublin 1. ⓒ **01/887-2400.** Fax 01/878-3185. www.morrison hotel.ie. 93 units. €270–€445 ($325–$536) double. AE, DC, MC, V. DART: Connolly. Bus: 70 or 80. **Amenities:** 2 restaurants (fusion, Asian); 2 bars; concierge; room service; babysitting; dry cleaning; video/CD library. *In room:* A/C, dataport, minibar, hair dryer, safe, CD player, voice mail.

MODERATE

Jurys Inn Custom House ✸✸ *Value* Ensconced in the grandiose new financial-services district and facing the quays, this Jurys Inn follows the successful formula of affordable comfort without frills.

Single rooms have a double bed and a pullout sofa, while double rooms offer both a double and a twin bed. Twenty-two especially spacious rooms, if available, cost nothing extra. Rooms facing the quays also enjoy vistas of the Dublin hills, but those facing the financial district are quieter. As occupancy runs at 100% from May to September and at roughly 95% for the rest of the year, be sure to book well in advance.

Custom House Quay, Dublin 1. (℃ **800/44-UTELL** in the U.S. or 01/607-5000. Fax 01/829-0400. www.jurys.com. 239 units. €108–€117 ($130–$141) double. Rates include service charge. Full Irish breakfast €9.50 ($11). AE, DC, MC, V. Discounted parking available at adjacent lot. DART: Tara St. Bus: 27A, 27B, or 53A. **Amenities:** Restaurant (Continental); bar; laundry/dry cleaning; nonsmoking rooms. *In room:* TV, dataport, tea/coffeemaker, hair dryer.

Royal Dublin Hotel ℛ Romantically floodlit at night, this five-story hotel is near Parnell Square at the north end of Dublin's main thoroughfare, within walking distance of all the main theaters and Northside attractions. The contemporary sky-lit lobby lies adjacent to lounge areas that were part of the original 1752 building. These Georgian-style rooms are elegant, with high molded ceilings, ornate cornices, crystal chandeliers, gilt-edged mirrors, and open fireplaces. Guest rooms are contemporary, featuring light woods, bold, checked bedspreads, and bay windows that extend over the busy street below.

40 Upper O'Connell St., Dublin 1. (℃ **800/528-1234** in the U.S. or 01/873-3666. Fax 01/873-3120. www.royaldublin.com. 120 units. €120–€185 ($145–$223) double. Rates include service charge, full Irish breakfast, and VAT. AE, DC, MC, V. Free parking. DART: Connolly. Bus: 36A, 40A, 40B, 40C, or 51A. **Amenities:** Restaurant (brasserie); lounge; bar; concierge; room service; babysitting; laundry; foreign-currency exchange. *In room:* TV, radio, tea/coffeemaker, hair dryer.

4

Where to Dine

You're here. You're famished. Where do you go? A formal, old-world hotel dining room? Perhaps a casual bistro or wine bar? Ethnic cuisine, maybe? Dublin has the goods, across a wide range of price categories. Expect generally higher prices than you'd pay for comparable fare in a comparable U.S. city. (Hey, Dublin's hip—you always pay for hip.) As befits a European capital, there's plenty of Continental cuisine, with a particular leaning toward French and Italian influences. But there's also a lot of exciting fusion cooking going on here these days, and chefs make excellent use of the wondrous Irish produce available at their doorsteps.

1 Historic Old City/Liberties Area

MODERATE

Lord Edward 🍴 SEAFOOD   Established in 1890 and situated in the heart of the Old City opposite Christ Church Cathedral, this cozy upstairs dining room claims to be Dublin's oldest seafood restaurant. A dozen preparations of sole, including au gratin and Veronique, are served; there are many variations of prawns, from thermidor to Provençal; and fresh lobster is prepared au naturel or in sauces. Fresh fish—from salmon and sea trout to plaice and turbot—is served grilled, fried, meunière, or poached. Vegetarian dishes are also available. At lunch, light snacks and simpler fare are served in the bar.

23 Christ Church Place, Dublin 8. ℂ 01/454-2420. Reservations required. Main courses €15–€24 ($18–$29); fixed-price dinner €35 ($42). AE, DC, MC, V. Mon–Fri noon–2:30pm; Mon–Sat 6–10:30pm. Closed Dec 24–Jan 3. Bus: 50, 54A, 56A, 65, 65A, 77, 77A, 123, or 150.

INEXPENSIVE

Govinda's VEGETARIAN   The motto here is healthy square meals on square plates for very good prices. The meals are generous, belly-warming concoctions of vegetables, cheese, rice, and pasta. Every day, 10 main courses are offered cafeteria-style. Some are always East Indian, and the others a variety of simple, European staples such as

Dublin Dining

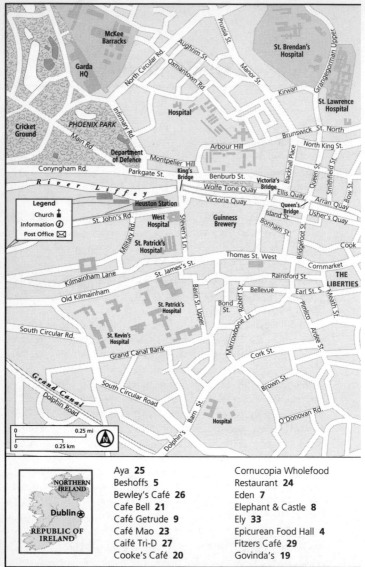

Aya **25**
Beshoffs **5**
Bewley's Café **26**
Cafe Bell **21**
Café Getrude **9**
Café Mao **23**
Caifé Tri-D **27**
Cooke's Café **20**

Cornucopia Wholefood
Restaurant **24**
Eden **7**
Elephant & Castle **8**
Ely **33**
Epicurean Food Hall **4**
Fitzers Café **29**
Govinda's **19**

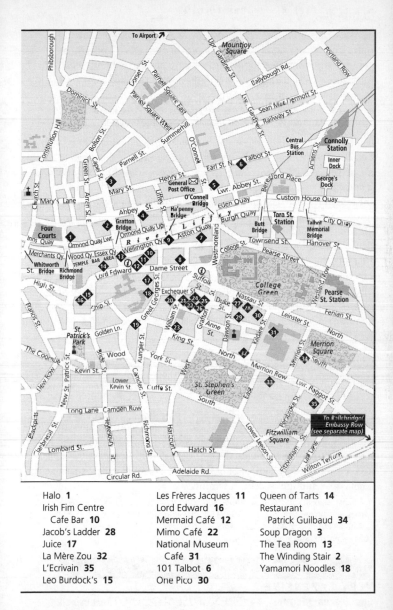

Halo **1**	Les Frères Jacques **11**	Queen of Tarts **14**
Irish Fim Centre	Lord Edward **16**	Restaurant
Cafe Bar **10**	Mermaid Café **12**	Patrick Guilbaud **34**
Jacob's Ladder **28**	Mimo Café **22**	Soup Dragon **3**
Juice **17**	National Museum	The Tea Room **13**
La Mère Zou **32**	Café **31**	The Winding Stair **2**
L'Ecrivain **35**	101 Talbot **6**	Yamamori Noodles **18**
Leo Burdock's **15**	One Pico **30**	

lasagna or macaroni and cheese. Veggie burgers are also prepared to order. All are accompanied by a choice of two salads and can be enjoyed unaccompanied by smoke—the restaurant is nonsmoking throughout. Desserts are healthy and huge, like a rich wedge of carrot cake with a dollop of cream or homemade ice cream.

4 Aungier St., Dublin 2. ℭ 01/475-0309. Main courses €8.45 ($10); soup and freshly baked bread €3.10 ($3.70). MC, V. Mon–Sat noon–9pm. Closed Dec 24–Jan 2. Bus: 16, 16A, 19, or 22.

Leo Burdock's 🐸 FISH AND CHIPS   Every visitor should go to a Dublin takeout "chipper" at least once, and you might as well do it at the best in town. Established in 1913 across from Christchurch, this quintessential Irish takeout shop remains a cherished Dublin institution, despite a devastating fire in 1998. Rebuilt from the ground up, Burdock's is back. Cabinet ministers, university students, and businesspeople alike can be found in the queue. They're waiting for fish bought fresh that morning and those good Irish potatoes, both cooked in "drippings" (none of that modern cooking oil!). There's no seating, but you can sit on a nearby bench or stroll down to the park at St. Patrick's Cathedral.

2 Werburgh St., Dublin 8. ℭ 01/454-0306. Main courses €6–€7 ($7.20–$8.45). No credit cards. Mon–Sat noon–midnight; Sun 4pm–midnight. Bus: 21A, 50, 50A, 78, 78A, or 78B.

Queen of Tarts 🐸🐸 TEA SHOP   This tiny tearoom is David to the Goliath of Irish tearooms (Bewley's, see later in this chapter). It's earned a reputation for the best cheap, home-cooked meals in town. Start with a gourmet sandwich, Greek salad, or savory tart of ham and spinach or cheddar cheese and chives. Then follow it up with the flaky sweetness of warm almond cranberry or blackberry pie. The scones here are tender and light, dusted with powdered sugar and accompanied by a little pot of fruit jam. The restaurant is small, smoke-free, and full of delicious aromas.

4 Corkhill, Dublin 2. ℭ 01/670-7499. Soup and fresh bread €3 ($3.60); sandwiches and savory tarts €5–€8 ($6–$9.60); baked goods and cakes €1.25–€4 ($1.50–$4.80). No credit cards. Mon–Fri 7:30am–7pm; Sat 9am–6pm; Sun 10am–6pm. Bus: Any city-center bus.

2 Temple Bar/Trinity College Area

VERY EXPENSIVE

Les Frères Jacques 🐸🐸 FRENCH/SEAFOOD   The business crowd loves this friendly, upmarket French restaurant, which brings a touch of haute cuisine to the lower edge of the trendy Temple Bar district. The dining room evokes old Paris, with its dark-green-and-cream backdrop. Start with something quintessentially French, such as the duck confit or ballotine of foie gras served with toasted brioche. The menu offers such entrees as Barbary duck with honey and red-wine sauce and a thyme-infused noisette of Wicklow lamb with gratin dauphinois. Chef Richard Reau is extremely talented with seafood and shellfish dishes, such as pan-fried Dover sole with lemon and parsley butter and grilled lobster flamed in Irish whiskey.

74 Dame St., Dublin 2. ℂ 01/679-4555. www.lesfreresjacques.com. Reservations recommended. Main courses average €33 ($40); fixed-price 4-course dinner €35 ($42). AE, DC, MC, V. Mon–Fri 12:15–2:30pm and 7:15–10:30pm; Sat 7–10:30pm. Closed Dec 24–Jan 4. Bus: 50, 50A, 54, 56, or 77.

The Tea Room 𝕲𝕲𝕲 INTERNATIONAL   This ultrasmart restaurant, ensconced in the very hip Clarence hotel, is virtually guaranteed to deliver one of your most memorable meals in Ireland. This gorgeous dining room's soaring yet understated lines are the perfect backdrop for Antony Ely's complex but controlled cooking. A classic such as beef filet with red-wine *jus* is downright zingy when served with arugula on a Dijon-infused potato-and-onion mash. Likewise, the *saucisson* of salmon becomes up-to-date and elegant astride teeny risoni pasta and chive dressing. Desserts, such as the caramelized peach with rice pudding pie, are heaven sent. Bono and the Edge, of U2, are part-owners of the hotel, so the celebrity-spotting quotient is always potentially high.

In The Clarence, 6–8 Wellington Quay, Dublin 2. ℂ 01/670-9000. Reservations required. Fixed-price 1-course dinner €31 ($37), 2-course dinner €41 ($49), 3-course dinner €53 ($64). AE, MC, V. Mon–Fri 12:30–2pm; Mon–Sun 6:30–9:45pm. Bus: 51B, 51C, 68, 69, or 79.

EXPENSIVE

Eden 𝕲𝕲 INTERNATIONAL/MEDITERRANEAN   This is one of Temple Bar's hippest eateries, a cool minimalist dining room with an open-plan kitchen and a vista overlooking Meeting House Square. Eleanor Walsh and Michael Dirkin are two of Ireland's most exciting young chefs, and here they offer a delicious menu of well-thought-out food at reasonable prices. The food is influenced by the global village, but there's a special penchant for Mediterranean flavors—the fresh hake comes served with black olives, sun-dried tomatoes, arugula (called rocket in Ireland), and pesto. On a cold day, opt for an updated Irish favorite such as a paper-thin smoked loin of pork (called kassler here) laid over an apple mash with port-infused gravy. Desserts are worth saving room for. The fixed-price lunch is a particularly good value.

Meeting House Sq. (entrance on Sycamore St.), Dublin 2. © 01/670-5372. Main courses €18–€28 ($22–$34); fixed-price lunch menu €19 ($23). AE, DC, MC, V. Daily 12:30–3pm and 6–10:30pm. Bus: 51B, 51C, 68, 69, or 79.

Jacob's Ladder ☆☆☆ ⟨Value⟩ MODERN IRISH   When a talented, confident chef knows what to do with the exceptional quality of Irish produce, the results can be superb. Inspired cooking by chef-owner Adrian Roche and a stylish dining room with great views overlooking Trinity College make this one of the most consistently packed places in town. Roche's forte is taking old Irish stalwarts and updating them into sublime signature dishes. His Dublin Coddle is a soupy seafood stew of onions, potatoes, mussels, clams, Dublin bay prawns, salmon, carrots, and turnips. He serves his excellent braised wood pigeon with colcannon—an old Irish favorite of potatoes and cabbage mashed together with plenty of butter—that is fluffier and more refined here than perhaps anywhere else on the island. Service is terrific and you get great value for your money, especially as this is one of the few upscale restaurants that hasn't upped its prices in the past year.

4–5 Nassau St., Dublin 2. © 01/670-3865. www.jacobsladder.ie. Reservations required. Main courses €20–€30 ($24–$36); fixed-price dinner €37 ($45). AE, DC, MC, V. Tues–Sat 12:30–2:30pm; Tues–Fri 6–10pm; Sat 7–10pm. Closed Dec 24–Jan 4. DART: Pearse. Bus: 7, 8, 10, 11, or 46A.

Mermaid Café ☆☆☆ MODERN   The Mermaid Café—known to locals as simply the Mermaid—has attained cult status in Dublin. Like a certain mild-mannered reporter for the *Daily Planet,* this could be something very ordinary. But it's not. Ben Gorman, who started the Mermaid back in 1996, now spends less time behind the stove. Not to worry: Chef Temple Garner's cooking is downright terrific in its own right—think classic cooking with a fresh, eclectic twist. As a starter, the orange, feta, and watercress salad with beetroot and mild chile dressing offers a good launch without threatening your appetite, though the Mermaid antipasti (especially when combined with the dangerously appealing assortment of freshly baked breads) may leave you with the will but not the way for the generous entrees soon to emerge from the kitchen. The New England crab cakes, grilled sword-fish with mango relish, roast duck breast on curried noodles, and chargrilled monkfish are all flawlessly prepared and quite memorable. On top of all that, the wine list is one of the best in Ireland and the desserts—especially the pecan pie—are divine.

70 Dame St., Dublin 2. ℭ 01/670-8236. www.mermaid.ie. Reservations required. Dinner main courses €19–€30 ($23–$36); Sun brunch €9–€15 ($11–$18). MC, V. Mon–Sat 12:30–2:30pm and 6–11pm; Sun 12:30–3:30pm (brunch) and 6–9pm. Bus: 50, 50A, 54, 56A, 77, 77A, or 77B.

MODERATE

Elephant & Castle 🍴🍴 AMERICAN   You'd be forgiven for thinking you could find this kind of food—burgers, chicken wings, omelets—at any old Yankee-style joint, but give it a chance and you won't be disappointed. The chicken wings are scrumptious, the burgers out of this world, the omelets "spot on," as the Irish would say. It's a buzzing, immensely popular place for breakfast, brunch, lunch, afternoon nibble, dinner, or late dinner.

18 Temple Bar, Dublin 2. ℭ 01/679-3121. Main courses €8–€22 ($9.20–$25). AE, MC, V. Mon–Fri 8am–11:30pm; Sat–Sun 10:30am–11:30pm. Bus: 51B, 51C, 68, 69, or 79.

Juice VEGETARIAN   Uh-oh. The V word. Don't worry, this place isn't about suffering for a higher principle. Truth is, if nobody told you that Juice was a vegetarian restaurant, you'd probably never notice. The menu is so interesting and the food so downright fabulous, just think of it as a bonus that everything on the menu is organic, healthy, and fresh. And what a hip room. Lofty, 30-foot ceilings softened by a suspended sailcloth and muted lighting. One entire wall is painted claret, with a net of tiny, white fairy lights twinkling in the distance. Along with pancakes, huevos rancheros, and French toast, topped with both fresh fruit and organic maple syrup, the menu takes you around the world. Sample the homemade dips—hummus, baba ghanouj, tapenade, roasted carrot pâté, smoked pimento pâté—served tapas-style with crudités and warm pita-bread strips. True to its name, there are about 30 kinds of juices and smoothies on offer. Desserts are good, too. After all, V is for value, too.

Castle House, 73 S. Great Georges St., Dublin 2. ℭ 01/475-7856. Reservations recommended Fri–Sat. Main courses €7–€10 ($8.45–$12); early-bird fixed-price dinner €14 ($17) (Mon–Fri 5–7pm). AE, MC, V. Daily 11am–11pm. Bus: 50, 50A, 54, 56, or 77.

Yamamori Noodles 🍴🍴 JAPANESE   If you're still skeptical about Japanese cuisine, Yamamori will make you an instant believer. In a pop, casual, and exuberant atmosphere, you may just be startled by how good the food is here. The splendid menu is a who's who of Japanese cuisine, and the prices range from budget to splurge. Regardless of the bottom line, however, everyone goes away feeling full and feted. On a raw, drizzly Dublin day, the chile chicken ramen is a pot of bliss, while the yamamori yaki soba offers, in a mound of wok-fried noodles, a well-rewarded treasure hunt for prawns, squid, chicken, and roast pork. Vegetarians aren't overlooked and the selective international wine list is well priced and well chosen. The lunch specials are outstanding. Even at 9:30pm on a Monday night, this place is jammed, not by tourists but by local Dubs, which tells you how good the food is.

71–72 S. Great George's St., Dublin 2. ℂ 01/475-5001. Reservations only for parties of 4 or more persons. Main courses €11–€18 ($13–$22). MC, V. Sun–Wed 12:30–11pm; Thurs–Sat 12:30–11:30pm. Bus: 50, 50A, 54, 56, or 77.

INEXPENSIVE

Café Gertrude *💉💉* MODERN CONTINENTAL   Here's an easygoing little oasis of calm amid boisterous Temple Bar. The interior is hip in an artsy kind of way—buttercup yellow walls, lilac trim on the doorjambs and window frames, simple pine floorboards, a folk guitar playing on the stereo, and a few pieces of modern art hung on the otherwise plain walls. The same menu runs all day—all simple stuff, executed with care: toasted bagel with fresh smoked salmon, cream cheese, and onion; potato cake grilled with herb and onion, topped with bacon, smoked cheese, and salsa; panini of chicken breast, roasted sweet peppers, and mozzarella on focaccia, grilled until it's a gloppy treat.

3–4 Bedford Row, Dublin 2. ℂ 01/677-9043. Main courses from €5 ($6). 2-course early-bird dinner €13 ($16). MC, V. Daily 9am–5pm. Bus: 21A, 78A, or 78B.

Irish Film Centre Cafe Bar *💉* IRISH/INTERNATIONAL One of the most popular drinking spots in Temple Bar, the hip Cafe Bar (in the lobby of the city's coolest place to grab a movie) features an excellent, affordable menu that changes daily. A vegetarian and Middle Eastern menu is available for both lunch and dinner. The weekend entertainment usually includes music or comedy.

6 Eustace St., Temple Bar, Dublin 2. ℂ 01/677-8788. Lunch and dinner €6–€10 ($7.20–$12). MC, V. Mon–Fri 12:30–3pm; Sat–Sun 1–3pm; daily 6–9pm. Bus: 21A, 78A, or 78B.

3 St. Stephen's Green/Grafton Street Area

VERY EXPENSIVE

One Pico *💉💉💉* MODERN EUROPEAN   About a 5-minute walk from Stephen's Green, on a wee lane off Dawson Street, is the restaurant (still in its infancy) that is launching an empire. Since opening One Pico, chef-owner Eamonn O'Reilly has opened two other popular Dublin bistros, but this one remains the most focused and best. (Let's hope his peripheral ventures don't distract him from the stove too often.) This is a sophisticated, grown-up, classy place, with excellent service and fantastic food. Favorite dishes include a starter of seared foie gras with pineapple tatin; memorable main dishes include scallops with baby beetroot and lime, confit of duck with fig tatin, and beef with Roquefort ravioli. For dessert, a caramelized lemon tart is the end to a near-perfect meal.

5–6 Molesworth Place, Schoolhouse Lane, Dublin 2. ⓒ 01/676-0300. www. onepico.com. Reservations required. Fixed-price 2-course lunch €25 ($30), 3-course lunch €30 ($36); dinner main courses €20–€30 ($24–$36). AE, DC, MC, V. Mon–Sat 12:30–2:30pm and 6–11pm. DART: Pearse. Bus: 10, 11A, 11B, 13, or 20B.

EXPENSIVE

Cooke's Café 🏩🏩 MODERN CLASSIC   Named for owner and chef Johnny Cooke, this shop-front restaurant is a longtime Dublin favorite. The food is all about classic dishes executed with just the right amount of originality. Specialties include a fabulous black-bean soup; grilled duck with pancetta, Marsala balsamic sauce, and wilted endive; sautéed brill and Dover sole with capers and croutons; and baked grouper with a ragout of mussels, clams, artichokes, and tomatoes. The open kitchen and Mediterranean murals dominate the cafe, and on weekend evenings they open the upstairs Rhino Room, where there's a terrific New York–grill atmosphere. In fine weather you can sit outside on the terrace.

14 S. William St., Dublin 2. ⓒ 01/679-0536. Reservations required. Fixed-price lunch menu €20 ($24); early-bird menu (6–7pm) €20 ($24); dinner main courses €14–€26 ($17–$31). AE, DC, MC, V. Daily 12:30–3pm; Mon–Sat 6–11pm; Sun 6–10pm. DART: Tara St. Bus: 16A, 19A, 22A, 55, or 83.

EXPENSIVE/MODERATE

Aya @ Brown Thomas 🏩🏩🏩 JAPANESE   This buzzy, fashionable annex to Dublin's poshest department store (actually, it's just across the street on Clarendon St.) is very much a good-time destination for chic Dubliners, with its conveyor-belt sushi bar. The good news is that, beyond the trendiness, the food here is damn good. Lunch offers all the classics—tempura, gyoza, toritatsuta, and, of course, plenty of sushi—while the dinner menu expands to include yakitori, steaks, and noodle salads. Come for dinner Sunday through Tuesday for the Sushi55 special: all you can eat, including one complimentary drink, for €24 ($29).

49–52 Clarendon St., Dublin 2. ⓒ 01/677-1544. Reservations recommended for dinner. Lunch averages €15 ($18); dinner averages €25 ($30). AE, DC, MC, V. Mon–Sat 10:30am–11pm; Sun noon–10pm. DART: Tara St. Bus: 16A, 19A, 22A, 55, or 83.

La Mère Zou 🍴 FRENCH   Imagine a country house in Provence where you could get superb Gallic cooking *en famille.* Chef Eric Tydgadt has created a warm, comfortable basement-level bistro in which to savor his fresh French country specialties. The emphasis is on perfectly cooked food accompanied by persuasive but "unarmed" sauces served in an unpretentious manner. Mussels are a house specialty, with an array of poultry, seafood, lamb, and game offerings. The quality of ingredients and attention to enhancing the flavor of all dishes is consistent from appetizers to dessert. The excellent wine list favors the French, and includes several €14 ($17) house wines.

22 St. Stephen's Green, Dublin 2. ☎ 01/661-6669. Reservations recommended. Fixed-price lunch €20 ($24); early-bird dinner menu €24 ($29); dinner main courses €20–€28 ($24–$34). AE, DC, MC, V. Mon–Fri 12:30–2:30pm; Mon–Thurs 6–10:30pm; Fri–Sat 6–11pm; Sun 6–9:30pm. DART: Pearse. Bus: 10, 11A, 11B, 13, or 20B.

MODERATE

Café Mao 🍴🍴🍴 ASIAN   Dubliners have beaten a path to this place since it opened a few years back, and it's already become something of an icon. This is where to go when you feel like Asian cooking laced with a fun and exhilarating attitude. An exposed kitchen lines an entire wall, and the rest of the space is wide open—fantastic for people-watching on weekends. The menu reads like a "best of Asia": Thai fish cakes, nasi goreng, chicken hoi sin, salmon ramen. Everything is well prepared and delicious, so you can't go wrong.

2 Chatham Row, Dublin 2. ☎ 01/670-4899. Reservations recommended. Main courses €13–€18 ($16–$22). AE, MC, V. Mon–Wed noon–10:30pm; Thurs–Sat noon–11:30pm; Sun 1–10pm. DART: Pearse. Bus: 10, 11A, 11B, 13, or 20B.

Fitzers Café 🍴 INTERNATIONAL   This is one branch of a chain of winning cafes that serve up excellent, up-to-date, and reasonably priced food. Nestled on a street known for its bookshops, this bright, airy Irish-style bistro has a multiwindowed facade and modern decor. Choices range from chicken breast with hot chile cream sauce or brochette of lamb tandoori with mild curry sauce to gratin of smoked cod. There are also tempting vegetarian dishes made from organic produce. Fitzers has two other Dublin locations: just a few blocks away at the National Gallery, Merrion Square West (☎ 01/661-4496), and at Temple Bar Square (☎ 01/679-0440). As with all chains, consistency is the operative word—the same menu, the same decor theme, and the same good service at each location.

51 Dawson St., Dublin 2. ☎ 01/677-1155. Dinner main courses €17–€25 ($21–$30). AE, DC, MC, V. Daily 11:30am–10:30pm. Closed Dec 24–27 and Good Friday. DART: Pearse. Bus: 10, 11A, 11B, 13, or 20B.

INEXPENSIVE
Bewley's Café *Overrated* TRADITIONAL CAFE/TEAROOM

Bewley's, a three-story landmark on Grafton Street, has been around forever (more specifically, since 1840) and is so ingrained in the Irish identity that you have to wonder whether people go out of habit rather than desire. Not that the place isn't busy. It's always bustling with the clink of teapots and hum of customers, but the atmosphere is somehow listless rather than buzzy. The interior is a traditional, mellow mix of dark wood, amber glass, and deep red velvet banquettes—a look that would be deemed welcoming if the food was great. Unfortunately, the scones, pies, and cakes are surprisingly mediocre, and the sandwiches, pasta dishes, sausages, chips, and casseroles are no better.

Go once, because Bewley's is a quintessential hit of real Dublin, and the people-watching is good. But go only once, and stick to coffee and tea.

78–79 Grafton St., Dublin 2. ℂ **01/679-4085.** Homemade soup €3 ($3.60); lunch main courses €4–€9 ($4.80–$11); lunch specials from €6.50 ($8.10); dinner main courses from €15 ($18). AE, DC, MC, V. Mon–Sat 7:30am–7pm; Sun 8:30am–6pm (continuous service for breakfast, hot food, and snacks). Bus: Any city-center bus.

Cafe Bell *Value* IRISH/SELF-SERVICE

In the cobbled courtyard of early-19th-century St. Teresa's Church, this serene little place is one of a handful of dining options springing up in historic or ecclesiastical surroundings. With high ceilings and an old-world decor, Cafe Bell is a welcome contrast to the bustle of Grafton Street a block away. The menu changes daily but usually includes very good homemade soups, sandwiches, salads, quiches, lasagna, sausage rolls, hot scones, and other baked goods.

St. Teresa's Courtyard, Clarendon St., Dublin 2. ℂ **01/677-7645.** All items €4–€8 ($4.80–$9.60). No credit cards. Mon–Sat 9am–5:30pm. Bus: 16, 16A, 19, 19A, 22A, 55, or 83.

Caifé Trí-D *Value* SANDWICHES

This unpretentious little eatery just steps from the wrought-iron rails of the Trinity College campus is a great find on a street known for its bookstores. This is a heart-on-its-sleeve Irish-language hangout with a bilingual menu half-written as *gaeilge* (in Irish Gaelic). *Ceapairí* and *filltéáin* (sandwiches and wraps) tempt with simple but interesting ingredients, like the winning combination of sharp Dubliner cheese, tomato relish, lettuce, and tomato. Try brie and cranberry sauce on toasted brown bread, and you'll be plotting a recreation in your own kitchen. The homemade soup of the day—maybe mushroom and spinach or carrot and coriander—comes with a chunky slab of homemade soda bread and butter.

3 Dawson St., Dublin 2. ℰ 01/474-1054. Soups, sandwiches, and wraps under €5 ($6). No credit cards. Mon–Sat 9am–6pm. Bus: Any city-center bus.

Cornucopia Wholefood Restaurant 🎯 *Value* ORGANIC/VEG-ETARIAN   This little cafe just off Grafton Street is one of the best vegetarian restaurants in the city, and also serves wholesome meals for people on various restricted diets (vegan, nondairy, low sodium, low fat). Soups are particularly good here, as is the baked lasagna made with eggplant. Predictably, the clientele is made up mainly of Birkenstock-wearing, backpack-toting 20-somethings.

Tips Picnic, Anyone?

The parks of Dublin offer plenty of sylvan settings for a picnic lunch; so feel free to park it on a bench, or pick a grassy patch and spread a blanket. In particular, try **St. Stephen's Green** at lunchtime (in the summer there are open-air band concerts), the **Phoenix Park,** and **Merrion Square.** You can also take a ride on the DART to the suburbs of **Dun Laoghaire, Dalkey, Killiney,** and **Bray** (to the south) or **Howth** (to the north) and picnic along a bayfront pier or promenade.

In recent years, some fine delicatessens and gourmet food shops—ideal for picnic fare—have sprung up. For the best selection of fixings, try any of the following. **Gruel,** 69 Dame St., Dublin 2 (ℰ **01/670-7119**), has a cult following for its hot roasted gourmet sandwiches that change daily. **Garlic Kitchen,** 49 Francis St., Dublin 8 (ℰ **01/454-4912**), has gourmet prepared food to go, from salmon en croûte to pastries filled with meats or vegetables, pâtés, quiches, sausage rolls, and homemade pies, breads, and cakes. **Magills Delicatessen,** 14 Clarendon St., Dublin 2 (ℰ **01/671-3830**), offers Asian and Continental delicacies, meats, cheeses, spices, and salads. For a fine selection of Irish cheeses, luncheon meat, and other delicacies, seek out **Sheridan's Cheesemongers,** 11 S. Anne St., Dublin 2 (ℰ **01/679-3143**), perhaps the best of Dublin's cheese emporiums, or the **Big Cheese Company,** St. Andrews Lane, Dublin 2 (ℰ **01/671-1399**).

19 Wicklow St., Dublin 2. ℰ **01/677-7583**. Main courses €4–€10 ($4.80–$12). MC, V. Mon–Thurs 8am–7pm; Fri–Sat 8am–10pm. Bus: Any city-center bus.

Mimo Cafe 𝕣𝕣 (Value) MODERN CONTINENTAL   Take a shopping break at this chic little cafe in the tony Powerscourt Townhouse minimall. It's a wonderfully classy and surprisingly budget-minded place to stop for terrific salads, pasta dishes, and inventive sandwiches. Plop down in one of the leather sofas or armchairs, and order the tasty salad of marinated flat mushrooms, piled high atop a bed of crisp green beans and Parmesan shavings with lemon-and-thyme dressing, and served with toasted *ciabatta* (bread). Or go for the warm goat's cheese crostini with caramelized figs, wild honey, and beetroot dressing. Everything is yummy and nicely presented. A piano player is a civilized touch on Thursday and Friday afternoons.

Powerscourt Townhouse, Dublin 2. ℰ **01/674-6712**. Main courses €8–€10 ($9.60–$12). MC, V. Daily noon–5:30pm. Bus: Any city-center bus.

4 Fitzwilliam Square/Merrion Square Area

VERY EXPENSIVE

L'Ecrivain 𝕣𝕣𝕣 FRENCH   This is one of Dublin's truly exceptional restaurants, from start to finish. The atmosphere is relaxed, welcoming, and unpretentious, and chef Derry Clarke's food is extraordinary. You can dine on the garden terrace, weather permitting, or in the chic dining rooms. Each course seems to receive the same devoted attention, and most consist of traditional "best of Irish" ingredients, prepared without dense sauces. The pan-flared wild sea bass with mango and red-pepper dressing and the entrecôte with caramelized onion are perfectly prepared and elegantly presented. Clarke's roast Barbary duck, served with honey and thyme navet and smoked bacon-infused mashed potatoes, is legendary. Of the out-of-this-world desserts, the crème brûlée here may be the best outside of France. The two-course lunch menu presents a particularly good opportunity to enjoy fabulous food without breaking your budget.

109 Lower Baggot St., Dublin 2. ℰ **01/661-1919**. www.lecrivain.com. Reservations required. Fixed-price 2-course lunch €30 ($36), 3-course lunch €40 ($48); fixed-price 4-course dinner €65 ($78); dinner main courses €37–€42 ($45–$51). 10% service charge. AE, DC, MC, V. Mon–Fri 12:30–2pm; Mon–Sat 7–10:30pm. Bus: 10.

Restaurant Patrick Guilbaud 𝕣𝕣 FRENCH   Ireland's most award-winning restaurant (including two Michelin stars) is ensconced in elegant quarters at the Merrion Hotel. The menu features such dishes as roasted West Cork turbot, honey-roasted quail, wild sea bass with ragout of mussels, and pan-fried foie gras with marinated red cabbage in a raspberry vinaigrette. If you're unde-cided, order the scrumptious ravioli of lobster with coconut cream, and finish with the *assiette gourmande au chocolat* (five small hot and cold chocolate desserts).

In the Merrion Hotel, 21 Upper Merrion St., Dublin 2. ℂ 01/676-4192. Reserva-tions required. Fixed-price 2-course lunch €30 ($36); fixed-price 3-course lunch €45 ($54); fixed-price dinner €110 ($133). Dinner main courses €35–€50 ($42–$60). AE, DC, MC, V. Tues–Sat 12:30–2:15pm and 7–10:15pm. DART: Westland Row. Bus: 10, 11A, 11B, 13, or 20B.

EXPENSIVE

Dobbins Wine Bistro 🕭🕭 BISTRO   This is a foodie's all-time favorite haunt. Almost hidden in a lane between Upper and Lower Mount streets, this hip, friendly bistro is a haven for inventive Con-tinental cuisine. The menu changes often, but usually includes such items as duckling with orange and port sauce; steamed *paupiette* of black sole with salmon, crab, and prawn filling; pan-fried veal kid-neys in pastry; and filet of beef topped with crispy herb bread crumbs with shallot and Madeira sauce. You'll have a choice of sit-ting in the bistro, with checkered tablecloths and sawdust on the floor, or on the atrium patio.

15 Stephen's Lane (off Upper Mount St.), Dublin 2. ℂ 01/676-4679. Reservations recommended. Dinner main courses €14–€23 ($17–$28). AE, DC, MC, V. Mon–Fri 12:30–2:30pm; Tues–Sat 7:30–10:30pm. DART: Pearse. Bus: 5, 7A, 8, 46, or 84.

Ely 🕭🕭 ORGANIC BISTRO   This is one of our favorite new entries this year: a cosmopolitan, clever place that does everything right. Erik Robson is originally from County Clare, and sources all its organic produce from his family farm there. The food is simple but expertly prepared, the crowd enthusiastic, the service attentive. Think fantastic "bangers and mash" (sausages and mashed spuds), delicious Clare oysters, superb Irish stew, and a great selection of cheeses from Sheridan's. Factor in a smashing wine list and you've got a winner.

22 Ely Place (off Merrion Row), Dublin 2. ℂ 01/676-8986. Reservations recom-mended. Dinner main courses €14–€23 ($17–$28). AE, DC, MC, V. Mon–Sat noon–3pm and 6–10:30pm. Bus: 7, 7A, 8, 10, 11, or 13.

INEXPENSIVE

National Museum Café 🕭 CAFETERIA   This is a great place to step out of the rain, warm yourself, and then wander among the nation's treasures. The cafe is informal but has a certain elegance, thanks to an elaborate mosaic floor, enameled fireplace, marble tabletops, chandelier, and tall windows that look across a cobbled yard toward the National Library. Everything is made fresh: beef salad, chicken salad, quiche, an abundance of pastries. The soup of the day is often vegetarian, and quite good. Admission to the museum is free, so you can visit at your own pace, as often as your curiosity (or appetite) demands.

National Museum of Ireland, Kildare St., Dublin 2. ℭ 01/677-7444. Soup €3 ($3.60); lunch main courses under €8 ($9.60). MC, V. Tues–Sat 10am–5pm; Sun 2–5pm. Bus: 7, 7A, 8, 10, 11, or 13.

5 Ballsbridge/Embassy Row Area

EXPENSIVE

Roly's Bistro 🕼🕼 IRISH/INTERNATIONAL Opened in 1992, this two-story shop-front restaurant quickly became an institution. The recent departure of Roly Saul, who pioneered the venture, spurred former head chef Colin O'Daly to step up as owner. Even with the changes, the Roly's magic is still palpable. The head chef, Paul Cartwright, cooks the same kind of excellent, tummy-warming food you never get tired of: confit of duck with garlic mash, roasted venison, chicken-and-bean-sprout spring roll, pan-fried Dublin Bay prawns, game pie with chestnuts, wild-mushroom risotto. The main dining room, with a bright and airy decor and lots of windows, can be noisy when the house is full, but the nonsmoking section has a quiet enclave of booths laid out in an Orient Express style for those who prefer a quiet tête-à-tête. There's also an excellent array of international wines offered.

7 Ballsbridge Terrace, Dublin 4. ℭ 01/668-2611. Reservations required. Main courses €20–€27 ($24–$33); set-price lunch €19 ($23). AE, DC, MC, V. Daily noon–3pm and 6–10pm. DART to Lansdowne Rd. Station. Bus: 5, 6, 7, 8, 18, or 45.

MODERATE

The French Paradox 🕼🕼 *Value* WINE BAR Just what tony Dublin 4 needed: A price-conscious, darling little bistro-cum–*bar de vin* that's endeared itself to everyone in the city. The wine's the thing here, so relax with a bottle of bordeaux or Côte du Rhone and whatever nibbles you like from the menu. There's a lovely cheese plate named for West Cork cheese maker Bill Hogan, superb Iberico hams from Spain, or, if you're more hungry, the delicious bistro stalwart of confit of duck with vegetables. Simply delicious.

53 Shelbourne Rd., Dublin 4. ℭ 01/660-4068. www.thefrenchparadox.com. Reservations recommended. All items €10–€20 ($12–$24). Main dishes come with glass of wine. AE, MC, V. Mon–Sat noon–3pm and 2 evening sittings at 6 and 9pm. DART: Lansdowne Rd. Bus: 5, 6, 7, 8, 18, or 45.

Ballsbridge/Embassy Row Area Dining

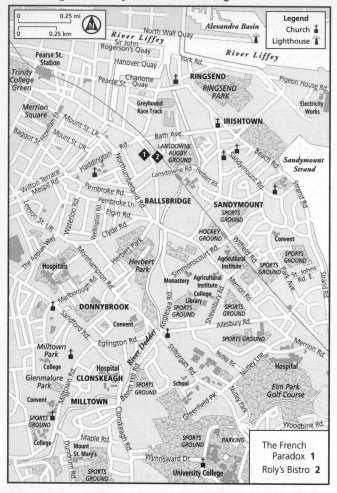

Legend

Church ✝
Lighthouse 🗼

The French Paradox 1
Roly's Bistro 2

6 O'Connell Street Area/North of the Liffey

EXPENSIVE

Halo 🎭🎭 FRENCH/FUSION   This is easily one of the hippest, hottest, coolest, most stylish places to eat in Dublin—so book your table before you leave home. In the early days, this place attracted a clientele that was snobbish and self-conscious, but thankfully the posers have disappeared. Now the room is buzzy and stylish without any pretentiousness—the perfect backdrop for chef Jean-Michel Poulot's fabulous cooking. The food is all about French fusion—snazzy, mind-blowing combinations of taste and texture that manage to be elegant instead of just far-flung. Consider the curried king scallops with lime potato, fennel, mizuna, and ginger vinaigrette. Or the baked goat's cheese wrapped in Parma ham with mizuna salad. Eating at Halo is an intense experience for all of your senses, and one that should be savored.

Morrison Hotel, Ormond Quay, Dublin 1. ℂ 01/878-2999. Reservations required. Dinner main courses €32–€45 ($39–$54). AE, MC, V. Daily 7–10:30pm; Sat–Sun noon–3:30pm. DART: Connolly. Bus: 70 or 80.

MODERATE

101 Talbot ☏☏ INTERNATIONAL This modest, friendly, second-floor eatery over a camping shop is a bright beacon of great cooking in a neighborhood that's otherwise culinarily challenged. The menu features light, healthy foods, with a strong emphasis on vegetarian dishes. Main dishes include seared filet of tuna with mango cardamom salsa, roast duck breast with plum-and-ginger sauce, Halloumi cheese and mushroom brochette served with couscous and raita, and a blue cheese and pistachio cream sauce on pasta. The dinner menu changes weekly. The dining room is bright and casually funky, with contemporary Irish art on display, big windows, yellow rag-rolled walls, ash-topped tables, and newspapers to read. Espresso and cappuccino are always available, and there is a full bar. The restaurant is convenient to the Abbey Theatre.

101 Talbot St. (at Talbot Lane near Marlborough St.), Dublin 1. ℂ 01/874-5011. Reservations recommended. Early-bird dinner €21 ($25); dinner main courses €14–€19 ($17–$23). AE, MC, V. Tues–Sat 5–11pm. DART: Connolly. Bus: 27A, 31A, 31B, 32A, 32B, 42B, 42C, 43, or 44A.

INEXPENSIVE

Beshoffs ☏ FISH AND CHIPS The Beshoff name is synonymous with fresh fish in Dublin. Ivan Beshoff emigrated here from Odessa, Russia, in 1913 and started a fish business that developed into this top-notch fish-and-chips eatery. Recently renovated in Victorian style, it has an informal atmosphere and a simple self-service menu. Crisp chips are served with a choice of fresh fish, from the original recipe of cod to classier variations using salmon, shark, prawns, and other local sea fare—some days as many as 20 varieties. The potatoes are grown on a 120-hectare (300-acre) farm in Tipperary and freshly cut each day. A second shop is just south of the Liffey at 14 Westmoreland St., Dublin 2 (ℂ 01/677-8026).

6 Upper O'Connell St., Dublin 1. ℭ **01/872-4400.** All items €3–€7 ($3.60–$8.45). No credit cards. Mon–Sat 10am–9pm; Sun noon–9pm. DART: Tara St. Bus: Any city-center bus.

Epicurean Food Hall ☆☆ GOURMET FOOD COURT   This wonderful food hall houses a wide variety of artisan produce, delicious local Irish delicacies, and regional specialties. Favorites include: Caviston's, Dublin's premier deli, for smoked salmon and seafood; Itsabagel, for its delicious bagels, imported from H&H Bagels in New York City; Crème de la Crème, for its French-style pastries and cakes; Missy and Mandy's, for its American-style ice cream; Nectar, for its plethora of healthy juice drinks; and Aroma Bistro for Italian paninis. There is limited seating but this place gets uncomfortably jammed during lunchtime midweek, so go midmorning or afternoon.

Middle Abbey St., Dublin 1. No phone. All items €2–€12 ($2.40–$14). No credit cards. Mon–Sat 10am–6pm. Bus: 70 or 80.

Soup Dragon ☆☆ SOUPS   Soup has become the healthy, hip alternative to stodgy sandwiches and fast food, and the Soup Dragon leads the way for cheap and cheerful chow-downs in Dublin. It's a tiny place, with less than a dozen stools alongside a bar, but big on drama. Think blue walls, black and red mirrors, orange slices and spice sticks flowing out of giant jugs, and huge flower-filled vases. The menu changes daily but usually features a few traditional choices (potato and leek, carrot and coriander) as well as the more exotic (curried parsnip and *sag aloo,* a spicy Indian spinach-and-potato concoction). It's also a good place for dessert. Try the bread-and-butter pudding or the yummy banana bread.

168 Capel St., Dublin 1. ℭ **01/872-3277.** All items €3–€8 ($3.60–$9.60). MC, V. Mon–Sat 8am–5:30pm; Sun 1–6pm. Bus: 70 or 80.

The Winding Stair ☆ HEALTH   Retreat from the bustle of the north side's busy quays into this darling bookshop's self-service cafe, and indulge in a snack while browsing for secondhand gems. There are three floors—one smoke-free, and each chock-full of used books (from novels, plays, and poetry to history, art, music, and sports) connected by a winding 18th-century staircase. (There's also an elevator available.) Tall, wide windows provide expansive views of the Ha'penny Bridge and River Liffey. The food is simple and healthy—sandwiches made with additive-free meats or fruits (such as banana and honey), organic salads, homemade soups, and natural juices. Evening events include poetry readings and recitals.

40 Lower Ormond Quay, Dublin 1. ℭ **01/873-3292.** All items €2–€8 ($2.40–$9.60). AE, MC, V. Mon–Sat 9:30am–6pm; Sun 1–6pm. Bus: 70 or 80.

5

Seeing the Sights

Dublin is a city of many moods and landscapes. There are medieval churches and imposing castles, graceful Georgian squares and lantern-lit lanes, broad boulevards and crowded bridges, picturesque parks and pedestrian walkways, intriguing museums and markets, gardens and galleries, and—if you have any energy left after all that—electric nightlife. Enjoy!

1 The Top Attractions

Áras an Uachtaráin (The Irish White House) 𝄐 Áras an Uachtaráin (Irish for "House of the President") was once the Viceregal Lodge, the summer retreat of the British viceroy, whose ordinary digs were in Dublin Castle. From what were never humble beginnings, the original 1751 country house was expanded several times, gradually accumulating splendor. President Mary McAleese recently opened her home to visitors; guided tours originate at the Phoenix Park Visitors Centre every Saturday. After an introductory historical film, a bus brings visitors to and from Áras an Uachtaráin. The focus of the tour is the state reception rooms. The entire tour lasts 1 hour. Only 525 tickets are given out, first-come, first-served; arrive before 1:30pm, especially in summer.

Note: For security reasons, no backpacks, travel bags, strollers, buggies, cameras, or mobile phones are allowed on the tour. No smoking, eating, or drinking are permitted, and no visitor toilets are available once the tour begins.

In Phoenix Park, Dublin 7. © 01/670-9155. Free admission. Sat 10:30am–4:30pm. Closed Dec 24–26. Same-day tickets issued at Phoenix Park (see later in this chapter). Bus: 10, 37, or 39.

The Book of Kells 𝄐𝄐𝄐 The jewel in Ireland's tourism crown is the Book of Kells, a magnificent manuscript of the four Gospels, from around A.D. 800, with elaborate scripting and illumination. This famous treasure and other early Christian manuscripts are on permanent public view at Trinity College, in the Colonnades, an exhibition area on the ground floor of the Old Library. Also housed

Dublin Attractions

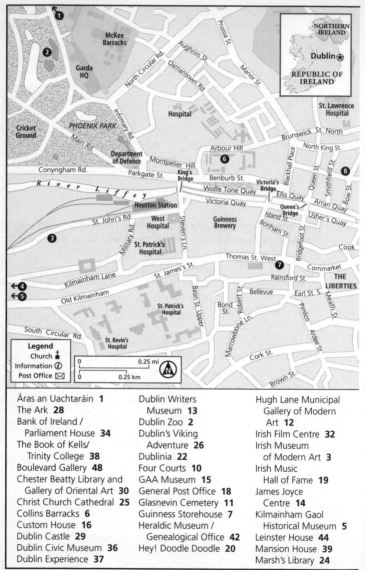

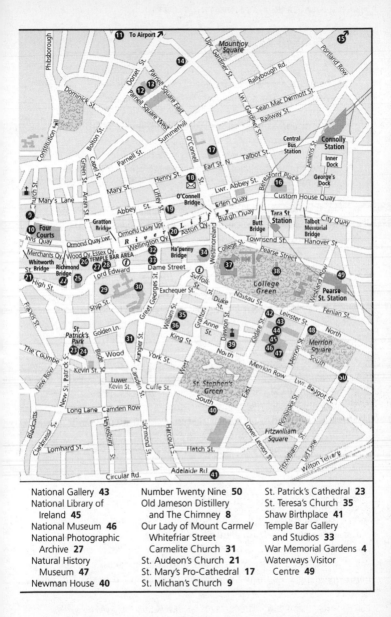

The Book of Kells

The Book of Kells is a large-format illuminated manuscript of the four Gospels in Latin, dated on comparative grounds to about A.D. 800. It's impossible to be more precise about its date because some leaves from the end of the book, where such information was normally recorded, are missing. It is the most majestic work of art to survive from the early centuries of Celtic Christianity, and has often been described as "the most beautiful book in the world." A team of talented scribes and artists working in a monastic scriptorium produced the book.

Its fascination derives from the dignified but elusive character of its main motifs, and the astonishing variety and complexity of the linear ornamentation that adorns every one of its 680 pages. Its creators managed to combine new artistic influences from Eastern Christendom with the traditional interlace patterning of Celtic metalwork to produce what Gerald of Wales, a 13th-century chronicler, called "the work not of men, but of angels." The message sometimes may not be easy to read, but everyone can admire the elegant precision of the standard script, the subtlety of the color harmonies, and the exuberant vitality of the human and animal ornamentation.

The book was certainly in the possession of the Columban monastery of Kells, a town in County Meath, during most of the Middle Ages. The Annals of Ulster record its theft from the western sacristy of the stone-built monastic church in 1007, and relate that it was recovered 2 to 3 months later from "under the sod," without the jewel-encrusted silver

in the Old Library is the **Dublin Experience** (p. 106), an excellent multimedia introduction to the history and people of Dublin. The oldest university in Ireland, Trinity was founded in 1592 by Queen Elizabeth I. It occupies a beautiful 16-hectare (40-acre) site just south of the River Liffey, with cobbled squares, gardens, a picturesque quadrangle, and buildings dating from the 17th to the 20th centuries.

College Green, Dublin 2. ℂ **01/608-2320.** http://www.tcd.ie/Library/Visitors/kells. htm. Free admission to college grounds. €7.20 ($9) adults, €6.50 ($7.85) seniors/ students, €11 ($13) families, free for children under 12. Combination tickets for the shrine in which such prestigious books were kept. Whether it was originally created in Kells remains an unresolved question. Some authorities think that it might have been begun, if not completed, in the great monastery founded by St. Columba himself (in about 561) on the island of Iona off the west coast of Scotland. Iona had a famous scriptorium and remained the headquarters of the Columban monastic system until the early years of the 9th century. It then became an untenable location because of repeated Viking raids, and in 807 a remnant of the monastic community retreated to the Irish mainland to build a new headquarters at Kells. It has been suggested that the great Gospel book that we call "of Kells" may have been started on Iona, possibly to mark the bicentenary of St. Columba's death in 797, and later transferred to Kells for completion. But it is also possible to argue that the work was entirely done in Kells, and that its object was to equip the monastery with a great new book to stand on the high altar of the new foundation.

In the medieval period, the book was (wrongly) regarded as the work of St. Columba himself and was known as the "great Gospel book of Colum Cille" (Colum of the Churches). The designation "Book of Kells" seems to have originated with the famous biblical scholar James Ussher, who made a study of its original Latin text in the 1620s. The gift shop in the Colonnades of the Old Library in Trinity College stocks a large selection of illustrative materials relating to the Book of Kells.

—*J. V. Luce, Trinity College and the Royal Irish Academy*

Library and Dublin Experience also available. Mon–Sat 9:30am–5pm; Sun noon–4:30pm (opens at 9:30am June–Sept).

Christ Church Cathedral ⊛⊛   Standing on high ground in the oldest part of the city, this cathedral is one of Dublin's finest historic buildings. It dates from 1038, when Sitric, Danish king of Dublin, built the first wooden Christ Church here. In 1171 the original simple foundation was extended into a cruciform and rebuilt in stone by Strongbow. The present structure dates mainly from 1871 to 1878, when a huge restoration took place. Highlights of the interior include magnificent stonework and graceful pointed arches, with delicately chiseled supporting columns. This is the mother church for the diocese of Dublin and Glendalough of the Church of Ireland. The Treasury in the crypt is open to the public, and you can hear bells pealing in the belfry.

Christ Church Place, Dublin 8. ✆ **01/677-8099**. Admission €5 ($6) adults, €2.50 ($3) students and children under 15. Daily 10am–5:30pm. Closed Dec 26. Bus: 21A, 50, 50A, 78, 78A, or 78B.

Collins Barracks   Officially part of the National Museum, Collins Barracks is the oldest military barracks in Europe. Even if it were empty, it would be well worth a visit for the structure itself, a splendidly restored early-18th-century masterwork by Colonel Thomas Burgh, Ireland's chief engineer and surveyor general under Queen Anne. The collection housed here focuses on the decorative arts. Most notable is the extraordinary display of Irish silver and furniture. Until the acquisition of this vast space, only a fraction of the National Museum's collection could be displayed, but that is changing, and more and more treasures find their way here. It is a prime site for touring exhibitions, so consult the *Event Guide* for details. There is also a cafe and gift shop on the premises.

Benburb St., Dublin 7. ✆ **01/677-7444**. Free admission. Tours (hours vary) €2 ($2.40) adults, free for seniors and children. Tues–Sat 10am–5pm; Sun 2–5pm. Bus: 34, 70, or 80.

Dublin Castle 👁👁   Built between 1208 and 1220, this complex represents some of the oldest surviving architecture in the city. It was the center of British power in Ireland for more than 7 centuries, until the new Irish government took it over in 1922. Film buffs might recognize the castle's courtyard as a setting in the Neil Jordan film *Michael Collins*. Highlights include the 13th-century Record Tower; the State Apartments, once the residence of English viceroys; and the Chapel Royal, a 19th-century Gothic building with particularly fine plaster decoration and carved oak gallery fronts and fittings. The newest developments are the Undercroft, an excavated site on the grounds where an early Viking fortress stood, and the Treasury, built between 1712 and 1715 and believed to be the oldest surviving office building in Ireland. Also here are a craft shop, heritage center, and restaurant.

Palace St. (off Dame St.), Dublin 2. ✆ **01/677-7129**. Admission €4.50 ($5.40) adults, €3.25 ($3.90) seniors and students, €2 ($2.40) children under 12. No credit cards. Mon–Fri 10am–5pm; Sat–Sun and holidays 2–5pm. Guided tours every 20–25 min. Bus: 50, 50A, 54, 56A, 77, 77A, or 77B.

Dublin Writers Museum ★★   Housed in a stunning 18th-century Georgian mansion with splendid plasterwork and stained glass, the museum is itself an impressive reminder of the grandeur of the Irish literary tradition. A fine collection of personal manuscripts and mementos that belonged to Yeats, Joyce, Beckett, Behan, Shaw, Wilde, Swift, and Sheridan are among the items that celebrate the written word. One of the museum's rooms is devoted to children's literature.

18–19 Parnell Sq. N., Dublin 1. Ⓒ **01/872-2077.** Admission €6.25 ($7.55) adults; €2.25 ($2.70) seniors, students, and children; €18 ($21) families (2 adults and up to 4 children). AE, DC, MC, V. Mon–Sat 10am–5pm (until 6pm June–Aug); Sun and holidays 11am–5pm. DART to Connolly Station. Bus: 11, 13, 16, 16A, 22, or 22A.

Dublinia ★   What was Dublin like in medieval times? This historically accurate presentation of the Old City from 1170 to 1540 is re-created through a series of theme exhibits, spectacles, and experiences. Highlights include an illuminated Medieval Maze, complete with visual effects, background sounds, and aromas that lead you on a journey through time from the arrival of the Anglo-Normans in 1170 to the closure of the monasteries in the 1530s. Another segment depicts everyday life in medieval Dublin with a diorama, as well as a prototype of a 13th-century quay along the banks of the Liffey. The medieval Fayre displays the wares of merchants from all over Europe. You can try on a flattering new robe, or, if you're feeling vulnerable, stop in at the armorer's and be fitted for chain mail.

St. Michael's Hill, Christ Church, Dublin 8. Ⓒ **01/679-4611.** www.dublinia.ie. Admission €5.75 ($6.90) adults; €4.50 ($5.40) seniors, students, and children; €15 ($18) families. AE, MC, V. Apr–Sept daily 10am–5pm; Oct–Mar Mon–Sat 11am–4pm, Sun 10am–4:30pm. Bus: 50, 78A, or 123.

Hugh Lane Municipal Gallery of Modern Art ★   Housed in a finely restored 18th-century building known as Charlemont House, this gallery is situated next to the Dublin Writers Museum. It is named after Hugh Lane, an Irish art connoisseur who was killed during the sinking of the *Lusitania* in 1915 and who willed his collection (including works by Courbet, Manet, Monet, and Corot) to be shared between the government of Ireland and the National Gallery of London. With the Lane collection as its nucleus, this gallery also contains paintings from the Impressionist and post-Impressionist traditions, sculptures by Rodin, stained glass, and works by modern Irish artists. In 2001 the museum opened the studio of Irish painter

Francis Bacon; it was moved piece by piece from Bacon's original studio and reconstructed at the museum. The bookshop is considered the best art bookshop in the city.

Parnell Sq. N., Dublin 1. ℂ 01/874-1903. Fax 01/872-2182. www.hughlane.ie. Free admission to museum; Francis Bacon studio €7 ($8.45) adults, €3.50 ($4.20) students. MC, V. Tues–Thurs 9:30am–6pm; Fri–Sat 9:30am–5pm; Sun 11am–5pm. DART to Connolly or Tara stations. Bus: 3, 10, 11, 13, 16, or 19.

Kilmainham Gaol Historical Museum 𝄞

This is a key sight for anyone interested in Ireland's struggle for independence from British rule. Within these walls political prisoners were incarcerated, tortured, and killed from 1796 until 1924, when President Eamon de Valera left as its final prisoner. To walk along these corridors, through the exercise yard, or into the main compound is a moving experience that lingers hauntingly in the memory. *Note:* The **War Memorial Gardens** (ℂ **01/677-0236**), along the banks of the Liffey, are a 5-minute walk from Kilmainham Gaol. The gardens were designed by the famous British architect Sir Edwin Lutyens (1869–1944), who completed a number of commissions for Irish houses and gardens. The gardens are fairly well maintained, and continue to present a moving testimony to Ireland's war dead. They are open weekdays 8am to dark, Saturday 10am to dark.

Kilmainham, Dublin 8. ℂ 01/453-5984. www.heritageireland.ie. Guided tour €5 ($6) adults, €3.50 ($4.20) seniors, €2 ($2.40) children, €11 ($13) families. AE, MC, V. Apr–Sept daily 9:30am–4:45pm; Oct–Mar Mon–Fri 9:30am–4pm, Sun 10am–4:45pm. Bus: 51B, 78A, or 79 at O'Connell Bridge.

National Gallery of Ireland 𝄞𝄞𝄞

This museum houses Ireland's national art collection, as well as a superb European collection of art spanning from the 14th to the 20th centuries. Every major European school of painting is represented, including fine selections by Italian Renaissance artists (especially Caravaggio's *The Taking of Christ*), French Impressionists, and Dutch 17th-century masters. The highlight of the Irish collection is the room dedicated to the mesmerizing works of Jack B. Yeats, brother of the poet W. B. Yeats. All public areas are wheelchair accessible. The museum has a fine gallery shop and an excellent self-service cafe run by Fitzers (p. 76 in chapter 4).

Merrion Sq. W., Dublin 2. ℂ 01/661-5133. Fax 01/661-5372. www.nationalgallery.ie. Free admission. Mon–Sat 9:30am–5:30pm; Thurs 9:30am–8:30pm; Sun noon–5pm. Free guided tours (meet in the Shaw Room) Sat 3pm, Sun 2, 3, and 4pm. Closed Good Friday and Dec 24–26. DART: Pearse. Bus: 5, 6, 7, 7A, 8, 10, 44, 47, 47B, 48A, or 62.

National Museum 𝄞𝄞𝄞

Established in 1890, this museum is a reflection of Ireland's heritage from 2000 B.C. to the present. It is the home of many of the country's greatest historical finds, including the Treasury exhibit, which toured the United States and Europe in the 1970s with the Ardagh Chalice, Tara Brooch, and Cross of Cong. Other highlights range from the artifacts from the Wood Quay excavations of the Old Dublin Settlements to "Or," an extensive exhibition of Irish Bronze Age gold ornaments dating from 2200 B.C. to 700 B.C. The museum has a shop and a cafe. *Note:* The National Museum encompasses two other attractions, Collins Barracks and the Natural History Museum; see their separate listings.

Kildare St. and Merrion St., Dublin 2. (C) **01/677-7444**. Free admission. Tours (hours vary) €2 ($2.40) adults, free for seniors and children. MC, V. Tues–Sat 10am–5pm; Sun 2–5pm. DART: Pearse. Bus: 7, 7A, 8, 10, 11, or 13.

Phoenix Park ★★ *(Kids)* Just 3.2km (2 miles) west of the city center, Phoenix Park, the largest urban park in Europe, is the playground of Dublin. A network of roads and quiet pedestrian walkways traverses its 704 hectares (1,760 acres), which are informally landscaped with ornamental gardens and nature trails. Avenues of trees, including oak, beech, pine, chestnut, and lime, separate broad expanses of grassland. The homes of the Irish president (see earlier in this chapter) and the U.S. ambassador are on the grounds, as is the Dublin Zoo (p. 107). Livestock graze peacefully on pasturelands, deer roam the forested areas, and horses romp on polo fields. The Phoenix Park Visitors Centre, adjacent to Ashtown Castle, offers exhibitions and an audiovisual presentation on the park's history. The cafe/restaurant is open 10am to 5pm weekdays, 10am to 6pm weekends. Free car parking is adjacent to the center.

Phoenix Park, Dublin 8. (C) **01/677-0095**. www.heritageireland.ie. Visitors Centre admission €2.75 ($3.30) adults, €2 ($2.40) seniors and students, €1.25 ($1.50) children, €9 ($11) families. June–Sept 10am–6pm (call for off-season hours). Bus: 37, 38, or 39.

St. Patrick's Cathedral ★ It is said that St. Patrick baptized converts on this site, and consequently a church has stood here since A.D. 450, making it the oldest Christian site in Dublin. The present cathedral dates from 1190, but because of a fire and 14th-century rebuilding, not much of the original foundation remains. It is mainly early English in style, with a square medieval tower that houses the largest ringing peal bells in Ireland, and an 18th-century spire. The 90m-long (300-ft.) interior makes it the longest church in the country. St. Patrick's is closely associated with Jonathan Swift, who was dean from 1713 to 1745 and whose tomb lies in the south aisle. Others memorialized within the cathedral include Turlough O'Carolan, a blind harpist and composer and the last of the great Irish bards; Michael William Balfe, the composer; and Douglas Hyde, the first president of Ireland. St. Patrick's is the national cathedral of the Church of Ireland.

21–50 Patrick's Close, Patrick St., Dublin 8. (✆ **01/475-4817.** Fax 01/454-6374. www.stpatrickscathedral.ie. Admission €4 ($4.80) adults, €3 ($3.60) students and seniors, €9 ($11) families. MC, V. Mon–Fri 9am–6pm year-round; Nov–Feb Sat 9am–5pm, Sun 9am–3pm. Closed except for services Dec 24–26 and Jan 1. Bus: 65, 65B, 50, 50A, 54, 54A, 56A, or 77.

2 More Attractions
ART GALLERIES & ART MUSEUMS

Boulevard Gallery   The fence around Merrion Square doubles as a display railing on summer weekends for an outdoor display of local art similar to those you'll find in Greenwich Village or Montmartre. Permits are given to local artists only for the sale of their own work, so this is a chance to meet an artist as well as to browse or buy.

Merrion Sq. W., Dublin 2. Free admission. May–Sept Sat–Sun 10:30am–6pm. DART: Pearse. Bus: 5, 7A, 8, 46, or 62.

Irish Film Centre ⅋   This art-house film institute is a hip hangout in Dublin's artsy Temple Bar district. The Irish Film Centre houses two cinemas, the Irish Film Archive, a library, a bookshop and cafe, and eight film-related organizations. Free screenings of *Flashback,* a history of Irish film since 1896, start at noon Wednesday to Sunday from June to mid-September. Follow with lunch in the cafe for a perfect midday outing.

6 Eustace St., Dublin 2. (✆ **01/679-5744,** or 01/679-3477 for cinema box office. www.irishfilm.ie. Free admission; cinema tickets €8 ($9.60). Centre daily 10am–11pm; cinemas daily 2–11pm; cinema box office daily 1:30–9pm. Bus: 21A, 78A, or 78B.

Irish Museum of Modern Art (IMMA) ⅋   Housed in the splendidly restored 17th-century edifice known as the Royal Hospital, IMMA is a showcase of Irish and international art from the latter half of the 20th century. The buildings and grounds also provide a venue for theatrical and musical events, overlapping the visual and performing arts. The galleries contain the work of Irish and international artists from the small but impressive permanent collection, with numerous temporary exhibitions. There's even a drawing room, where kids and parents can record their impressions of the museum with the crayons provided. The formal gardens, an important early feature of this magnificent structure, have been restored and are open to the public during museum hours. In 2000 a series of new galleries opened in the restored Deputy Master's House, in the northeast corner of the Royal Hospital site.

Military Rd., Kilmainham. ℂ **01/612-9900**. www.modernart.ie. Free admission. Tues–Sat 10am–5:30pm; Sun noon–5:30pm. Bus: 79 or 90.

Irish Music Hall of Fame The draw here is the exhaustive collection of memorabilia—much of it exclusive—chronicling the history of Irish music, from traditional and folk through pop, rock, and dance. There's loads of great stuff about U2, Van Morrison, Christy Moore, the Chieftains, the Dubliners, Thin Lizzy, Bob Geldof, Enya, the Cranberries, and Sinéad O'Connor, right up to BoyZone, Westlife, and Samantha Mumba.

57 Middle Abbey St., Dublin 1. ℂ **01/878-3345**. Free admission. Daily 10am–5:30pm. DART: Connolly. Bus: 25, 26, 34, 37, 38A, 39A, 39B, 66A, or 67A.

Temple Bar Gallery and Studios Founded in 1983 in the heart of Dublin's "Left Bank," this is one of the largest studio and gallery complexes in Europe. More than 30 Irish artists work here at a variety of contemporary visual arts, including sculpture, painting, printing, and photography. Only the gallery section is open to the public, but you can make an appointment in advance to view individual artists at work.

5–9 Temple Bar, Dublin 2. ℂ **01/671-0073**. Fax 01/677-7527. Free admission. Tues–Wed 11am–6pm; Thurs 11am–7pm; Sun 2–6pm. Bus: 21A, 46A, 46B, 51B, 51C, 68, 69, or 86.

BREWERIES/DISTILLERIES

Guinness Storehouse Founded in 1759, the Guinness Brewery is one of the world's largest breweries, producing a distinctive dark stout, famous for its thick, creamy head. Although tours of the brewery itself are no longer allowed, visitors are welcome to explore the adjacent Guinness Hopstore, a converted 19th-century four-story building. It houses the World of Guinness Exhibition, an audiovisual presentation showing how the stout is made; the Cooperage Gallery, displaying one of the finest collections of tools in Europe; the Gilroy Gallery, dedicated to the graphic design work of John Gilroy; and last but not least a bar where visitors can sample a glass of the famous brew. The brewery recently became home to the largest glass of stout in the world, roughly 60m (200 ft.) tall, whose head is in fact an observatory restaurant offering spectacular views of the city.

St. James's Gate, Dublin 8. © 01/408-4800. www.guinness-storehouse.com. Admission €14 ($16) adults, €9 ($11) seniors and students, €5 ($6) children 6–12, €30 ($36) families. AE, MC, V. Daily 9:30am–5pm. Guided tours every half-hour. Bus: 51B, 78A, or 123.

The Old Jameson Distillery ☆   This museum illustrates the history of Irish whiskey, known in Irish as *uisce beatha* (the water of life). Housed in a former distillery warehouse, it consists of a short introductory audiovisual presentation, an exhibition area, and a whiskey-making demonstration. At the end of the tour, visitors can sample whiskey at an in-house pub, where an array of fixed-price menus (for lunch, tea, or dinner) is available.

Note: A new added attraction here at Smithfield Village is **"The Chimney"** (see "The Bird's-Eye View" on p. 34), a ride to the top of a 56m (185-ft.) brick chimney built in 1895 and converted to support an observation chamber from which you'll enjoy unparalleled views of the city.

Bow St., Smithfield Village, Dublin 7. © 01/807-2355. Admission €8 ($9.60) adults, €6.25 ($7.55) students and seniors, €3.50 ($4.20) children, €20 ($24) families. Mon–Sat 9:30am–6pm (last tour at 5pm); Sun 11am–7pm. Bus: 67, 67A, 68, 69, 79, or 90.

CATHEDRALS & CHURCHES

St. Patrick's Cathedral and Christ Church Cathedral are listed earlier in section 1, "The Top Attractions."

Our Lady of Mount Carmel/Whitefriar Street Carmelite Church   One of the city's largest churches, this edifice was built between 1825 and 1827 on the site of a pre-Reformation Carmelite priory (1539) and an earlier Carmelite abbey (13th c.). It has since been extended, with an entrance from Aungier Street. This is a favorite place of pilgrimage, especially on February 14, because the body of St. Valentine is enshrined here (Pope Gregory XVI presented it to the church in 1836). The other highlight is the 15th-century black oak Madonna, Our Lady of Dublin.

56 Aungier St., Dublin 2. © 01/475-8821. Free admission. Mon and Wed–Fri 8am–6:30pm; Sat 8am–7pm; Sun 8am–7:30pm; Tues 8am–9:30pm. Bus: 16, 16A, 19, 19A, 83, 122, or 155.

St. Audoen's Church   Situated next to the only remaining gate of the Old City walls (dating from 1214), this church is said to be the only surviving medieval parish in Dublin. Although it is partly in ruins, significant parts have survived, including the west doorway, which dates from 1190, and the 13th-century nave. In addition, the 17th-century bell tower houses three bells cast in 1423, making them the oldest in Ireland. It's a Church of Ireland property, but nearby is another St. Audoen's Church, this one Catholic and dating from 1846. It was in the latter church that Father Flash Kavanagh used to say the world's fastest mass so that his congregation was out in time for the football matches. Since 1999, entrance to the ancient church is through the visitor center. The center's exhibition, relating the history of St. Audoen's, is self-guided, while visits to the church itself are by guided tour only.

Cornmarket (off High St.), Dublin 8. (𝄐 01/677-0088. Admission and tour €2 ($2.40) adults, €1.25 ($1.50) seniors, €1 ($1.20) children and students, €5.50 ($6.60) families. June–Sept daily 9:30am–5:30pm. Last admission 45 min. prior to closing. Bus: 21A, 78A, or 78B.

St. Mary's Pro-Cathedral   Because Dublin's two main cathedrals (Christ Church and St. Patrick's) belong to the Protestant Church of Ireland, St. Mary's is the closest the Catholics get to having their own. Tucked into a corner of a rather-unimpressive back street, it is in the heart of the city's north side and is considered the main Catholic parish church of the city center. Built between 1815 and 1825, it is of the Greek Revival Doric style, providing a distinct contrast to the Gothic Revival look of most other churches of the period. The exterior portico is modeled on the Temple of Theseus in Athens, with six Doric columns, while the Renaissance-style interior is patterned after the Church of St. Philip de Reule of Paris. The church is noted for its Palestrina Choir, which sings a Latin Mass every Sunday at 11am.

Cathedral and Marlborough sts., Dublin 1. (𝄐 01/874-5441. Free admission. Mon–Fri 8am–6pm; Sat–Sun 8am–7pm. DART: Connolly. Bus: 28, 29A, 30, 31A, 31B, 32A, 32B, or 44A.

St. Michan's Church   Built on the site of an early Danish chapel (1095), this 17th-century edifice claims to be the only parish church on the north side of the Liffey surviving from a Viking foundation. Now under the Church of Ireland banner, it has some fine interior woodwork and an organ (dated 1724) on which Handel is said to have played his *Messiah*. The church was completely and beautifully restored in 1998. A unique (and, let it be noted, most macabre) feature of this church is the underground burial vault. Because of the dry atmosphere, bodies have lain for centuries without showing signs of decomposition. The church is wheelchair accessible, but the vaults are not.

Church St., Dublin 7. (*C*) 01/872-4154. Free admission. Guided tour of church and vaults €3.50 ($4.20) adults, €3 ($3.60) seniors and students, €2.50 ($3) children under 12. Nov–Feb Mon–Fri 12:30–2:30pm, Sat 10am–1pm; Mar–Oct Mon–Fri 10am–12:45pm and 2–4:45pm, Sat 10am–1pm. Bus: 134 (from Abbey St.).

St. Teresa's Church   The foundation stone was laid in 1793, and the church was opened in 1810 by the Discalced Carmelite Fathers. After continuous enlargement, it reached its present form in 1876. This was the first post–Penal Law church to be legally and openly erected in Dublin, following the Catholic Relief Act of 1793. Among the artistic highlights are John Hogan's *Dead Christ,* a sculpture displayed beneath the altar, and Phyllis Burke's seven beautiful stained-glass windows.

Clarendon St., Dublin 2. (*C*) 01/671-8466. Free admission; donations welcome. Daily 8am–8pm or longer. Bus: 16, 16A, 19, 19A, 22, 22A, 55, or 83.

A CEMETERY
Glasnevin Cemetery 𝕲𝕲   Situated north of the city center, the Irish National Cemetery was founded in 1832 and covers more than 50 hectares (124 acres). Most people buried here were ordinary citizens (especially poignant are the sections dedicated to children who died young), but there are also many famous names on the headstones. They range from former Irish presidents such as Eamon de Valera and Sean T. O'Kelly to other political heroes such as Michael Collins, Daniel O'Connell, Roger Casement, and Charles Stewart Parnell. Literary figures also have their place here, including poet Gerard Manley Hopkins and writers Christy Brown and Brendan Behan. Though open to all, this is primarily a Catholic burial ground, with many Celtic crosses. A heritage map, on sale in the flower shop at the entrance, serves as a guide to who's buried where, or you can take a free 2-hour guided tour.

Finglas Rd., Dublin 11. (*C*) 01/830-1133. Free admission. Daily 8am–4pm. Free guided tours Wed and Fri 2:30pm from main gate. Map: €3.50 ($4.20). Bus: 19, 19A, 40, 40A, 40B, or 40C.

MORE HISTORIC BUILDINGS
Although it's not open to the public, one building whose exterior is worth a look is **Mansion House,** Dawson Street, Dublin 2 ((*C*) 01/ 676-1845). Built by Joshua Dawson, the Queen Anne–style building has been the official residence of Dublin's lord mayors since 1715. Here the first Dáil Éireann (House of Representatives) assembled, in

1919, to adopt Ireland's Declaration of Independence and ratify the Proclamation of the Irish Republic by the insurgents of 1916. Ride the DART to Pearse, or take bus no. 10, 11A, 11B, 13, or 20B.

Bank of Ireland Centre/Parliament House 🕭 Although it's now a busy bank, this building was erected in 1729 to house the Irish Parliament. It became superfluous when the British and Irish parliaments were merged in London. In fact, the Irish Parliament voted itself out of existence, becoming the only recorded parliament in history to do so. Highlights include the windowless front portico, built to avoid distractions from the outside when Parliament was in session, and the unique House of Lords chamber. The room is famed for its Irish oak woodwork, 18th-century tapestries, golden mace, and a sparkling Irish crystal chandelier of 1,233 pieces, dating from 1765.

This is also the home of the **Bank of Ireland Arts Centre,** which plays host to an impressive program of art exhibitions, concerts, and poetry readings. Entry to readings, lunchtime recitals, and exhibitions is free.

2 College Green, Dublin 2. 🕿 **01/661-5933**, ext. 2265. Free admission. Mon–Wed and Fri 10am–4pm; Thurs 10am–5pm. Guided 45-min. tours of House of Lords chamber Tues 10:30am, 11:30am, and 1:45pm (except holidays). DART: Tara St. Bus: Any city-center bus.

Custom House   The Custom House, which sits prominently on the Liffey's north bank, is one of Dublin's finest Georgian buildings. Designed by James Gandon and completed in 1791, it is beautifully proportioned, with a long classical facade of graceful pavilions, arcades, and columns, and a central dome topped by a 5m (16-ft.) statue of Commerce. The 14 keystones over the doors and windows are known as the Riverine Heads, because they represent the Atlantic Ocean and the 13 principal rivers of Ireland. Although burned to a shell in 1921, the building has been masterfully restored and its bright Portland stone recently cleaned. The visitor center's exhibitions and audiovisual presentation unfold the remarkable history of the structure from its creation by James Gandon to its reconstruction after the War of Independence.

Custom House Quay, Dublin 1. 🕿 **01/888-2538.** €1.25 ($1.50) adults, €4 ($4.80) families. Mid-Mar to Oct Mon–Fri 10am–12:30pm, Sat–Sun 2–5pm; Nov to mid-Mar Wed–Fri 10am–12:30pm, Sun 2–5pm. DART: Tara St.

Four Courts   Home to the Irish law courts since 1796, this fine 18th-century building overlooks the north bank of the Liffey on Dublin's west side. With a sprawling 132m (440-ft.) facade, it was

Fun Fact **Monumental Humor**

Dublin boasts countless public monuments, some modest, others boldly evident. The Irish make a sport of naming them, giving their irrepressible wit and ridicule yet another outlet. A sampler:

Sweet **Molly Malone,** a figment of Irish imagination—inspiring poetry, song, and most recently sculpture—appears complete with her flower cart, all larger than life, at the intersection of Nassau and Grafton streets, across from the Trinity College Provost's house. Ms. Malone's plunging neckline may explain why she is known as "the tart with the cart."

Just around the corner from Molly on Dame Street stands another sculpture, a silent frenzy of **trumpeters** and streaming columns of water, proclaiming "You're a nation again"—popularly transliterated as "urination again."

Then there's Dublin's testimonial to arguably Ireland's greatest patriot and Dublin's most eminent native son, **Theobald Wolfe Tone.** Born at 44 Stafford St. in 1763 and graduated from Trinity College, Tone went on to spark a revolutionary fervor among the Irish. His timeless contribution to Ireland and the world is commemorated in a semicircular assemblage of rough-hewn columns on the north side of Stephen's Green—better known as "Tonehenge."

designed by James Gandon and is distinguished by its graceful Corinthian columns, massive dome (192m/64 ft. in diameter), and exterior statues of Justice, Mercy, Wisdom, and Moses (sculpted by Edward Smyth). The building was severely burned during the Irish Civil War of 1922, but has been artfully restored. The public is admitted only when court is in session, so phone in advance.

Inns Quay, Dublin 8. 🕐 **01/872-5555.** Free admission. Mon–Fri 11am–1pm and 2–4pm, but only if court is in session. Bus: 34, 70, or 80.

General Post Office (GPO) 🕊 With a facade of Ionic columns and Greco-Roman pilasters 60m (200 ft.) long and 17m (56 ft.) high, this is more than a post office; it is the symbol of Irish freedom. Built between 1815 and 1818, it was the main stronghold of the Irish Volunteers in 1916. Set afire, the building was gutted and

Across the Liffey, on Dublin's north side, are two theaters, the **Gate** and the **Abbey,** that have set the standard for Irish theater in this century. The Gate was founded by and flourished for decades under Michael MacLiammoir and Hilton Edwards, a respected gay couple. The Abbey, for its part, gained a reputation for stage-Irish productions served up for overseas tourists. Their stature makes them not immune from but prey to Irish irreverence—they were collectively known as "Sodom and Begorrah."

The city's newest monument is the **Millennium Spire,** a 120m-high (394-ft.) conical spire made of stainless steel, designed by London architect Ian Ritchie. The new spire is hoped to reflect Dublin of the 21st century and replaces Nelson's Pillar, which was erected by the British during colonial times. Dubliners have had great fun coming up with a suitable nickname for its latest monument. So far, the front runner is simply "The Spike."

Anna Livia, Joyce's mythical personification of the River Liffey, used to be found cast in bronze on O'Connell Street across from the General Post Office. Reclining in a pool of streaming water, Anna had been nicknamed by locals "the floozie in the Jacuzzi." But she was moved to make room for the Millennium Spire and hasn't found a new home yet.

abandoned after the surrender and execution of many of the Irish rebel leaders. It reopened as a post office in 1929 after the formation of the Irish Free State. In memory of the building's dramatic role in Irish history, an impressive bronze statue of Cuchulainn, the legendary Irish hero, is on display. Look closely at the pillars outside— you can still see bullet holes from the siege.

O'Connell St., Dublin 1. ✆ **01/705-8833.** www.anpost.ie. Free admission. Mon–Sat 8am–8pm; Sun 10:30am–6:30pm. DART: Connolly. Bus: 25, 26, 34, 37, 38A, 39A, 39B, 66A, or 67A.

Leinster House   Dating from 1745 and originally known as Kildare House, this building is said to have been the model for Irishborn architect James Hoban's design for the White House in Washington, D.C. It was sold in 1815 to the Royal Dublin Society, which developed it as a cultural center. The National Museum,

Library, and Gallery all surround it. In 1924, however, it took on a new role when the Irish Free State government acquired it as a parliament house. Since then, it has been the meeting place for the Dáil Éireann (Irish House of Representatives) and Seanad Éireann (Irish Senate), which together constitute the Oireachtas (National Parliament). Tickets for a guided tour when the Dáil is in session (Oct–May, Tues–Thurs) must be arranged in advance from the Public Relations Office (✆ **01/618-3066**).

Kildare St. and Merrion Sq., Dublin 2. ✆ **01/618-3000**. Free admission. By appointment only, Oct–May Mon and Fri 10am–4:30pm. DART: Pearse. Bus: 5, 7A, or 8.

Newman House ✎   In the heart of Dublin on the south side of St. Stephen's Green, this is the historic seat of the Catholic University of Ireland. Named for Cardinal John Henry Newman, the 19th-century writer and theologian and first rector of the university, it consists of two of the finest Georgian town houses in Dublin. They date from 1740 and are decorated with outstanding Palladian and rococo plasterwork, marble tiled floors, and wainscot paneling. No. 85 has been magnificently restored to its original splendor. *Note:* Every other Sunday, Newman House hosts an antiques-and-collectibles fair, where dealers from throughout Ireland sell a wide range of items, including silver, rare books, paintings and prints, coins, stamps, and so forth.

85–86 St. Stephen's Green, Dublin 2. ✆ **01/706-7422**. Fax 01/706-7211. Guided tours €5 ($6) adults; €4 ($4.80) seniors, students, and children under 12. June–Aug Tues–Fri noon–5pm, Sat 2–5pm, Sun 11am–2pm; Oct–May by appointment only. Bus: 10, 11, 13, 14, 14A, 15A, or 15B.

LIBRARIES
Chester Beatty Library and Gallery of Oriental Art ✎
Bequeathed to the Irish nation in 1956 by Sir Alfred Chester Beatty, this extraordinary collection contains approximately 22,000 manuscripts, rare books, miniature paintings, and objects from Western, Middle Eastern, and Far Eastern cultures. There are more than 270 copies of the Koran to be found here, and the library has especially impressive biblical and early Christian manuscripts. There's a gift shop on the premises.

Clock Tower Building, Dublin Castle, Dublin 2. ✆ **01/407-0750**. Free admission. Tues–Fri 10am–5pm; Sat 11am–5pm; Sun 1–5pm. Free guided tours Wed and Sat 2:30pm. DART: Sandymount. Bus: 5, 6, 6A, 7A, 8, 10, 46, 46A, 46B, or 64.

Marsh's Library   This is Ireland's oldest public library, founded in 1701 by Narcissus Marsh, Archbishop of Dublin. It is a repository of more than 25,000 scholarly volumes, chiefly on theology, medicine, ancient history, maps, and Hebrew, Syriac, Greek, Latin, and French literature. In his capacity as dean of St. Patrick's Cathedral, Jonathan Swift was a governor of Marsh's Library. The interior—a magnificent example of a 17th-century scholar's library—has remained very much the same for 3 centuries. Special exhibits are designed and mounted annually.

St. Patrick's Close, Upper Kevin St., Dublin 8. (℗ 01/454-3511. www.marshllibrary.ie. Donation of €1.25 ($1.50) requested, free for children. Mon and Wed–Fri 10am–12:45pm and 2–5pm; Sat 10:30am–12:45pm. Bus: 50, 54A, or 56A.

National Library of Ireland   If you're coming to Ireland to research your roots, this library should be one of your first stops (along with the Heraldic Museum; see below). It has thousands of volumes and records that yield ancestral information. Opened at this location in 1890, this is the principal library of Irish studies. It's particularly noted for its collection of first editions and the papers of Irish writers and political figures, such as W. B. Yeats, Daniel O'Connell, and Patrick Pearse. It also has an unrivaled collection of maps of Ireland.

Kildare St., Dublin 2. (℗ 01/603-0200. Fax 01/676-6690. www.nli.ie. Free admission. Mon–Wed 10am–9pm; Thurs–Fri 10am–5pm; Sat 10am–1pm. DART: Pearse. Bus: 10, 11A, 11B, 13, or 20B.

National Photographic Archive   The newest member of the Temple Bar cultural complex, the National Photographic Archive houses the extensive (more than 300,000 items) photo collection of the National Library, and serves as its photo exhibition space. In addition to the exhibition area, there is a library and a small gift shop. Admission to the reading room is by appointment.

Meeting House Sq., Temple Bar, Dublin 2. (℗ 01/603-0200. www.nli.ie. Free admission. Mon–Fri 10am–5pm. DART: Tara St. Bus: 21A, 46A, 46B, 51B, 51C, 68, 69, or 86

LITERARY LANDMARKS

See also "Libraries," above, and the listing for the Dublin Writers Museum on p. 91. You might also be interested in the James Joyce Museum, in nearby Sandycove; it's described on p. 144 in chapter 8.

James Joyce Centre 𝒜   Near Parnell Square and the Dublin Writers Museum, the Joyce Centre is in a restored 1784 Georgian town house, once the home of Denis J. Maginni, a dancing instructor who appears briefly in *Ulysses.* The Ulysses Portrait Gallery on the second floor has a fascinating collection of photographs and drawings of characters from *Ulysses* who had a life outside the novel. The recently opened Paul Leon Exhibition Room holds the writing table used by Joyce in Paris when he was working on *Finnegan's Wake*. The room is named after Paul Leon, an academic who aided Joyce in literary, business, and domestic affairs and salvaged many of the author's papers after Joyce and his family left Paris. There are talks and audiovisual presentations daily. Guided walking tours through the neighborhood streets of "Joyce Country" in Dublin's north inner city are offered daily.

35 N. Great George's St., Dublin 1. ℭ 01/878-8547. www.jamesjoyce.ie. Admission €5 ($6) adults; €4 ($4.80) seniors, students, and children under 10; €13 ($15) families. Separate fees for walking tours and events. AE, MC, V. Mon–Sat 9:30am–5pm; Sun 12:30–5pm. Closed Dec 24–26. DART: Connolly. Bus: 3, 10, 11, 11A, 13, 16, 16A, 19, 19A, 22, or 22A.

Shaw Birthplace   This simple two-story terraced house, built in 1838, was the birthplace in 1856 of George Bernard Shaw, one of Dublin's three winners of the Nobel Prize for Literature. Recently restored, it has been furnished in Victorian style to re-create the atmosphere of Shaw's early days. Rooms on view are the kitchen, the maid's room, the nursery, the drawing room, and a couple of bedrooms, including young Bernard's. The house is off South Circular Road, a 15-minute walk from St. Stephen's Green.

33 Synge St., Dublin 2. ℭ 01/475-0854. Admission €6 ($7.20) adults, €5 ($6) seniors and students, €3.50 ($4.20) children, €17 ($20) families. Discounted combination ticket with Dublin Writers Museum and James Joyce Museum available. May–Oct Mon–Tues and Thurs–Fri 10am–1pm and 2–5pm, Sat–Sun 2–5pm. Closed Nov–Apr. Bus: 16, 19, or 22.

MORE MUSEUMS

See also "Art Galleries & Art Museums," earlier in this section. The National Gallery, the National Museum, the Dublin Writers Museum, and Kilmainham Gaol Historical Museum are all listed earlier in section 1, "The Top Attractions."

Dublin Civic Museum   In the old City Assembly House, a fine 18th-century Georgian structure next to the Powerscourt Townhouse Centre, this museum focuses on the history of the Dublin area from medieval to modern times. In addition to old street signs, maps, and prints, you can see Viking artifacts, wooden water mains, coal covers—and even the head from the statue of Lord Nelson, which stood in O'Connell Street until it was blown up in 1965. Exhibits change three or four times a year.

58 S. William St., Dublin 2. ℭ 01/679-4260. Free admission. Tues–Sat 10am–6pm; Sun 11am–2pm. Bus: 10, 11, or 13.

GAA Museum On the grounds of Croke Park, principal stadium of the Gaelic Athletic Association, this museum dramatically presents the athletic heritage of Ireland. The Gaelic Games (Gaelic football, hurling, handball, and camogie) have long been contested on an annual basis between teams representing the various regions of Ireland. Test your skills with interactive exhibits, and peruse the extensive video archive of football finals dating back to 1931. The 12-minute film *A Sunday in September* captures admirably the hysteria of the final match. Note that the museum is open only to new stand ticket holders on match days.

Croke Park, Dublin 3. ℭ **01/855-8176.** Fax 01/855-8104. www.gaa.ie. Admission €5 ($6) adults, €3.50 ($4.20) students, €3 ($3.60) children, €13 ($16) families. May–Sept daily 9:30am–5pm; Oct–Apr Tues–Sat 10am–5pm, Sun noon–5pm. Bus: 3, 11, 11A, 16, 16A, 51A, or 123.

Heraldic Museum/Genealogical Office The only one of its kind in the world, this museum focuses on the uses of heraldry. Exhibits include shields, banners, coins, paintings, porcelain, and stamps depicting coats of arms. In-house searches by the office researcher are billed at the rate of €56 ($67) per hour. This is the ideal place to start researching your roots.

2 Kildare St., Dublin 2. ℭ **01/603-0200.** Fax 01/662-1062. Free admission. Mon–Wed 10am–8:30pm; Thurs–Fri 10am–4:30pm; Sat 10am–12:30pm. DART: Pearse. Bus: 5, 7A, 8, 9, 10, 14, or 15.

Natural History Museum A division of the National Museum of Ireland, the recently renovated Natural History Museum is considered one of the finest traditional Victorian-style museums in the world. In addition to presenting the zoological history of Ireland, it contains examples of major animal groups from around the world, including many that are rare or extinct. The Blaschka glass models of marine animals are a big attraction.

Merrion St., Dublin 2. ℭ **01/677-7444.** Free admission. Tues–Sat 10am–5pm; Sun 2–5pm. DART: Pearse. Bus: 7, 7A, 8, or 13A.

Number Twenty Nine This unique museum is in the heart of one of Dublin's fashionable Georgian streets. The restored four-story town house is designed to reflect the lifestyle of a middle-class Georgian family during the heyday period from 1790 to 1820. The exhibition ranges from artifacts and artwork of the time to carpets, curtains, decorations, plasterwork, and bell pulls. The nursery holds dolls and toys of the era.

29 Lower Fitzwilliam St., Dublin 2. 𝄢 **01/702-6165**. Admission €3.50 ($4.20) adults; €1.50 ($1.80) seniors, students, and children under 16. MC, V. Tues–Sat 10am–5pm; Sun 2–5pm. Closed 2 weeks before Christmas. DART: Pearse. Bus: 7, 8, 10, or 45.

Waterways Visitor Centre   Heading south from Dublin on the DART, you may notice the tiny Waterways Visitor Centre, a brilliant white cube floating on the Grand Canal Basin amidst massive derelict brick warehouses. This intriguing modern building is home to a fascinating exhibit describing the history of Ireland's inland waterways, a network of canals connecting Dublin westward and northward to the Shannon watershed. The center's shiny white exterior gives way inside to the subdued tones of Irish oak wall panels and a hardwood ship's floor. A series of exhibits describes aspects of canal design, and several interactive models attempt to demonstrate dynamically the daily operations of the canals. No longer used for transporting goods, the canals of Ireland are now popular with boaters and hikers, and there's some information here for those interested in these activities.

Grand Canal Quay, Ringsend Rd., Dublin 2. 𝄢 **01/677-7510**. Admission €2.50 ($3) adults, €1.90 ($2.30) seniors, €1.20 ($1.45) students, €1.50 ($1.80) children, €6.35 ($7.85) families. No credit cards. June–Sept daily 9:30am–5:30pm; Oct–May Wed–Sun 12:30–5pm. DART: Pearse. Bus: 1 or 3.

A SIGHT & SOUND SHOW

Dublin Experience 𝒜𝒜   An ideal orientation for first-time visitors to the Irish capital, this 45-minute multimedia sight-and-sound show traces the history of Dublin from the earliest times to the present. It takes place in the Davis Theatre of Trinity College, on Nassau Street.

Trinity College, Davis Theatre, Dublin 2. 𝄢 **01/608-1688**. €4.20 ($5) adults, €3.50 ($4.20) seniors and students, €2.20 ($2.65) children, €8.40 ($10) families. Daily late May to early Oct, hourly shows 10am–5pm. DART: Tara St. Bus: 5, 7A, 8, 15A, 15B, 15C, 46, 55, 62, 63, 83, or 84.

3 Especially For Kids

The Ark: A Cultural Centre for Children 𝒜𝒜𝒜 *(Kids)*   If you've got kids, make this place a top priority on your itinerary. Every year more than 20,000 children visit this unique cultural center where they are the makers, thinkers, doers, listeners, and watchers. Age-specific programs are geared to small groups of kids from 4 to 14 years old. There are organized minicourses (1–2 hr. long) designed around themes in music, visual arts, and theater, as well as workshops in photography, instrument making, and the art of architecture. The custom-designed arts center has three modern floors that house a theater, a gallery, and a workshop for hands-on learning sessions. The wonderful semicircular theater can be configured to open onto either of the other spaces, or outdoors onto Meeting House Square. Weekdays are often booked for school groups, but Saturdays (and sometimes Sun) are kept open for families. Check the current themes and schedule, and book accordingly.

Eustace St., Temple Bar, Dublin 2. © 01/670-7788. Fax 01/670-7758. www.ark.ie. Individual activities €6.50 ($7.85) per child. Daily 10am–4pm. Closed mid-Aug to mid-Sept. DART: Tara St. Bus: 37, 39, 51, or 51B.

Dublin's Viking Adventure 𝄐 *Kids* Much like Colonial Williamsburg does, this popular attraction brings you back in time with the help of actors playing citizens of Viking-era Dublin. The "Vikings" who populate the village create a lively, authentic atmosphere in their period houses and detailed costumes. The townspeople engage in the activities of daily life in the Wood Quay area along the Liffey, while you watch and interact with them.

Temple Bar (enter from Essex St.), Dublin 8. © 01/679 6040. Fax 01/679-6033. Admission €6 ($7.20) adults, €5 ($6) seniors and students, €4 ($4.80) children, €18 ($22) families AE, MC, V. Mar–Oct Tues–Sat 10am–4:30pm; Nov–Feb Tues–Sat 10am–1pm and 2–4:30pm. DART: Tara St., then no. 90 bus. Bus: 51, 51B, 79, or 90.

Dublin Zoo 𝄐𝄐𝄐 *Kids* Established in 1830, this is the third-oldest zoo in the world (after those in London and Paris), nestled in the city's largest playground, the Phoenix Park, about 3.2km (2 miles) west of the city center. In the past few years, the zoo has doubled in size to about 24 hectares (60 acres) and provides a naturally landscaped habitat for more than 235 species of wild animals and tropical birds. Highlights for youngsters include the Children's Pets' Corner and a train ride around the zoo. You can visit purpose-specific exhibits such as "African Plains," "Fringes of the Arctic," the "World of Primates," the "World of Cats," and the "City Farm and Pets Corner." There are playgrounds interspersed throughout the zoo, and there are also several gift shops. A downside: The restaurants within the zoo serve fast food that's nothing short of awful, but there are plenty of picnic areas for folks who want to bring their own meals.

Phoenix Park, Dublin 8. © 01/677-1425. www.dublinzoo.ie. Admission €13 ($16) adults, €10 ($12) seniors and children 3–16, free for children under 3, €29–€34 ($35–$41) families, depending on number of children. V. Summer Mon–Sat 9:30am–6pm, Sun 10:30am–6pm. Bus: 10, 25, or 26.

Hey! Doodle Doodle 𝄐𝄐 *Kids* *Finds* If your child likes arts and crafts, make a point of stopping into Temple Bar's paint-it-yourself ceramics studio. Kids of all ages can choose from a wide range of

Kids Family Favorites

There is so much for families to see and do in Dublin that it's hard to know where to begin, but here are a few child- and parent-tested favorites:

Dublin's parks give families on the go a respite from the city's ruckus. In **Merrion Square** and **St. Stephen's Green,** you will find lawns for picnicking, ducks for feeding, play-grounds for swinging, and gardens for viewing. Horse-lov-ing youngsters will especially enjoy taking a family carriage tour around the parks (see "Organized Tours," below).

West of Dublin's city center, the vast **Phoenix Park** entices visitors and locals alike (p. 93). Phoenix Park is home to the **Dublin Zoo** (see above), myriad trails, amazing trees, sports fields, playgrounds, and herds of lovely free-roaming deer. You will discover mansions, castles, and many secret gar-dens. Ice-cream vendors and teahouses spring up in all the right places to keep you going. Those weary of walking can take a trail ride through the park thanks to the nearby **Ash-town Riding Stables** (see section 5, "The Great Outdoors").

If a day with Vikings appeals to your family, don't miss **Dublin's Viking Adventure** (see above) or the lively **Viking Splash Tour** in a reconditioned World War II amphibious "duck" vehicle. You'll see Dublin from land and water with a Viking tour guide who will keep the whole family dry and well entertained (see "Organized Tours," below).

Interactive creative activities for families can be found in the **Temple Bar** area. **The Ark** (see above) offers unique arts classes and cultural experiences for children, while **Hey! Doodle Doodle** (see above) is a paint-it-yourself pottery stu-dio for the whole family.

Day excursions out of town are great fun, especially when there are beaches to run on and treasures to discover. North of the city is the **Malahide Castle Demesne** (see "Dublin's Northern Suburbs" in chapter 8). This great estate features not only the beautiful **Malahide Castle** but also the fasci-nating **Fry Model Railway** exhibit, a display of exquisite antique dollhouses and toys at **Tara's Palace,** acres of park-land, playgrounds, and picnic areas.

The towns south of Dublin are best explored by DART light rail from the city center. You might stop in Monkstown to see a puppet show at the famous **Lambert Puppet Theatre and Museum** (see below), or, if the kids need a little seaside adventure, go on a few more stops to the charming heritage village of Dalkey. **The Ferryman** of Coliemore Harbor (see "Dublin's Southern Suburbs" in chapter 8), just a 10-minute walk from the train, can take the family out to explore **Dalkey Island** and return you to shore. After your adventure, you can reward your daring with a creamy soft-serve ice-cream cone in the village. The park at the top of **Dalkey Hill** offers a memorable view of the town and bay beyond.

One stop after Dalkey on the DART lies the long pebbled beach of **Killiney.** This is just the place to find the perfect stone for your family collection or to take a beachcombing stroll along the strand. Farther on down the line is the seaside resort town of **Bray.** Irish water creatures, from starfish to sharks, can be found in the **National Sea Life Centre** (p. 159 in chapter 8). Along with the aquarium, Bray also sports arcades, games, and other family amusements along its boardwalk. If you get to Bray with energy and daylight to spare, the hike up **Bray Head** will give you a spectacular view of the Dublin coastline. In season the purple heather and yellow gorse are stunning, and you might see rabbits inquiring around the bushes.

Even with so much out there for families to do together, there may be some events—a romantic dinner, perhaps—to which you'd rather not bring the kids. So where do you turn for a babysitter? Dublin parents swear by **Minder Finders** (www.minderfinders.ie), a clued-in agency that uses only certified child minders (many are former nannies or teachers) who arrive armed with a bag full of kid-friendly activities. Each sitter is matched with your kids' ages and interests in mind, to alleviate any "new babysitter" jitters.

white ready-to-paint pieces—including mugs, plates, wine coolers, pasta dishes, cups, and dinnerware—and personalize each with their own artwork. Paints, stencils, stamps, and inspiration are all provided along with a little instruction for novices. The finished pieces are kiln-fired and ready to pick up a few days later (so it makes sense to visit on one of your first days in town). All paints are nontoxic, and the pottery is all dishwasher proof. Painting time is charged per hour with a minimum time of 1 hour. Items start at €8 ($9.60). Discounts are available for groups.

14 Crown Alley, Dublin 2. ℂ 01/672-7382. Mon–Sat 11am–6pm. DART: Tara St. Bus: 37, 39, 51, or 51B.

Lambert Puppet Theatre and Museum *(Kids*   Founded by master ventriloquist Eugene Lambert, this 300-seat suburban theater presents puppet shows designed to delight audiences both young and young at heart. During intermission you can browse in the puppet museum or look for a take-home puppet in the shop.

5 Clifden Lane, Monkstown, County Dublin. ℂ 01/280-0974. www.lambertpuppet theatre.com. No box office; call for same-day reservations. Admission €9.50 ($11) adults, €8.50 ($10) children. Shows Sat–Sun 3:30pm. DART: Salthill. Bus: 7, 7A, or 8.

4 Organized Tours

BUS TOURS

The city bus company, **Dublin Bus** (℃ 01/873-4222; www.dublin bus.ie), operates four different tours, all of which depart from the Dublin Bus office at 59 Upper O'Connell St., Dublin 1. Free pickup from many hotels is available for morning tours. You can buy your ticket from the bus driver or book in advance at the Dublin Bus office or at the Dublin Tourism ticket desk on Suffolk Street.

The 75-minute guided **Dublin City Tour** operates on a hop-on, hop-off basis, connecting 10 major points of interest, including museums, art galleries, churches and cathedrals, libraries, and historic sites. Rates are €13 ($15) for adults, €6 ($7.20) for children under 14, and €17 ($21) for a family of four. Tours operate daily from 9:30am to 6:30pm.

The 2-hour-15-minute **Dublin Ghost Bus** is an evening tour, departing Tuesday to Friday at 8pm and Saturday and Sunday at 7 and 9:30pm. The tour highlights Dublin's troubled history of felons, fiends, and phantoms. You'll see haunted houses, learn of Dracula's Dublin origins, and even get a crash course in body snatching. Fares are €22 ($27) for adults only (not recommended for under-14s).

The 3-hour **Coast and Castle Tour** departs daily at 10am, traveling up the north coast to Malahide and Howth. Fares, which include free admission to Malahide Castle, are €20 ($24) for adults, €10 ($12) for children under 14.

The 3-hour-45-minute **South Coast Tour** departs daily at 11am and 2pm, traveling south through the seaside town of Dun Laoghaire, through the upscale "Irish Riviera" villages of Dalkey and Killiney, and farther south to visit the Avoca Handweavers in County Wicklow. Fares are €20 ($24) for adults, €10 ($12) for children under 14.

Gray Line (© 01/605-7705; www.guidefriday.com), the world's largest sightseeing organization, operates its own hop-on, hop-off city tour, covering all the same major sights as the Dublin Bus's Dublin City Tour. The tours are identical, so there's no reason to pay more for Gray Line.

The first tours leave at 10am from 14 Upper O'Connell St., and at 10am from the Dublin Tourism Center on Suffolk Street, Dublin 2, and run every 10 to 15 minutes thereafter. The last departures are 4pm from Suffolk Street, 4:30pm from O'Connell Street. You can also join the tour at any of a number of pickup points along the route and buy your ticket from the driver. Gray Line's Dublin city tour costs €14 ($17) for adults, €12 ($14) for seniors and students, €5 ($6) for children, and €32 ($39) for families.

Gray Line also offers a range of full-day excursions from Dublin to such nearby sights as Glendalough, Newgrange, and Powerscourt. Adult fares for their other tours range from €20 to €30 ($24–$36)

Kids Horse-Drawn-Carriage Tours

You can tour Dublin in style in a handsomely outfitted horse-drawn carriage with a driver who will comment on the sights as you travel the city's streets and squares. To arrange a ride, consult one of the drivers stationed with carriages at the Grafton Street side of St. Stephen's Green. Rides range from a short swing around the green to an extensive half-hour Georgian tour or an hour-long Old City tour. It's slightly touristy, but kids (and romantics) love it.

Rides are available on a first-come, first-served basis from approximately April to October (weather permitting) and will run you between €15 and €50 ($18–$60) for one to four passengers, depending on the duration of the ride.

HELICOPTER TOURS

Want a bird's-eye view of Dublin's fair city? **First Flight Aviation Ltd.,** Dublin, Helicopter Centre NSC, Cloghran, County Dublin (© **1800/471147** toll-free or 01/890-0222; www.firstflight.ie), offers 20-minute helicopter tours over the center city, with more distant views of Dublin Bay and the north and south coastlines. The cost is from €150 ($181) per person.

LAND & WATER TOURS

The immensely popular **Viking Splash Tour** ★★ (© **01/707-6000;** www.vikingsplashtours.com) is an especially fun way to see Dublin. Aboard a reconditioned World War II amphibious landing craft, or "duck," this tour starts on land (from Bull Alley St. beside St. Patrick's Cathedral) and eventually splashes into the Grand Canal. Passengers wear horned Viking helmets (a reference to the original settlers of the Dublin area) and are encouraged to issue war cries at appropriate moments. One of the ducks even has bullet holes as evidence of its military service. Tours depart roughly every half-hour every day 9:30am to 5pm and last an hour and 15 minutes. It costs €14 ($17) for adults, €8 ($9.60) for children under 12, and €47 ($57) for a family of five.

WALKING TOURS

Small and compact, Dublin lends itself to walking tours. If you prefer to set off on your own, the **Dublin Tourism Office,** St. Andrew's Church, Suffolk Street, Dublin 2, has been stellar in the development of self-guided walking tours around Dublin. To date, four tourist trails have been mapped out and signposted throughout the city: Old City, Georgian Heritage, Cultural Heritage, and Rock 'n Stroll/Music Theme. For each trail, the tourist office has produced a handy booklet that maps out the route and provides commentary about each place along the trail.

If you'd like some guidance, some historical background, or just some company, you might want to consider one of the following options.

Historical Walking Tours of Dublin ★★ *Value*   This award-winning outfit has recently expanded its repertoire to include six terrific introductory walks, all 2-hour primers on Dublin's historic landmarks, from medieval walls and Viking remains around Wood Quay to Christ Church, to the architectural splendors of Georgian Dublin, to highlights of Irish history. All guides are history graduates of Trinity College, and participants are encouraged to ask questions. Tours assemble just inside the front gate of Trinity College; no reservations are needed.

From Trinity College. ℂ 01/878-0227. www.historicalinsights.ie. Tickets €10 ($12) adults, €8 ($9.60) seniors and students. May–Sept Mon–Fri 11am and 3pm, Sun 11am, noon, and 3pm; Oct–Apr Fri–Sun noon.

Literary Pub Crawl   Walking in the footsteps of Joyce, Behan, Beckett, Shaw, Kavanagh, and other Irish literary greats, this guided tour, winner of the "Living Dublin Award," visits a number of Dublin's most famous pubs with literary connections. Actors provide humorous performances and commentary between stops. Throughout the night there is a Literary Quiz with prizes for the winners. The tour assembles nightly at 7:30pm and Sunday at noon, upstairs at the Duke Pub on Duke Street (off Grafton St.).

37 Exchequer St., Dublin 2. ℂ 01/670-5602. www.dublinpubcrawl.com. Tickets €11 ($13) per person.

Traditional Irish Musical Pub Crawl   This tour explores and samples the traditional music scene, and the price includes a songbook. Two professional musicians, who sing as you make your way from one famous pub to another in Temple Bar, lead the tour. The evening is touristy, but the music is good and thankfully free from clichés. It lasts 2½ hours. The "crawl" better describes the way back to your hotel.

Leaves from Oliver St. John Gogarty pub and restaurant, 57–58 Fleet St. (at Anglesea St.), Temple Bar. ℂ 01/478-0193. Tickets €10 ($12) adults, €8 ($9.60) students and seniors. Mid-May to Oct daily 7:30pm; Nov and Feb to mid-May Fri–Sat 7:30pm. Tickets on sale at 7pm or in advance from Dublin Tourist Office.

Walk Macabre   The Trapeze Theatre Company offers this 90-minute walk past the homes of famous writers around Merrion Square, St. Stephen's Green, and Merrion Row, while reconstructing old scenes of murder and intrigue. The tour includes reenactments from some of the darker pages of Yeats, Joyce, Bram Stoker, and Oscar Wilde. This one would be rated "R" for violent imagery, so it's not for children or light sleepers. Advance booking is essential. Tours leave from the main gates of St. Stephen's Green.

ℂ 087/677-1512 or 087/271-1346. Tickets €12 ($14) adults, €10 ($12) students. Daily 7:30pm.

The Zosimus Experience 𝓐   This is the latest rage on the walking-tour circuit. Its creators call it a "cocktail mix" of ghosts, murderous tales, horror stories, humor, circus, history, street theater, and whatever's left, all within the precincts of medieval Dublin. With the blind and aging Zosimus as your storyteller, you help guide him down the ascetic alleyways. It's essential to book in advance, when you'll receive the where (outside the pedestrian gate of Dublin Castle, opposite the Olympia Theatre) and the when (time varies according to nightfall). The experience lasts approximately 1½ hours.

28 Fitzwilliam Lane, Dublin 2. ℰ 01/661-8646. www.zozimus.com. €10 ($12) per person. Daily at nightfall, by appointment.

5 The Great Outdoors

BEACHES Dublin has a good selection of fine beaches accessible by either city bus or DART, since the tramway follows the coast from Howth, north of the city, to Bray, south of the city in County Wicklow. Some popular beaches include **Dollymount,** 5.6km (3½ miles) away; **Sutton,** 11km (7 miles) away; **Howth,** 15km (9 miles) away; and **Portmarnock** and **Malahide,** each 11km (7 miles) away. In addition, the southern suburb of **Dun Laoghaire,** 11km (7 miles) away, offers a beach (at Sandycove) and a long bayfront promenade that's ideal for strolling in the sea air. For more details, inquire at the Dublin Tourism Office.

BIRD-WATCHING The many estuaries, salt marshes, sand flats, and islands near Dublin Bay provide a varied habitat for a number of species. **Rockabill Island,** off the coast at Skerries, is home to an important colony of roseate terns; there is no public access to the island, but the birds can be seen from the shore. **Rogerstown and Malahide estuaries,** on the north side of Dublin, are wintering grounds for large numbers of brent geese, ducks, and waders. **Sandymount Strand,** on Dublin's south side, has a vast intertidal zone; around dusk in July and August, you can often see large numbers of terns, including visiting roseate terns from Rockabill Island.

But for top birding and convenient location, your all-around best bet is a bird sanctuary called Bull Island, also known as the **North Bull,** which lies just north of Dublin city harbor. Actually, it's a misnomer—not an island, but rather a 3km (2-mile) spit of land connected to the mainland by a bridge. It comprises dunes, a salt marsh, and extensive intertidal flats on the side facing the mainland. Because of this unique environment, the North Bull attracts thousands of seabirds—nearly 200 different species have been recorded, and up to 40,000 birds shelter and nest here. In winter these figures are boosted by tens of thousands of visiting migrants from the Arctic Circle, as well as North American spoonbills, little egrets, and sandpipers. Together, they all make a delightfully deafening racket. A visitor center is open daily 10:15am to 4:30pm.

FISHING The greater Dublin area offers a wide range of opportunities for freshwater angling on local rivers, reservoirs, and fisheries. A day's catch might include perch, rudd, pike, salmon, sea trout, brown trout, or freshwater eel. The **Irish Tourist Board** operates a good website dedicated to fishing (**www.angling.travel.ie**); just run the search engine for County Dublin and out will pop possibilities ranging from angling for brown trout with the River Dodder Anglers' Club (© **01/298-2112**) in southwest County Dublin to sea fishing on Charles Weston's 11m (35-ft.) ketch (© **01/843-6239**) off the shores of Malahide, just north of the city. In addition, the **Dublin Angling Initiative**, Balnagowan, Mobhi Boreen, Glasnevin, Dublin 9 (© **01/837-9209**), offers a guide—the *Dublin Freshwater Angling Guide*, available for €2 ($2.40)—to tell you everything you'll need to know about local fishing.

GOLF Dublin is one of the world's great golfing capitals. A quarter of Ireland's courses—including 5 of the top 10—lie within an hour's drive of the city. Visitors are welcome, but be sure to phone ahead and make a reservation. The following four courses—two parkland and two links—are among the best 18-hole courses in the Dublin area.

Elm Park Golf Club *Æ*, Nutley Lane, Donnybrook, Dublin 4 (© **01/269-3438**), is in the residential, privileged south side of Dublin. The beautifully manicured parkland par-69 course is especially popular with visitors because it is within 5.6km (3½ miles) of the city center and close to the Jurys, Berkeley Court, and Four Seasons hotels. Greens fees are €80 ($96) on weekdays, €100 ($120) on weekends.

Portmarnock Golf Club *ÆÆÆ*, Portmarnock, County Dublin (© **01/846-2968;** www.portmarnockgolfclub.ie), is one of the finest links courses in Europe, not to mention Ireland. The course is located 16km (10 miles) from the city center on Dublin's north side, on a spit of land between the Irish Sea and a tidal inlet. Opened in 1894, the par-72 championship course has been the scene of leading tournaments, including the Dunlop Masters (1959, 1965), Canada Cup (1960), Alcan (1970), St. Andrews Trophy (1968), and many an Irish Open. Greens fees are €165 ($199) on weekdays, €190 ($229) on weekends.

Royal Dublin Golf Club *ÆÆ*, Bull Island, Dollymount, Dublin 3 (© **01/833-6346;** www.theroyaldublingolfclub.com), is often compared to St. Andrews. The century-old par-73 championship seaside links is on an island in Dublin Bay, 4.8km (3 miles) north-east of the city center. Like Portmarnock, it has been rated among the world's top courses and has played host to several Irish Opens. The home base of Ireland's legendary champion Christy O'Connor, Sr., the Royal Dublin is well known for its fine bunkers, close lies, and subtle trappings. Greens fees are €120 ($145) daily.

St. Margaret's Golf Club ✦, Skephubble, St. Margaret's, County Dublin (℗ **01/864-0400;** www.st-margarets.net), is a stunning, par-72 parkland course 4.8km (3 miles) west of Dublin Airport. Though one of Dublin's newest championship golf venues, St. Margaret's has already hosted three international tournaments, including the Irish Open in 2004. Greens fees are €75 ($90) Monday to Thursday, €90 ($108) Friday to Sunday.

HORSEBACK RIDING   For equestrian enthusiasts of any experience level, almost a dozen riding stables are within easy reach. Prices average about €25 ($30) an hour, with or without instruction. Many stables offer guided trail riding, as well as courses in show jumping, dressage, prehunting, eventing, and cross-country riding. For trail riding through Phoenix Park, **Ashtown Riding Stables** (℗ **01/838-3807**) is ideal. They're located in the village of Ashtown, adjoining the park and only 10 minutes by car or bus (no. 37, 38, 39, or 70) from the city center. Among the other riding centers within easy reach of downtown Dublin are **Calliaghstown Riding Centre,** Calliaghstown, Rathcoole, County Dublin (℗ **01/458-8322**), and **Carrickmines Equestrian Centre,** Glenamuck Road, Foxrock, Dublin 18 (℗ **01/295-5990**).

WALKING   For casual walking, the Royal Canal and Grand Canal, which skirt the north and south city centers, respectively, are ideal for seeing both the city and neighboring areas. Both have been restored as marked trails for serious walkers, so you can't get lost. And because they stick to the towpaths of the canals, they are flat and easy. Moreover, both routes pass through a range of small towns and villages that can be used as starting or stopping points. For more information, contact the Waterways Service at **Duchas the Heritage Service** (℗ **01/647-6000**).

The walk from Bray (the southern terminus of the DART) to Greystones along the rocky promontory of **Bray Head** is a great excursion, with beautiful views back toward Killiney Bay, Dalkey Island, and Bray. It's readily accessible from Dublin. Follow the beachside promenade south through town; at the outskirts of town,

Tips These Boots Are Made for Hiking . . .

Does Dublin leave you yearning for the great outdoors? Then get out of town with **Dirty Boots Treks** (☎ 01/623-6785; www.dirtybootstreks.com), a fantastic, brand-new outfit offering full-day excursions into the mountains south of Dublin. Dirty Boots has thought of everything. After a 9am pickup at the gates of Trinity College, your group (maximum eight people) will be transported in a 4×4 Land Rover into Wicklow Mountains National Park, deep in "the Garden of Ireland." Highlights of the easy-to-moderate hike might include spotting a herd of wild deer or taking a dip in a mountain stream. Treks are typically 4 to 5 hours of trail walking, with plenty of stops for conversation, photo opportunities, admiring the scenery, and a homemade picnic lunch. The day is capped off with a drink in a local country pub before returning to Dublin around 6pm. Later on, you can download photos from your trek from the Dirty Boots website and send them to friends back home. A full-day trek, including round-trip transportation and lunch (but not an after-trek pub stop) costs €45 ($54) for adults, €39 ($47) for students. Didn't pack your hiking gear? No worries. For €9 ($11), Dirty Boots will provide a trekking backpack with hiking boots, gaiters, and waterproofs—all in your size. It's essential to book ahead, either by phone or online.

the promenade turns left and up, beginning the ascent of Bray Head. Shortly after the ascent begins, a trail branches to the left—this is the cliff-side walk, which continues another 5.6km (3.5 miles) along the coast to Greystones. From the center of Greystones, a train will take you back to Bray. This is an easy walk, about 2 hours each way.

Dalkey Hill and **Killiney Hill** drop steeply into the sea and command great views of Killiney Bay, Bray Head, and Sugarloaf Mountain. To get there, leave the Dalkey DART station, head into the center of Dalkey and then south on Dalkey Avenue (at the post office). About .8km (half a mile) from the post office, you'll pass a road ascending through fields on your left—this is the entrance to the Dalkey Hill Park. From the parking lot, climb a series of steps to the top of Dalkey Hill; from here you can see the expanse of the bay, the Wicklow Hills in the distance, and the obelisk topping nearby Killiney Hill. If you continue on to the obelisk, there is a trail leading from there down on the seaward side to Vico Road, another lovely place for a seaside walk. It's about .8km (half a mile) from the parking lot to Killiney Hill.

WATERSPORTS   Certified level-one and level-two instruction and equipment rental for three watersports—kayaking, sailing, and wind-surfing—are available at the **Surfdock Centre,** Grand Canal Dock Yard, Ringsend, Dublin 4 (℗ **01/668-3945;** fax 01/668-1215; www.surfdock.ie). The center has 17 hectares (42 acres) of enclosed fresh water for its courses. It's open from June to September.

6 Spectator Sports

GAELIC SPORTS   If your schedule permits, try to get to a **Gaelic football** or **hurling** match—the only indigenously Irish games and two of the fastest-moving sports in the world. Gaelic football is vaguely a cross between soccer and American football; you can move the ball with either your hands or feet. **Hurling** is a lightning-speed game in which 30 men use heavy sticks to fling a hard leather ball called a *sliotar*—think field hockey meets lacrosse. Both amateur sports are played every weekend throughout the summer at various local fields, culminating in September with the **All-Ireland Finals,** the Irish version of the Super Bowl. For schedules and admission fees, phone the **Gaelic Athletic Association,** Croke Park, Jones Road, Dublin 3 (℗ **01/836-3222;** www.gaa.ie).

GREYHOUND RACING   Watching these lean, swift canines is one of the leading spectator sports in the Dublin area. Races are held throughout the year at **Shelbourne Park Greyhound Stadium,** Southlotts Road, Dublin 4 (℗ **01/668-3502**), and **Harold's Cross Stadium,** 151 Harold's Cross Rd., Dublin 6 (℗ **01/497-1081**). For a complete schedule and details for races throughout Ireland, contact **Bord na gCon (the Greyhound Board),** Limerick (℗ **061/315788;** www.igb.ie).

HORSE RACING   The closest racecourse to the city center is the **Leopardstown Race Course,** off the Stillorgan road (N11), Foxrock, Dublin 18 (℗ **01/289-2888;** www.leopardstown.com). This modern facility with all-weather glass-enclosed spectator stands is 9.7km (6 miles) south of the city center. Racing meets—mainly steeplechases, but also a few flats—are scheduled throughout the year, two or three times a month.

POLO With the Dublin Mountains as a backdrop, polo is played from May to mid-September on the green fields of Phoenix Park, on Dublin's west side. Matches take place on Wednesday evenings and Saturday and Sunday afternoons. Admission is free. For full details, contact the **All Ireland Polo Club,** Phoenix Park, Dublin 8 (© 01/ 677-6248), or check the sports pages of the newspapers.

6

Shopping

Ireland is known the world over for its handmade products and fine craftsmanship, and Dublin is a one-stop source for the country's best wares. Also, due to Ireland's wholehearted membership in the European Union, Irish shops are brimming with imported goods from the Continent. In broad terms (though, obviously, there are exceptions) most of the trendy shops and upscale designer stores are located south of the Liffey, while north of the Liffey is a bit more downscale and serviceable.

VAT REFUNDS

First, the bad news: In Ireland, almost all consumer products are subject to value-added tax—better known as VAT—of 21% on the net price of goods, which is roughly 17% of the selling price. Now, the good news: If you're not a citizen of an E.U. country, you are entitled to this money back.

The first thing you should know is that VAT is a "hidden tax"— it's already added into the purchase price of any items you see in shops. (The two notable exceptions: no VAT on books and no VAT on children's clothing and footwear.)

There are two ways to get your money back:

Global Refund (© **800/566-9828;** www.globalrefund.ie) is the world's largest private company offering VAT refunds, with more than 5,000 stores in Ireland displaying TAX FREE FOR TOURISTS stickers in their front windows. Unlike all other E.U. countries, Ireland requires no minimum purchase in a single store. The system works like this:

> **Step 1:** Collect refund checks at every store where you make a purchase.
> **Step 2:** Fill in the blanks (name, address, passport number, and so on) on the checks, noting whether you'd like your refund in cash or on a credit card.
> **Step 3:** Hand in your completed checks to the VAT-refund desk at the airport just before departing Ireland. The VAT desk is in

the departures hall at Dublin Airport. If you're running late at the airport, you can have the checks stamped by Customs and mail them to Global Refund in an international prepaid envelope. Finally, if you forget to get your checks stamped at Customs, all is not lost. Just get them stamped by a notary public, justice of the peace, or a police officer (with a badge number) in your home country, and mail them back.

What if the shop isn't part of the Global Refund network? For a **store refund,** get a full receipt at the time of purchase that shows the shop's name, address, and VAT paid. (Customs does not accept generic cash-register tally slips.) Save your receipts until you're ready to depart Ireland, then go to the Customs Office at the airport or ferry port to have your receipts stamped and your goods inspected. A passport and other forms of identification (a driver's license, for example) may be required. Then send your stamped receipts back to the store where you made the purchase, which will then issue a VAT refund check to you by mail to your home address. Most stores deduct a small handling fee for this service.

AVOIDING THE VAT HASSLE

Don't want to fill out those forms? Hate the thought of lining up at the airport refund desk? There are three ways to pay no VAT from the beginning.

- **Mail your purchases home.** Arrange for the store to ship your purchases home, and the VAT will be subtracted at the point of sale. You save having to fill out those forms, and you don't have to lug around your stuff. But you still have to pay shipping costs, which may outweigh any hassle you save.
- **Buy at the airport.** When returning home from Ireland, non-E.U. citizens are entitled to shop in the duty-free shops at Dublin Airport. If you're flying on Aer Lingus, you can also shop onboard at the airline's "Duty-Free Sky Shop." These shops offer prices that are free of duty or tax. There are no forms to fill out and no lines to reclaim money. The main drawback is the very limited variety of goods compared to the shops around Ireland.
- **Support a good cause.** Ireland's nonprofit organizations that sell goods operate as charitable trusts and are not subject to VAT, so all their prices are VAT-free. Check out **Oxfam** shops (www.oxfamireland.org) for pottery and other trendy housewares.

1 The Shopping Scene

Generally, Dublin shops are open from 9am to 6pm Monday to Saturday, and Thursday until 9pm. Many of the larger shops also have Sunday hours from noon to 6pm.

The hub of shopping south of the Liffey is **Grafton Street,** crowned by the city's most fashionable department store, Brown Thomas (known simply as BT), and most exclusive jeweler, Weirs. Sadly, many Irish specialty shops on Grafton Street have been displaced over the years by British chain shops (Principles, Jigsaw, Monsoon, Oasis, A–Wear, Next, Boots, Mothercare) so that it now resembles the average High Street in England. Since it's pedestrianized, Grafton Street tends to have a festive atmosphere thanks to

---

Tips **New Kid on the Block: The Old City**

Shoppers take note: Dublin's latest "it" shopping district is **Old City,** located just west of Temple Bar and roughly comprising the area between Castle Street and Fishamble Street. Though still under development, there's already a good mix of hip fashion, modern interior design, crafts, and leisure shops, as well as a bakery, Internet cafe, and a hair salon. The center of the action is a cobbled, pedestrianized street called Cow's Lane, which links Lord Edward Street with Essex Street West. Granted, the name may not immediately conjure up a cool image, but it's become a destination in itself for style mongers who like to get their retail therapy away from the crush of Grafton and Henry streets. On Cow's Lane, don't miss **Whichcraft** (see "Craft Emporiums," below), contemporary pieces for the home at **2cooldesign,** postwar home accessories from **20th Century Furniture,** and the latest looks in glasses at the swish London eyewear outlet **Kirk Originals.**

North of the Liffey, the **O'Connell Street** area is the main inner-city shopping nucleus, along with its nearby offshoots—Abbey Street for crafts, Moore Street for its open-air market, and most notably, Henry Street, a pedestrian-only strip of chain stores, department stores, and indoor malls such as the ILAC Centre and the Jervis Shopping Centre. Roches Store, on Henry Street, is a great place to find Irish linens at lower prices.

street performers and sidewalk artists. But you'll find better shopping on the smaller streets radiating out from Grafton—Duke, Dawson, Nassau, and Wicklow—which have more Irish shops that specialize in small books, handcrafts, jewelry, gifts, and clothing.

A 2-minute walk toward the river brings you to **Temple Bar,** the hub of Dublin's colorful bohemian district and the setting for art and music shops, vintage-clothing stores, and a host of other increasingly fine and interesting boutiques, cafes, and restaurants.

Major department stores include **Arnotts,** 12 Henry St., Dublin 1 (© **01/805-0400**); the most exclusive of them all, **Brown Thomas,** 15–20 Grafton St., Dublin 2 (© **01/605-6666**); and **Clerys,** Lower O'Connell Street, Dublin 1 (© **01/878-6000**).

Dublin also has several clusters of shops in **multistory malls** or ground-level arcades, ideal for indoor shopping on rainy days. These include the **ILAC Centre,** off Henry Street, Dublin 1; the **Jervis Shopping Centre,** off Henry Street, Dublin 1; and **Royal Hibernian Way,** 49–50 Dawson St., Dublin 2. Our favorite of these is the **Powerscourt Townhouse,** where Grafton Street meets St. Stephen's Green, Dublin 2, and the **St. Stephen's Green Centre,** at the top of Grafton Street, Dublin 2. You'll find an American-style cafe on the second floor that offers free refills of coffee.

2 Shopping A to Z
ART
Combridge Fine Arts   In business for more than 100 years, this shop features works by modern Irish artists as well as quality reproductions of classic Irish art. 17 S. William St., Dublin 2. © **01/677-4652.** www.cfa.ie. DART: Pearse. Bus: 15A, 15B, 15C, 55, or 83.

Davis Gallery   One block north of the Liffey, this shop offers a wide selection of Irish watercolors and oil paintings, with emphasis on Dublin scenes, wildlife, and flora. 11 Capel St., Dublin 1. © **01/872-6969.** www.liviaarts.com. Bus: 34, 70, or 80.

M. Kennedy and Sons Ltd.   If you are looking for a souvenir that reflects Irish art, try this interesting shop, established more than 100 years ago. It's a treasure trove of books on Irish artists and works, and it stocks a lovely selection of fine-art greeting cards, postcards, and bookmarks. There are all types of artists' supplies as well, and an excellent art gallery on the upstairs level. 12 Harcourt St., Dublin 2. © **01/475-1740.** Bus: 62.

BOOKS

Greene's Bookshop Ltd.   Established in 1843, this shop near Trinity College is one of Dublin's treasures for scholarly bibliophiles. It's chock-full of new and secondhand books on every topic from religion to the modern novel. The catalog of Irish-interest books is issued five to six times a year. 16 Clare St., Dublin 2. ✆ 01/676-2554. www.greenesbookshop.com. DART: Pearse. Bus: 5, 7A, 8, or 62.

CERAMICS

Louis Mulcahy   The ceramic creations of Louis Mulcahy are internationally renowned. For years he has been exporting his work throughout Ireland and the rest of the world from his studio on the Dingle Peninsula. This modest shop across from the Shelbourne hotel gives him a base in Dublin. In addition to pottery, he designs furniture, lighting, and hand-painted silk and cotton lampshades. 46 Dawson St., Dublin 2. ✆ 01/670-9311. DART: Pearse. Bus: 10, 11A, 11B, 13, or 20B.

CHINA & CRYSTAL

If you're specifically looking for Waterford Crystal, don't bother shopping around because it has fixed pricing. You'll find the best selections at **Brown Thomas** (Grafton St., Dublin 2), **Weirs** (Grafton St., Dublin 2), and **House of Ireland** (Nassau St., Dublin 2). If brand names aren't important, check out other native crystal makers, including Galway, Tipperary, Cavan, and Tyrone. Don't forget to get your cash-back forms if you want to reclaim the VAT (see "VAT Refunds," earlier in this chapter for more information on VAT reclamation).

The China Showrooms   Established in 1939, this is Ireland's oldest china-and-crystal shop in continuous operation. It's a one-stop source for fine china such as Belleek, Aynsley, Royal Doulton, and Rosenthal; hand-cut crystal from Waterford, Tipperary, and Tyrone; and handmade Irish pottery. Worldwide shipping is available. 32–33 Abbey St., Dublin 1. ✆ 01/878-6211. www.chinashowrooms.ie. DART: Connolly. Bus: 27B or 53A.

Dublin Crystal Glass Company   This is Dublin's own distinctive hand-cut-crystal business, founded in 1764 and revived in 1968. Visitors are welcome to browse in the factory shop and see the glass being made and engraved. Brookfield Terrace, Carysfort Ave., Blackrock, County Dublin. ✆ 01/288-7932. www.dublincrystal.ie. DART: Blackrock. Bus: 114.

CRAFT EMPORIUMS

Craft Centre of Ireland   Perched on the top floor of a popular shopping mall, this place offers an exquisite collection of ceramics, wood turning, glassware, and more—all by top Irish artisans. Unit 214 (top floor), St. Stephen's Green Centre, Dublin 2. ℭ 01/475-4526. Bus: All cross-city buses.

Powerscourt Townhouse Centre   Housed in a restored 1774 town house, this four-story complex consists of a central sky-lit courtyard and more than 60 boutiques, craft shops, art galleries, snack bars, wine bars, and restaurants. The wares include all kinds of crafts, antiques, paintings, prints, ceramics, leather work, jewelry, clothing, hand-dipped chocolates, and farmhouse cheeses. 59 S. William St., Dublin 2. ℭ 01/679-4144. Bus: 10, 11A, 11B, 13, 16A, 19A, 20B, 22A, 55, or 83.

Tower Craft Design Centre   Alongside the Grand Canal, this beautifully restored 1862 sugar refinery now houses a nest of craft workshops where you can watch the artisans at work. The merchandise ranges from fine-art greeting cards and hand-marbled stationery to pewter, ceramics, pottery, knitwear, hand-painted silks, copper-plate etchings, all-wool wall hangings, silver and gold Celtic jewelry, and heraldic gifts. Pearse St. (off Grand Canal Quay), Dublin 2. ℭ 01/677-5655. Limited free parking. DART: Pearse. Bus: 2 or 3.

Whichcraft   If you're serious about taking home quality, contemporary Irish crafts, this is an essential stop for finding out what the best contemporary artisans from all over Ireland are doing. All kinds of crafts are represented, from wooden bowls to basketry to rocking horses to pottery to jewelry to ironmongery to batiks. There's a second Whichcraft shop on Cow's Lane in the burgeoning Old City. 5 Castlegate, Lord Edward St., Dublin 2. ℭ 01/670-9371. Bus: 50, 54A, 56A, 65, 65A, 77, 77A, 123, or 150.

FASHION
See also "Knitwear," below.

MEN'S FASHION
Alias Tom   This was Dublin's best small, men's designer shop until BT2 opened. The emphasis is Italian (Gucci, Prada, Armani), but the range covers other chic designers from the rest of Europe and America. Prices are exorbitant. Duke House, Duke St., Dublin 2 ℭ 01/671 5443. DART: Pearse. Bus: 10, 11A, 11B, 13, or 20B.

BT2   This offshoot of Brown Thomas, located across the street on Grafton, is the best shop in Dublin for the hippest designer labels for both men and women. The look is sportier, more casual, and geared to the younger, hopelessly cool set. The prices are nearly as crazy as in BT. Grafton St., Dublin 2 ℭ 01/605-6666. Bus: All cross-city buses.

Kevin & Howlin   Open for more than a half-century, this is the best place in town for hand-woven Donegal tweed garments. The selection includes suits, overcoats, jackets, scarves, vests, and myriad hats—everything from Patch caps and Gatsby fedoras to Sherlock Holmes–style deerstalkers and the ubiquitous Paddy hats. 31 Nassau St., Dublin 2. ℂ 01/677-0257. DART: Pearse. Bus: 7, 8, 10, 11, or 46A.

Louis Copeland and Sons   Behind a distinctive old-world shop front, this is where well-dressed insiders, from Pierce Brosnan to Prime Minister Bertie Ahern, buy their suits. Louis Copeland is a tailor known for high-quality work in made-to-measure suits, but also carries ready-to-wear men's suits, coats, and shirts. The look here is conservative and classic, not trendy. 39–41 Capel St., Dublin 1. ℂ 01/872-1600. Bus: 34, 70, or 80. Branches at 30 Pembroke St., Dublin 2 (ℂ 01/661-0110); 18 Wicklow St., Dublin 2 (ℂ 01/677-7038).

WOMEN'S FASHION

BT2   Brown Thomas's sister shop, located right across the street, is the best place in town for A-list designer labels. BT2 targets a younger but no less label-conscious crowd than BT—think style-obsessed Trustifarians and yuppies and you've got the clientele in a nutshell. Grafton St., Dublin 2. ℂ 01/605-6666. Bus: All cross-city buses.

Claire Garvey   The brightest luminary in Old City is a 34-year-old Dublin native with a talent for creating romantic, dramatic, and feminine clothing with Celtic flair. A favorite designer of Irish divas Enya and Sinéad O'Connor, Garvey transforms hand-dyed velvet and silk into sumptuous garments that beg to be worn on special occasions. Her one-of-a-kind bijou handbags are a white-hot fashion accessory. 6 Cow's Lane, Old City, Dublin 8. ℂ 01/671-7287. Bus: 50, 54A, 56A, 65, 65A, 77, 77A, 123, or 150.

Design Centre   This is the city's best one-stop shop if you want to find all of Ireland's hottest contemporary designers—including Louise Kennedy, Mary Gregory, Karen Millen, Mary Grant, and Sharon Hoey—under one roof. Prices are generally high, but there are good bargains to be had during sale seasons and on the seconds rack. Powerscourt Townhouse, Dublin 2. ℂ 01/679-5863. DART: Pearse. Bus: 10, 11A, 11B, 13, or 20B.

Jenny Vander   This is where actresses and supermodels come to find extraordinary and stylish antique clothing. There's plenty of jeweled frocks, vintage day wear, and stunning costume jewelry filling the clothing racks and display cases. Overall, it's a fabulous place to shop for one-of-a-kind pieces. 20 Georges St. Arcade, S. Great Georges St., Dublin 2. © **01/677-0406.** DART: Pearse. Bus: 10, 11A, 11B, 13, or 20B.

Louise Kennedy   This glamorous and sophisticated designer is a longtime favorite of Meryl Streep, British first lady Cherie Blair, and Carol Vorderman, and recently Dublin native and popstress/actress/model Samantha Mumba has signed on to be the body and face of Kennedy's sumptuous collection. Her elegant showroom carries her clothing, accessories, and home collections, as well as Philip Treacy hats, Lulu Guinness handbags, Lindley furniture, and other items of perfect taste. 56 Merrion Sq., Dublin 2. © **01/662-0056.** DART: Pearse. Bus: 5, 7A, or 8.

GIFTS & IRISH KEEPSAKES

House of Ireland   This shop opposite Trinity College is a happy blend of European and Irish products, from Waterford and Belleek to Wedgwood and Lladró. It also carries high-quality tweeds, linens, knitwear, Celtic jewelry, mohair capes, shawls, kilts, blankets, and dolls. 37–38 Nassau St., Dublin 2. © **01/677-1111.** www.houseofireland.com. DART: Pearse. Bus: 5, 7A, 15A, 15B, 46, 55, 62, 63, 83, or 84.

Kilkenny Design Centre   A sister operation of the Blarney Woollen Mills (see "Knitwear," below), this modern multilevel shop is also a showplace for original Irish designs and quality products, including pottery, glass, candles, woolens, pipes, knitwear, jewelry, books, and prints. The pleasant cafe is ideal for coffee and pastries or a light lunch. 6–10 Nassau St., Dublin 2. © **01/677-7066.** DART: Pearse. Bus: 5, 7A, 15A, 15B, 46, 55, 62, 63, 83, or 84.

HERALDRY

Heraldic Artists   For more than 20 years, this shop has been known for helping visitors locate their family roots. In addition to tracing surnames, it sells all the usual heraldic items, from family crest parchments, scrolls, and mahogany wall plaques to books on researching ancestry. 3 Nassau St., Dublin 2. © **01/679-7020.** www.heraldicartists.com. DART: Pearse. Bus: 5, 7A, 8, 15A, 15B, 46, 55, 62, 63, 83, or 84.

House of Names   As its name implies, this company offers a wide selection of Irish, British, and European family names affixed—along with their attendant crests and mottoes—to plaques, shields, parchments, jewelry, glassware, and sweaters. 26 Nassau St., Dublin 2. © **01/679-7287.** DART: Pearse. Bus: 5, 7A, 8, 15A, 15B, 46, 55, 62, 63, 83, or 84.

JEWELRY

DESIGNyard   The ground-floor studio of this beautiful emporium showcases exquisite, often affordable work from the very best contemporary Irish jewelry designers. Upstairs in the same building, the Crafts Council Gallery displays and sells Irish-made crafts, including furniture, ceramics, glass, lighting, and textiles. All exhibited pieces are for sale, and you may also make an appointment to commission an original work of Irish applied art and design. 12 E. Essex St., Temple Bar, Dublin 2. ✆ 01/677-8453. DART: Tara St. Bus: 21A, 46A, 46B, 51B, 51C, 68, 69, or 86.

Weir and Sons   Established in 1869, this is the granddaddy of Dublin's fine jewelry shops. It sells new and antique jewelry as well as silver, china, and crystal. There is a second branch at the ILAC Centre, Henry Street (✆ **01/872-9588**). 96 Grafton St., Dublin 2. ✆ 01/677-9678. DART: Pearse. Bus: 10, 11A, 11B, 13, or 20B.

KNITWEAR

Blarney Woollen Mills   This branch of the highly successful Cork-based enterprise stands opposite the south side of Trinity College. Known for its competitive prices, it stocks a wide range of woolen knitwear made at the home base in Blarney, as well as Irish-made crystal, china, pottery, and souvenirs. Always check the label or ask a sales assistant to verify whether a sweater is hand-knit or made by machine. 21–23 Nassau St., Dublin 2. ✆ 01/671-0068. www.blarney.ie. DART: Pearse. Bus: 5, 7A, 8, 15A, 15B, 46, 55, 62, 63, 83, or 84.

Brown Thomas   This is the only place in town to find Dubliner Lainey Keogh's creative and sensuous knitwear—a far cry from the chunky Aran sweaters you see everywhere else. The creator of what *Vogue* magazine calls "amazingly organic knitwear" had her first, rapturously received show in 1997, and has been a staple in the closets of Hollywood celebrities such as Demi Moore and Isabella Rosselini ever since. She works mostly with cashmere and her pieces are predominantly made by expert hand-knitters, so prices are high. Grafton St., Dublin 2. ✆ 01/605-6666. Bus: All cross-city buses.

Dublin Woollen Mills   Since 1888, this shop has been a leading source of Aran sweaters, vests, hats, jackets, and scarves, as well as lamb's-wool sweaters, kilts, ponchos, and tweeds at competitive prices. As at Blarney Woollen Mills, always verify whether a sweater is hand-knit. The shop is on the north side of the River Liffey next to the Ha'penny Bridge. There is a 5% discount for those with current international student cards. 41–42 Lower Ormond Quay, Dublin 1. ✆ 01/677-5014. www.woollenmills.com. Bus: 70 or 80.

Monaghan's Established in 1960 and operated by two generations of the Monaghan family, this store is a prime source of cashmere sweaters for men and women. It boasts the best selection of
colors, sizes, and styles anywhere in Ireland. Other items include
traditional Aran knits, lamb's wool, crochet, and Shetland wool
products. There's another store at 4–5 Royal Hibernian Way, off
Dawson Street (C **01/679-4451**). 15–17 Grafton Arcade, Grafton St.,
Dublin 2. C **01/677-0823.** DART: Pearse. Bus: 10, 11A, 11B, 13, or 20B.

MARKETS

Blackrock Market More than 60 vendors run stalls that offer
everything from gourmet cheese to vintage clothing in an indoor/out-
door setting. As at most markets, prices range from very reasonable to
highway robbery. Open Saturday from 11am to 5:30pm and Sunday
from noon to 5:30pm, including holidays. 19a Main St., Blackrock.
C **01/283-3522.** DART: Blackrock. Bus: 5, 7, 7A, 8, 17, 45, or 114.

Book Market Temple Bar This weekend market has enough of
everything to make for excellent browsing—old and new titles, classics and contemporary novels, science fiction and mysteries, serious
biographies, and pulp fiction. Open Saturday and Sunday only, from
11am to 4pm. Temple Bar Sq., Dublin 2. No phone. Bus: 50, 50A, 54, 56, or 77.

Food Market Temple Bar Like Moore Street, this is another
great picnic shopping spot. Everything here is organic, from fruits
and veggies to a delicious selection of homemade cheeses, chutneys,
breads, and jams. Open Saturday and Sunday only, from 10am to
5pm. Meeting House Sq., Dublin 2. No phone. Bus: 50, 50A, 54, 56, or 77.

Moore Street Market For a walk into the past, the Moore
Street Market is full of street-side barrow vendors plus plenty of
local color and chatter. It's the city's principal open-air fruit, flower,
fish, and vegetable market and a great stop for stocking up on picnic provisions. Open daily from 10am to 4pm. Moore St., Dublin 1. No
phone. DART: Connolly. Bus: 25, 34, 37, 38A, 66A, or 67A.

Mother Red Caps Market In the heart of Old Dublin, this
enclosed market calls itself the "mother of all markets." The stalls
offer the usual garage-sale junk mixed in with the occasional treasure (some more in hiding than others), including antiques, used
books, coins, silver, handcrafts, leather products, knitwear, music
tapes, and furniture. There's even a fortuneteller! The pickings can
be hit-or-miss, but do make a point of popping by the Ryefield
Foods stall (farm-made cheeses, baked goods, marmalades, and

jams). Open Friday to Sunday only, from 10am to 5:30pm. Back Lane (off High St.), Dublin 8. ℂ **01/453-8306.** Bus: 21A, 78A, or 78B.

TRADITIONAL IRISH MUSIC

The Celtic Note   Second only to Claddagh Records, this is a terrific source of recorded Irish music in Dublin. The staff is experienced and helpful, and you can listen to a CD before purchasing it. You'll pay full price here, but you're likely to find what you're looking for. 14–15 Nassau St., Dublin 2. ℂ **01/670-4157.** www.celticnote.ie. DART: Pearse. Bus: 5, 7A, 15A, 15B, 46, 55, 62, 63, 83, or 84.

Claddagh Records   Renowned among insiders in traditional Irish music circles, this is where to find "the genuine article" in traditional music and perhaps discover a new favorite. Not only is the staff knowledgeable and enthusiastic about turning you on to new artists, but they're able to tell you which venues and pubs are hosting the best sessions of live traditional music that week. Dame St., Dublin 2. ℂ **01/677-3664.** www.claddaghrecords.com. Bus: 50, 50A, 54, 56, or 77.

7

Dublin After Dark

A more appropriate title for this chapter might be "Dublin Almost Dark," because during high season, Dublin's nightlife takes place mostly in daylight. Situated roughly 53 degrees north of the equator, Dublin in June gets really dark only as the pubs are closing. Night, then, is just a state of mind.

One general fact to keep in mind concerning Dublin's nightlife is that there are very few fixed points. Apart from a handful of established institutions, venues come and go, change character, open their doors to ballet one night and cabaret the next. *In Dublin* and the *Event Guide* offer the most thorough and up-to-date listings. They can be found on almost any magazine stand.

The award-winning website of the *Irish Times* (**www.ireland.com**) offers a "what's on" daily guide to cinema, theater, music, and whatever else you're up for. The **Dublin Events Guide,** at www.dublinevents. com, also provides a comprehensive listing of the week's entertainment possibilities. *Time Out* now covers Dublin as well; check their website at **www.timeout.com/dublin**.

Advance bookings for most large concerts, plays, and so forth can be made through **Ticketmaster Ireland** (✆ **01/886-0996;** www. ticketmaster.ie), with ticket centers in most HMV stores, as well as at the Dublin Tourism Centre, Suffolk Street, Dublin 2.

1 The Pub Scene

The mainstay of Dublin social life is unquestionably the pub. More than 1,000 specimens spread throughout the city, on every street, at every turn. In *Ulysses,* James Joyce referred to the puzzle of trying to cross Dublin without passing a pub; his characters quickly abandoned the quest as fruitless, preferring to sample a few in their path. You will need no assistance finding a pub, but here are recommendations of some of the city's most distinctive.

PUBS FOR CONVERSATION & ATMOSPHERE

Ba Mizu   This new bar draws the young, glamorous set. The clientele includes a regular smattering of models (both male and female) and trendy urbanites. Powerscourt Townhouse Centre, S. William St., Dublin 2. © 01/674-6712.

Davy Byrnes   Referred to as a "moral pub" by James Joyce in *Ulysses,* this imbibers' landmark has drawn poets, writers, and literature lovers ever since. It dates from 1873, when Davy Byrnes first opened the doors. He presided for more than 50 years, and visitors can still see his likeness on one of the turn-of-the-20th-century murals hanging over the bar. 21 Duke St. (off Grafton St.), Dublin 2. © 01/677-5217. www.davybyrnes.com.

Doheny and Nesbitt   The locals call this Victorian-style pub simply "Nesbitt's." The place houses two fine old "snugs"—small rooms behind the main bar where women could have a drink out of the sight of men in days of old—and a restaurant. 5 Lower Baggot St., Dublin 2. © 01/676-2945.

The Long Hall   This is one of the city's most photographed pubs, with a beautiful Victorian decor of filigree-edged mirrors, polished dark woods, and traditional snugs. The hand-carved bar is said to be the longest counter in the city. 51 S. Great George's St., Dublin 2. © 01/475-1590.

The Mercantile   Try for one of the comfy booths in the back of this ultratrendy watering hole, which draws a mixed crowd of locals and in-the-know out-of-towners. Despite being very big, it's always buzzing and tends to get overjammed on weekends, so midweek nights are best. U2 members The Edge and Larry Mullen are regulars. Dame St., Dublin 2. © 01/679-0522.

Neary's   Adjacent to the back door of the Gaiety Theatre, this celebrated enclave is a favorite with stage folk and theatergoers. Its trademarks are the pink-and-gray marble bar and the brass hands that support the globe lanterns adorning the entrance. 1 Chatham St., Dublin 2. © 01/677-7371 or 01/677-8596.

Palace Bar   This old charmer is decorated with local memorabilia, cartoons, and paintings that tell the story of Dublin through the years. 21 Fleet St., Dublin 2. © 01/677-9290.

River Club   Converted from an old merchant's warehouse, this wine bar–cum–supper club combines soaring ceilings, an enviable position overlooking the river, and contemporary furnishings for an overall feeling of easygoing sophistication. It's a favorite of Ireland's film glitterati for a late drink, so don't be surprised to spy author-screenwriter Roddy Doyle, Pierce Brosnan, or director Jim Sheridan. Ha'penny Theatre, 48 Wellington Quay, Dublin 2. © 01/677-2382. www.riverclub.ie.

Ryan's of Parkgate Street   This Victorian gem also houses a fine gourmet restaurant. You'll see some of Dublin's best traditional pub features, including a metal ceiling, a domed skylight, beveled mirrors, etched glass, brass lamp holders, a mahogany bar, and four old-style snugs. It's on the north side of the Liffey, near Phoenix Park. 28 Parkgate St., Dublin 7. ℰ **01/677-6097.**

Searson's   This formerly down-at-its-heels rugby pub underwent a face-lift and has a new lease on life, thanks to hordes of Ballsbridge yupsters who pack the place every evening after work. The weekday crowd is wall-to-wall suits; Saturdays are more relaxed. Actor Gabriel Byrne is a regular. 42 Upper Baggot St., Dublin 4. ℰ **01/660-0330.**

Stag's Head   Mounted stags' heads and eight stag-themed stained-glass windows dominate the decor, and there are wrought-iron chandeliers, polished Aberdeen granite, old barrels, skylights, and ceiling-high mirrors. Look for the stag sign inlaid into the sidewalk. This place is a classic. 1 Dame Court (off Dame St.), Dublin 2. ℰ **01/679-3701.**

PUBS FOR TRADITIONAL & FOLK MUSIC

Brazen Head   Sure it's touristy, but it's an institution. This brass-filled, lantern-lit pub claims to be the city's oldest, and it might very well be, considering that it was licensed in 1661 and occupies the site of an even earlier tavern dating from 1198. Nestled on the south bank of the River Liffey, it is at the end of a cobblestone courtyard and was once the meeting place of Irish freedom fighters such as Robert Emmet and Wolfe Tone. A full a la carte menu is offered and traditional music sessions start at 9:30pm nightly. 20 Lower Bridge St., Dublin 8. ℰ **01/677-9549.**

The Castle Inn   Situated between Dublin Castle and Christ Church Cathedral, this recently rejuvenated bi-level pub exudes an "old city" atmosphere. It has stone walls, flagstone steps, suits of armor, big stone fireplaces, beamed ceilings, and lots of early Dublin memorabilia. From May to September it is also the setting for an Irish ceili (traditional music and dance session) and banquet. 5 Lord Edward St., Dublin 2. ℰ **01/475-1122.**

Chief O'Neill's   One of the city's best haunts for gimmick-free traditional music, in the hotel of the same name. Smithfield Village, Dublin 7. ℰ **01/817-3838.** www.chiefoneills.com. Bus: 25, 25A, 66, 67, or 90.

Mother Red Caps Tavern   A former shoe factory in the heart of the Liberties section of the city, this large two-story pub exudes Old Dublin atmosphere. It has eclectic mahogany and stripped pine furnishings, antiques and curios on the shelves, and walls lined with old paintings and 19th-century newspaper clippings. On Sunday there is usually a midday session of traditional Irish music; everyone is invited to bring an instrument and join in. On many nights there is traditional music on an informal basis or in a concert setting upstairs. Back Lane, Dublin 8. ℭ 01/453-8306. No cover except for concerts.

O'Donoghue's *Overrated* Tucked between St. Stephen's Green and Merrion Street, this much-touristed, smoke-filled enclave is widely heralded as the granddaddy of traditional music pubs. A spontaneous session is likely to erupt at almost any time of the day or night. 15 Merrion Row, Dublin 2. ℭ 01/676-2807.

Oliver St. John Gogarty Situated in the heart of Temple Bar and named for one of Ireland's literary greats, this pub has an inviting old-world atmosphere, with shelves of empty bottles, stacks of dusty books, a horseshoe-shaped bar, and old barrels for seats. There are traditional-music sessions most every night from 9 to 11pm, as well as Saturday at 4:30pm, and Sunday from noon to 2pm. 57–58 Fleet St., Dublin 2. ℭ 01/671-1822.

LATE-NIGHT PUBS

If you're still going strong when the pubs shut down (11pm in winter, 11:30pm in summer), you might want to crawl to a "late-night pub"—one with a loophole allowing it to remain open after hours, perhaps 3am or thereabouts. Late-nighters for the 18-to-25 set include **The Capital,** 2 Aungier St., Dublin 2 (ℭ 01/475-7166), **Hogans,** 35 S. Great George's St., Dublin 2 (ℭ 01/677-5904), and the **Club Mono** (see "Smaller Concert Venues," later in this chapter). After-hours pubs that attract the young and hip but are still congenial for those over 25 include **Whelans,** 25 Wexford St.,

Beware: Late-Night Crime

Crime in Dublin—and most specifically late-night crime—has been on the ascent in recent years. What's most alarming about these aggressions are the random, senseless acts of violence that can occur on any street in Dublin after dark. These attacks are often booze-fueled and happen on streets that are perfectly safe during the day. Be especially on your guard in the areas around O'Connell Street and Grafton Street after pubs' closing time (see above). Never walk back to your hotel alone after this hour.

Dublin 2 (© **01/478-0766**), and the second-oldest pub in Dublin, the **Bleeding Horse,** 24–25 Camden St., Dublin 2 (© **01/475-2705**). For the over-30 late crowd, try **Break for the Border,** Lower Stephen's Street, Dublin 2 (© **01/478-0300**), **Bad Bob's Backstage Bar,** East Essex Street, Dublin 2 (© **01/677-0945**), **Major Tom's,** South King Street, Dublin 2 (© **01/478-3266**), or **Sinnotts,** South King Street, Dublin 2 (© **01/478-4698**).

2 The Club & Music Scene

Dublin's club and music scene is confoundingly complex and volatile. Jazz, blues, folk, country, traditional, rock, and comedy move from venue to venue, night by night. The same club could be a gay fetish scene one night and a techno-pop dance hall the next, so you have to stay on your toes to find what you want. The first rule is to get the very latest listings and see what's on and where (see the introduction to this chapter for a couple of suggested resources). Keeping all this in mind, a few low-risk generalizations might prove helpful to give you a sense of what to expect.

One fact unlikely to change is that the after-hours scene in Dublin is definitively young, averaging about 25. The hottest clubs have a "strict" (read unfriendly) door policy of admitting only "regulars." It helps if you're a celebrity or a supermodel—or just look like one. But barring that, your chances of getting past the door increase if you go in smallish groups and wear your hippest clothes and your coolest attitude.

Most trendy clubs have DJs or live music, with the current genre of choice being "rave." Cover charges tend to fluctuate not only from place to place, but from night to night and from person to person (some people can't buy their way in, while others glide in gratis). Cover charges range from nominal to €15 ($18).

HIPPER THAN THOU

Wear your designer duds and a big attitude to these cutting-edge clubs, where Europe's best DJs are the prime entertainers:

Lillie's Bordello   Open more than a decade and still the hippest of them all, Lillie's breaks the rule that you've got to be new to be hot. Paintings of nudes hanging on whorehouse-red walls is the look that's made Lillie's a surprisingly unraunchy icon of kitsch. There's a well-deserved reputation for posers and boy-band celebrities, and the door policy can best be described as callous, except on Sundays. If you don't feel like dancing, head for "The Library," whose floor-to-ceiling

---

> ## *Tips* Late-Night Bites
>
> Although Dublin is keeping later and later hours, it is still
> nearly impossible to find anything approaching 24-hour din-
> ing. One place that comes close is the **Coffee Dock at Jurys
> Hotel,** Ballsbridge, Dublin 4 (✆ 01/660-5000). It's open Mon-
> day 7am to 4:30am, Tuesday to Saturday 6am to 4:30am, and
> Sunday 6am to 10:30pm. **Bewley's,** 78–79 Grafton St., Dublin 2
> (✆ 01/677-6761), is open until 1am on Friday and Saturday.

bookcases and well-worn leather Chesterfields evoke a Victorian gentlemen's club. Open daily from 11pm to 3am. Adam Court, off Grafton St.,
Dublin 2. ✆ 01/679-9204.

Renards　This quasi–jazz club is the see-and-be-seen choice of the
highlife set. Regulars include Bono of U2, actors Colin Farrell and
Gabriel Byrne, and the Corrs, while out-of-towners like Mick Jagger
pop in when they're in town. The look is modern (think glass and
chrome) on all three floors: the upstairs piano bar with its small tables
and comfy armchairs; the bustling ground-floor cafe-bar; and the basement Plus club, which pulls in the crowd with live music—everything
from acid jazz to Latin beats—Sunday to Thursday. Renards is open
nightly from 11pm to 3am. 23–25 Frederick St. S., Dublin 2. ✆ 01/648-1099.

Ri-Rá　The name means "uproar" in Irish. Though trendy, Rí-Rá
has a friendlier door policy than most of its competition, so this may
be the place to try first. Open nightly from 11:30pm to 4am or later.
1 Exchequer St., Dublin 2. ✆ 01/677-4835.

Spy Club　Fashionable 30-somethings love this lounge bar, where
the emphasis is off dance and firmly on socializing. The look begins
with a classical, 18th-century town house with mile-high, corniced
ceilings. Next, add Greco-Roman friezes and pared-down, contemporary furnishings. Need more drama? The VIP room's focal point
is a photo of a woman in the buff riding a tiger pelt—an in-your-
face wink at the Celtic tiger. Saturday is electric pop night; Sunday
is gay night. Open nightly from 7pm to 3am. Powerscourt Townhouse
Centre, S. William St., Dublin 2. No phone.

Traffic　Located opposite Arnott's department store, this urban-cool
bar and club covers three floors. Music is provided by a mix of Dublin
DJs and international talent. By day, the mood is fresh and funky;
after hours things get hotter. 54 Middle Abbey St., Dublin 1. ✆ 01/873-4800.

KINDER & GENTLER CLUBS

These established clubs, while they attract young singles and couples, have friendly door policies and are places where people of almost any age and ilk are likely to feel comfortable.

Annabel's Just south of the Lower Leeson Street nightclub strip, this club is one of the longest-lasting in town. It welcomes a mix of tourists and locals of all ages with a disco party atmosphere. Open Tuesday to Saturday from 10pm to 2am. Burlington hotel, Upper Leeson St., Dublin 4. ℂ 01/660-5222.

Club M In the basement of Blooms hotel, in the trendy Temple Bar district close to Trinity College, this club boasts Ireland's largest laser-lighting system. It offers DJ-driven dance or live music for the over-23 age bracket. Open Tuesday to Sunday from 11pm to 2am. Blooms hotel, Anglesea St., Dublin 2. ℂ 01/671-5622.

3 Comedy Clubs

The Irish comedy circuit is relatively new and quite popular. The timing, wit, and twist of mind required for comedy seems to me so native to the Irish that it's difficult to draw a line between those who practice comedy for a living and those who practice it as a way of life. You'll find both in the flourishing Dublin comedy clubs. Besides the favorite clubs listed below, **Vicar Street** (see "Smaller Concert Venues," below) tends to get many of the international comics who happen to be in town. As always, check the latest listings magazines for details. Admission ranges from €5 to €20 ($6–$24) depending on the act and the night.

Comedy Club A very small, packed venue, full of enthusiastic exchange. This is up-close, in-your-face improv, with nowhere to hide, so stake out your turf early. International Bar, 23 Wicklow St., Dublin 2. ℂ 01/677-9250.

Ha'Penny Laugh Comedy Club Ha'Penny plays host to some of Ireland's funniest people, many of whom are in theater. The Battle of the Axe is a weekly show in which comedians, singers, songwriters, musicians, actors, and whoever storm the open mic in pursuit of the Lucky Duck Award. Ha'penny Bridge Inn, Merchant's Arch, Wellington Quay, Dublin 2. ℂ 01/677-0616.

Murphy's Laughter Lounge This 400-seat comedy venue is the current prime-time king of the Irish comedy circuit. It attracts the most popular stand-ups on the Irish scene as well as top international acts. Middle Abbey St., Dublin 1. ℂ 1-800/COMEDY.

4 Dinner Shows & Traditional Irish Entertainment

These shows are outside the city center and aimed at tourists, although locals also attend and enjoy them.

Abbey Tavern   After you've ordered an a la carte dinner, the show—authentic Irish ballad music, with its blend of fiddles, pipes, tin whistles, and spoons—costs an extra €4.50 ($5.40). The price of a full dinner and show is €50 ($60). The box office is open Monday to Saturday from 9am to 5pm. Dinner is at 7pm, and shows start at 9pm. There are shows nightly in the summer; in the off season, call ahead to find out which nights shows will be offered. Abbey Rd., Howth, County Dublin. ⓒ 01/839-0307.

Cultúrlann na hÉireann   This is the home of Comhaltas Ceoltoiri Éireann, an Irish cultural organization that has been the prime mover in encouraging a renewed appreciation of and interest in Irish traditional music. The year-round entertainment programs include old-fashioned ceili dances (Fri 9pm–midnight) and informal music sessions (Fri–Sat 9:30–11:30pm). From mid-June to early September, there's an authentic fully costumed show featuring traditional music, song, and dance (Mon–Thurs 9–10:30pm). No reservations are necessary for any of the events. 32 Belgrave Sq., Monkstown, County Dublin. ⓒ 01/280-0295. www.comhaltas.com. Tickets for ceilis €7 ($8.45); informal music €2 ($2.40); stage show €15 ($18). DART: Monkstown. Bus: 7, 7A, or 8.

Jurys Irish Cabaret   Ireland's longest-running show (more than 30 years) offers a unique mix. You'll see and hear traditional Irish and international music, rousing ballads and Broadway classics, toe-tapping set dancing and graceful ballet, humorous monologues and telling recitations, plus audience participation. The show takes place May through October, Tuesday to Sunday. Dinner is served at 7:15pm; the show starts at 8pm. In Jurys Hotel and Towers, Pembroke Rd., Ballsbridge, Dublin 4. ⓒ 01/660-5000. Tickets €50 ($60). AE, DC, MC, V. Free parking. DART: Lansdowne Rd. Bus: 5, 7, 7A, or 8.

5 The Gay & Lesbian Scene

New gay and lesbian bars, clubs, and venues appear monthly, it seems, and many clubs and organizations, such as the Irish Film Centre, have special gay events or evenings once a week to once a month. The social scene ranges from quiet pub conversation and dancing to fetish nights and hilarious contests. Cover charges range from €5 to €15 ($5.75–$18), depending on the club or venue, with discounts for students and seniors.

Check the *Gay Community News, In Dublin,* or the *Event Guide* to find out what's going on in town. The most comprehensive websites for gay organizations, events, issues, and information are **Gay Ireland Online** (www.gay-ireland.com), **Outhouse** (www.outhouse.ie; click on the "Ireland's Pink Pages" link), and **Dublin's Queer Guide** (www. dublinqueer.com). Folks on the help lines **Lesbians Organizing Together** (© 01/872-7770) and **Gay Switchboard Dublin** (© 01/872-1055) are also extremely helpful in directing you to activities of particular interest. (See "Specialized Travel Resources," in chapter 1, for details on many of these resources.)

The Front Lounge This Temple Bar hangout is one of the coolest, chicest pubs in Dublin, with every drink under the sun, and great big loungey couches to chill in. Go early, get a nice seat, and relax with a G and T. The crowd is mixed, but definitely more gay than straight. Every Tuesday night there's a cabaret hosted by a drag queen—one of the most popular gay nights out in Dublin. 32 Parliament St., Dublin 2. © 01/670-4112. Bus: 54 or 65.

The George The George is Dublin's largest gay bar, covering two floors where both the decor and clientele can be described as camp. Theme nights include "Carwash," a 1970s disco night every Thursday, and bingo in the bar Sundays at 5pm. 89 S. Great George's St., Dublin 2. © 01/478-2983. Admission for theme nights, usually 10pm–2am, €7 ($8.05). DART: Tara St. Bus: 22A.

Out on the Liffey This relaxed, friendly pub caters to a balance of gays and lesbians (except for Sat, which is men only) and serves up pub food with good conversation. In 1998, "Out" expanded to include a happening late-night venue, Oscar's, where you can dance (or drink) until you drop. 27 Upper Ormond Quay, Dublin 1. © 01/872-2480. DART: Tara St. Walk up the Liffey and cross at Parliament Bridge. Bus: 34, 70, or 80.

6 The Performing Arts
THEATER
Dublin has a venerable and vital theatrical tradition, in which imagination and talent have consistently outstripped funding. Apart from some mammoth shows at the Point, production budgets and ticket prices remain modest, even minuscule, compared with those in New York or any other major U.S. city. With the exception of a handful of houses that offer a more-or-less uninterrupted flow of productions, most theaters mount shows only as they find the funds and

opportunity to do so. A few venerable (or at least well-established) theaters offer serious drama more-or-less regularly.

The online booking site **Ticketmaster** (www.ticketmaster.ie) is an excellent place to get a quick look at what's playing where and also to buy tickets. In addition to the major theaters listed below, other venues present fewer, although on occasion quite impressive, productions. They also book music and dance performances. They include the **Focus Theatre,** 12 Fade St., Dublin 2 (✆ **01/671-2417**), the **Gaiety Theatre,** South King Street, Dublin 2 (✆ **01/677-1717**), the **Olympia,** 72 Dame St., Dublin 2 (✆ **01/679-3323**), **Project: Dublin,** 39 E. Essex St., Dublin 2 (✆ **01/679-6622**), and the **Tivoli,** 135–138 Francis St., opposite Iveagh Market, Dublin 8 (✆ **01/ 454-4472**).

Abbey Theatre   For more than 90 years, the Abbey has been the national theater of Ireland. The original theater, destroyed by fire in 1951, was replaced in 1966 by the current functional, although uninspired, 600-seat house. The Abbey's artistic reputation in Ireland has risen and fallen many times, but is reasonably strong at present. Lower Abbey St., Dublin 1. ✆ 01/878-7222. www.abbeytheatre.ie. Tickets €15–€26 ($18–$31). Senior, student, and children's discounts available Mon–Thurs evening and Sat matinee.

Andrews Lane Theatre   This relatively new venue has an ascending reputation for fine theater. It consists of a 220-seat main theater where contemporary work from home and abroad is presented, and a 76-seat studio geared for experimental productions. 9–17 St. Andrews Lane, Dublin 2. ✆ 01/679-5720. Tickets €13–€20 ($16–$24).

The City Arts Centre   The City Arts Centre is an affiliate of Trans Europe Halles, the European network of independent arts centers. It presents a varied program, from dramatic productions, theatrical discussions, and readings by local writers to shows by touring companies from abroad. 23–25 Moss St., at City Quay. ✆ 01/677-0643. Tickets €10–€12 ($12–$14).

The Gate   Just north of O'Connell Street off Parnell Square, this recently restored 370-seat theater was founded in 1928 by Hilton Edwards and Michael MacLiammoir to provide a venue for a broad range of plays. That policy prevails today, with a program that includes a blend of modern works and the classics. Although less known by visitors, The Gate is easily as distinguished as the Abbey. 1 Cavendish Row, Dublin 1. ✆ 01/874-4368. Tickets €21–€25 ($25–$30) or €15 ($18) for previews. AE, DC, MC, V.

Smaller Concert Venues

If you prefer smaller, more intimate settings, check out the listings magazines for who's performing at these favorite venues:

- **Temple Bar Music Centre,** Temple Bar, Dublin 2 (✆ 01/670-9202)
- **Vicar Street,** 99 Vicar St., Dublin 8 (✆ 01/454-5533; www.vicarstreet.com)
- **Whelans,** 25 Wexford St., Dublin 2 (✆ 01/478-0766)
- **Eamonn Doran's,** 3A Crown Alley, Temple Bar, Dublin 2 (✆ 01/679-9114)
- **Club Mono,** 26 Wexford St., Dublin 2 (✆ 01/475-8555)
- **Midnight at the Olympia,** 74 Dame St., Dublin 2 (✆ 01/677-7744)

The Peacock   In the same building as the Abbey, this 150-seat theater features contemporary plays and experimental works. It books poetry readings and one-person shows, as well as plays in the Irish language. Lower Abbey St., Dublin 1. ✆ **01/878-7222.** www.abbeytheatre.ie. Tickets €10–€20 ($12–$24).

CONCERTS

Dublin is a great town for live music. On a given night, you can find almost anything—rock, pop, jazz, blues, traditional Irish, country, or folk—so check listings magazines to find out what's on and where. Music and dance concerts take place in a range of Dublin venues—theaters, churches, clubs, museums, sports stadiums, castles, parks, and universities. Again, the online booking site **Ticketmaster** (www.ticketmaster.ie) is an excellent place to get a quick look at who's playing where and buy your tickets. While you're probably more likely to choose your entertainment based on the performer rather than the venue, these institutions stand out as venues where most international performers play.

The Helix   This massive auditorium at University College Dublin hosts many concerts throughout the year. The box office is open Monday to Saturday 10am to 6pm. Collins Ave., Glasnevin, Dublin 9. ✆ **01/700-7077.** www.helix.ie. Tickets €13–€60 ($16–$75). AE, MC, V.

National Concert Hall   This magnificent 1,200-seat hall is home to the National Symphony Orchestra and Concert Orchestra, and host to an array of international orchestras and performing artists. In addition to classical music, there are evenings of Gilbert and Sullivan, opera, jazz, and recitals. The box office is open Monday to Friday from 10am to 3pm and from 6pm to close of concert. Open weekends 1 hour before concerts. Parking is available on the street. Earlsfort Terrace, Dublin 2. (✆ 01/417-0000. www.nch.ie. Tickets €10–€32 ($12–$39). Lunchtime concerts €5 ($6). DC, MC, V.

The Point Depot   With a seating capacity of 3,000, The Point is one of Dublin's larger indoor theater/concert venues, attracting top Broadway-caliber shows and international stars such as Justin Timberlake and Tom Jones. The box office is open Monday to Saturday 10am to 6pm. Parking is €4 ($4.80) per car. East Link Bridge, North Wall Quay. (✆ 01/836-3633. Tickets €13–€65 ($16–$78). AE, DC, MC, V.

Royal Dublin Society (RDS)   Although best known as the venue for the Dublin Horse Show, this huge indoor arena also hosts major concerts (Bruce Springsteen, Paul McCartney, and The Eagles were recent performers), with seating and standing room for more than 6,000 people. Merrion Rd., Ballsbridge, Dublin 2. (✆ 01/668-0866. www.rds.ie. Most tickets €13–€40 ($16–$48).

8

Side Trips from Dublin

Fanning out a little over 19km (12 miles) in each direction, Dublin's southern and northern suburbs offer a variety of interesting sights and experiences. All are easy to reach by public transportation or rental car.

Further out is County Wicklow. This area is within easy distance from Dublin city, has less rain, less bog, and more history than any other region of comparable concentration on the island. County Wicklow presents a panorama of gardens, lakes, mountains, and seascapes.

1 Dublin's Southern Suburbs

Stretching southward along Dublin Bay from Ballsbridge is the harbor town of Dun Laoghaire, followed by Dublin's poshest suburbs, the seaside towns of **Dalkey** 🅐🅐 and **Killiney**—nicknamed "Bel Eire" for their beauty and density of celebrity residents. All three towns offer lovely seaside views and walks. Dun Laoghaire has a long promenade and a bucolic park, Killiney has a stunning, cliff-backed expanse of beach. The prettiest is Dalkey, a heritage town with a lovely medieval streetscape and something for just about everyone.

Thanks to DART service, these towns are easily accessible from downtown Dublin. They offer a good selection of restaurants and fine places to stay. A hillside overlooking Dublin Bay outside the village of Killiney is the setting for the Dublin area's only authentic deluxe castle hotel, Fitzpatrick Castle (p. 146).

If you're traveling to Ireland by ferry from Holyhead, Wales, your first glimpse of Ireland will be the port of Dun Laoghaire. Many people decide to base themselves here and commute into downtown Dublin each day. As a base, it is less expensive than Dalkey, but less attractive, too.

ATTRACTIONS
Dalkey Castle and Heritage Centre   Housed in a 16th-century tower house, the center and its fascinating exhibitions unfold

this venerable town's remarkable history. After taking in the exhibit, you can visit the battlements to put it all in place and enjoy vistas of the Dublin area coastline. Adjoining the center is a medieval grave-yard and the Church of St. Begnet, Dalkey's patron saint, whose foundations may be traced to Ireland's Early Christian period. Booklets sketching the history of the town, the church, and the graveyard are available at the Heritage Centre. You'll see and appreciate more of this landmark town if you purchase these and take them next door to the Queens Bar for a pint and quick scan. "Those who are patient," wrote the playwright Hugh Leonard, "and will sit, wait and listen or will linger along the tree-shaded roads running down to the sea, can hear the centuries pass."

Castle St., Dalkey, County Dublin. © 01/285-8366. Admission €6 ($7.20) adults, €5 ($6) seniors and students, €4 ($4.80) children, €16 ($19) families. Apr–Oct Mon–Fri 9:30am–5pm, Sat–Sun 11am–5pm; Nov–Mar Sat–Sun 11am–5pm. DART: Dalkey. Bus: 8.

The Ferryman 🎯 *Kids* Young Aidan Fennel heads the third generation of Fennels to ferry visitors to nearby Dalkey Island, whose only current inhabitants are a small herd of wild goats and the occasional seal. Aidan is a boat builder, and his brightly painted fleet comes mostly from his hand. The island, settled about 6000 B.C., offers three modest ruins: a church that's over 1,000 years old, ramparts dating from the 15th century, and a Martello tower constructed in 1804 to make Napoleon think twice. Now the island is little more than a lovely picnic spot. If you want to build up an appetite and delight your children or sweetheart, row out in one of Aidan's handmade boats.

Coliemore Rd. (at stone wharf, adjacent to a seaside apt complex). © 01/283-4298. Island ferry round-trip €10 ($12) adults, €5 ($6) children; rowboat rental €15 ($18)/hour June–Aug, weather permitting.

James Joyce Museum 🎯🎯 Sitting on the edge of Dublin Bay about 9.7km (6 miles) south of the city center, this 12m (40-ft.) granite monument is one of a series of Martello towers built in 1804 to withstand an invasion threatened by Napoleon. The tower's great claim to fame is that James Joyce lived here in 1904. He was the guest of Oliver Gogarty, who rented the tower from the Army for an annual fee of IR£8 (€10/$12). Joyce, in turn, made the tower the setting for the first chapter of *Ulysses,* and it has been known as Joyce's Tower ever since. Its collection of Joycean memorabilia includes letters, documents, first and rare editions, personal possessions, and photographs.

Side Trips from Dublin

Balbriggan

Bernageara h Bay

St. Patrick's Island

Skerries **7 8 9**

Shenick's Island

6
R127

0   5 mi
0   5 km

NORTHERN IRELAND

Area of detail

REPUBLIC OF IRELAND

N1

R127

R128

R108

R126 Donabate
10

Lambay Island

Swords **11**
R106

Malahide

12 13

R106

R122

N1

Dublin Airport ✈   M1

Portmarnock

Irish Sea

R107

R104

Sutton

Ireland's Eye

15 16

N2 **3 4**
2 R103 **5**

N3

1 Clontarf

North Bull Island

Howth
▲ *Ben of Howth*

14

R105

N4 ✈ **Dublin**

Liffey   *Royal Canal*

Dublin Bay

N7   R110

N11

R117

R112

17 18 19

Dun Laoghaire

20 21

Sandycove

Dalkey
Dalkey Hill ▲
Killiney Hill ▲

22 *Dalkey Island*

23 24 25

R113

26

Killiney

To Shankill ↓   **27**

ATTRACTIONS ●
Ardgillan Castle **6**
Casino Marino **5**
Dalkey Castle Heritage Centre **25**
The Ferryman **22**
Fry Model Railway **12**
Howth Castle Rhododendron Gardens **14**
James Joyce Museum **20**
Malahide Castle **13**
National Botanic Gardens **2**
Newbridge House & Park **10**
Skerries Mills **7**

ACCOMMODATIONS ■
Clontarf Castle Hotel **1**
The Court Hotel **27**
Egan's House **3**
Fitzpatrick Castle Hotel **26**
Forte Travelodge **11**
The Gresham Royal Marine **17**
Iona House **4**
Red Bank House **8**

DINING ◆
Abbey Tavern **15**
Brasserie na Mara **18**
Caviston's **19**
Dee Gee's Wine & Steak Bar **16**
Munkberrys **24**
Nosh **23**
P.D.'s Woodhouse **21**
The Red Bank **9**

Sandycove, County Dublin. ℂ 01/280-9265. Admission €6 ($7.20) adults, €5 ($6) seniors and students, €3.75 ($4.95) children, €18 ($21) families. Apr–Oct Mon–Sat 10am–1pm and 2–5pm, Sun 2–6pm. Closed Nov–Mar. DART: Sandycove. Bus: 8.

WHERE TO STAY
EXPENSIVE
The Court Hotel   Situated on 1.6 hectares (4 acres) of gardens and lawns, this three-story Victorian hotel enjoys a splendid location overlooking Killiney Bay and convenient access to Dublin with the nearby DART. The hotel's multiple lounges and popular restaurants show off their Victorian origins with corniced ceilings and old wood, and are bright and welcoming. The guest rooms are comfortably, though unremarkably, furnished, so it pays to request a room with a view of the bay. The real draw of this hotel is its lovely setting, which is convenient for excursions to Dublin as well as evening strolls on one of the most beautiful beaches on Ireland's east coast.

Killiney Bay Rd., Killiney, County Dublin. ℂ **800/221-2222** in the U.S. or 01/285-1622. Fax 01/285-2085. www.killineycourt.ie. 86 units. €175–€230 ($211–$277) double. Rates include service charge and full Irish breakfast. AE, DC, MC, V. DART: Killiney. Bus: 59. **Amenities:** 2 restaurants (Continental, grill); lounge; bar; concierge; room service; laundry service. *In room:* TV, hair dryer, radio.

Fitzpatrick Castle Hotel ⚔   With a fanciful Victorian facade of turrets, towers, and battlements, this restored 1741 gem is an ideal choice for those who want to live it up a bit. A 15-minute drive from the center of the city, it is between the villages of Dalkey and Killiney, on 3.6 hectares (9 acres) of gardens and hilltop grounds with romantic vistas of Dublin Bay. Two generations of the Fitzpatrick family pamper guests with 21st-century comforts in a regal setting of medieval suits of armor, Louis XIV–style furnishings, Irish antiques, original oil paintings, and specially woven shamrock-pattern green carpets. Most of the guest rooms have four-poster or canopy beds, and many have balconies with sweeping views of Dublin and the surrounding countryside. In spite of its size and exacting standards, the castle never fails to exude a friendly, family-run atmosphere.

Killiney Hill Rd., Killiney, County Dublin. ℂ 01/230-5400. Fax 01/230-5430. www.fitzpatrickcastle.ie. 113 units. €210 ($253) double. Breakfast €17 ($20). AE, DC, MC, V. DART: Dalkey. Bus: 59. **Amenities:** 2 restaurants (Continental, grill); 2 bars; indoor swimming pool; guest privileges at nearby 18-hole golf course; gym; saunas; concierge; salon; room service; laundry service; nonsmoking rooms. *In room:* TV, tea/coffeemaker, hair dryer, garment press.

MODERATE
The Gresham Royal Marine   A landmark since 1870, this five-story hotel sits on a hill overlooking the harbor, 11km (7 miles)

south of Dublin City. It's a good place to stay for ready access to the ferry across the Irish Sea to and from Wales. Basically a Georgian building with a wing of modern rooms, the Royal Marine has public areas that have been beautifully restored and recently refurbished, with original molded ceilings and elaborate cornices, crystal chandeliers, marble-mantled fireplaces, and antique furnishings. The older rooms, many of which offer wide-windowed views of the bay, carry through the Georgian theme, with dark woods, traditional floral fabrics, and four-poster or canopy beds. Newer rooms are less atmospheric, with more contemporary light woods and pastel tones.

Marine Rd., Dun Laoghaire, County Dublin. (℘ **800/44-UTELL** in the U.S. or 01/280-1911. Fax 01/280-1089. www.ryan-hotels.com. 103 units. €150 ($181) double. Rates include service charge and full breakfast. AE, DC, MC, V. DART: Dun Laoghaire. Bus: 7, 7A, or 8. **Amenities:** Restaurant (International); bar; concierge; room service; laundry service; nonsmoking rooms. *In room:* TV, tea/coffeemaker, hair dryer, garment press, radio, voice mail.

WHERE TO DINE
EXPENSIVE

Brasserie na Mara ✸ SEAFOOD   Award-winning chef Adrian Spelman keeps this fine seafood restaurant high on the charts, despite ever-steepening competition. Set squarely in the bustle of Dun Laoghaire's busy seafront, this restaurant, elegantly converted from the old Kingstown terminal building, has been a benchmark for South Dublin cuisine since 1971. In addition to a wide selection of fish and shellfish, you can count on an array of poultry and meat dishes, from guinea fowl to Irish beef, as well as vegetarian options. Flaming desserts—another specialty—provide both high drama and suitable closure to a memorable meal.

1 Harbour Rd., Dun Laoghaire, County Dublin. (℘ **01/280-6767.** Reservations required. 4-course fixed-price lunch €25 ($30); 4-course fixed-price dinner €35 ($42); main courses €17–€27 ($21–$32). Mon–Fri 12:30–2:30pm; Mon–Sat 6:30–10pm. DART: Dun Laoghaire. Bus: 7, 7A, 8, or 46A.

MODERATE

Caviston's ✸✸ SEAFOOD   Fresh, fresh fish is the hallmark of this tiny lunch spot in Sandycove, run by the Caviston family, whose neighboring delicatessen and fish shop is legendary. There's no doubt that having the inside track on fresh produce transfers to the preparation of fish in the restaurant itself; chef Noel Cusack checks out the daily catch before creating the menu of simply prepared dishes, relying on just one or two well-chosen ingredients to bring out the seafood's delicate flavors. The daily menu might include roast monkfish with pasta in a saffron-and-basil sauce, chargrilled salmon with béarnaise, or marinated red mullet with roasted red peppers. Unfortunately, the three lunchtime sittings can make for frantic service, so your best bet is to arrive at noon sharp before things get too hectic, or else aim for the last sitting and enjoy your meal without feeling like your table has been earmarked for somebody else.

59 Glasthule Rd., Sandycove, County Dublin. ℂ 01/280-9120. Reservations recommended. Main courses €13–€28 ($16–$34). DC, MC, V. Tues–Fri 3 sittings: noon, 1:30pm, 3pm; Sat: noon, 1:45pm, and 3:15pm.

Munkberrys ℛ MODERN CONTINENTAL   Crisp linens, candlelight, and tasteful contemporary art lend an immediate calm to this intimate restaurant on Dalkey's most animated street. The excitement here lies in the food, which provokes both the eye and the palate. The crostini of goat's cheese with fresh figs and spicy tomato chutney arrives on a swirl of delicious and mysterious sauces. The spinach ricotta tortellini with a Stilton, pistachio, and cognac sauce is perfectly prepared and elegant to behold. It's a struggle to decide between desserts: The lemon crème brûlée with hazelnut biscuit? Or perhaps the steamed date pudding with butterscotch? Or—sigh—the Italian ice cream. While the service is especially attentive, there is no true separation of smokers and nonsmokers, who are potentially at arm's length from each other.

Castle St., Dalkey, County Dublin. ℂ 01/284-7185. Reservations recommended. 4-course fixed-price dinner €30 ($36); main courses €13–€23 ($16–$28); early-bird fixed-price dinner (Mon–Sat 5:30–7pm) €20 ($24). AE, DC, MC, V. Mon–Fri noon–2:30pm and 5:30–10pm; Sat 5:30–10:30pm; Sun noon–6pm. DART: Dalkey.

Nosh ℛℛ INTERNATIONAL   Call it a rich man's diner or a poor man's bistro, if you must, but Nosh delivers the sort of hit-the-spot food that you wish you could get in your own neighborhood. The point is: It ain't what they do, it's the way that they do it. French toast with bacon, bananas, and maple syrup is terrifically satisfying; there are wonderful soups, and big, well-constructed club sandwiches. If you're in the mood for something more elitist, go for one of the fish dishes, such as the sautéed brill with ratatouille, and choose one of the wines from the short-but-sweet list. The place is friendly, the food is top-notch, and brunch on weekends is simply fabulous.

111 Coliemore Rd., Dalkey, County Dublin. ℂ 01/284-0666. Reservations recommended. Main courses €17–€25 ($21–$30). MC, V. Tues–Sun noon–4pm and 6–10pm. DART: Dalkey.

P. D.'s Woodhouse IRISH/MEDITERRANEAN   The first and only oak-wood barbecue bistro in Ireland, P. D.'s Woodhouse cooks everything over chips from oaks ripped up by Hurricane Charlie, the worst tropical storm to hit Ireland in recent memory. The wild Irish salmon in caper-and-herb butter is fabulous, as is the white sole. And whatever you do, don't miss the Halumi cheese kabobs—conversation-stopping grilled Greek goat's cheese. On the other hand, the nut kabobs, one of several vegetarian entrees, are unnecessarily austere.

1 Coliemore Rd., Dalkey center, County Dublin. © 01/284-9399. Reservations recommended. Main courses €10–€23 ($12–$28). AE, DC, MC, V. Mon–Sat 6–11pm; Sun 4–9:30pm. DART: Dalkey.

PUBS

P. McCormack and Sons   This popular pub offers three distinctive atmospheres. The main bar has an old-world feel, with globe lamps, stained-glass windows, books and jugs on the shelves, and lots of nooks and crannies for a quiet drink. In the sky-lit, plant-filled conservatory area, classical music fills the air, and outdoors you'll find a festive courtyard beer garden. The pub grub here is top-notch, with a varied buffet table of lunchtime salads and meats. 67 Lower Mounttown Rd. (off York Rd.), Dun Laoghaire, County Dublin. © 01/280-5519.

The Purty Kitchen   Housed in a building that dates from 1728, this old pub has a homey atmosphere, with an open brick fireplace, cozy alcoves, a large fish mural, and pub poster art on the walls. There's always something going on—be it a session of Irish traditional music in the main bar area, blues upstairs in the Loft, or a DJ spinning dance music. Call ahead for entertainment details. Old Dunleary Rd., Dun Laoghaire, County Dublin. © 01/284-3576. No cover for traditional music; cover €6–€8 ($7.20–$9.60) for blues in the Loft.

2 Dublin's Northern Suburbs

Dublin's northern suburbs make a convenient base to **Dublin International Airport**, and they're also home to a delightful assortment of castles, historic buildings, gardens, and other attractions. In addition, the residential suburbs of **Drumcondra** and **Glasnevin** offer many good lodgings.

Just north of Dublin, the picturesque suburbs of **Howth** and **Malahide** offer panoramic views of Dublin Bay, beautiful hillside gardens, and many fine seafood restaurants. Best of all, they are easily reached on the DART. Farther north along the coast, but only 20 minutes from Dublin Airport, lies the bustling and attractive harbor town of **Skerries** 𝒞. Skerries is a convenient and appealing spot to spend your first or last night in Ireland; or stay longer and explore all this area has to offer, including a resident colony of gray seals and the lowest annual rainfall in Ireland.

ATTRACTIONS

Ardgillan Castle and Park 🔥   Between Balbriggan and Skerries, this exquisitely restored 18th-century castellated country house sits right on the coastline on sumptuously manicured lawns. The house was built in 1738 and contains some fine period furnishings and antiques. But the real draw is the setting, right on the edge of the Irish Sea, with miles of walking paths and coastal views as well as a rose garden and an herb garden. Behind the lavish rose garden, there's also a nice cafe for grabbing a quick bite or some ice cream.

Balbriggan, County Dublin. ℂ **01/849-2212.** Admission to house €5 ($6) adults, €3 ($3.60) seniors and students, €10 ($12) families. Castle Oct–Dec and Feb–Mar Tues–Sun 11am–4:30pm; Apr–June and Sept Tues–Sun 11am–6pm; July–Aug daily 11am–6pm. Park daily dawn to dusk. Closed Jan. Free parking year-round. Sign-posted off N1. Bus: 33.

Casino Marino   Standing on a gentle rise 4.8km (3 miles) north of the city center, this 18th-century building is considered one of the finest garden temples in Europe. Designed in the Franco-Roman neoclassical style by Scottish architect Sir William Chambers, it was constructed in the garden of Lord Charlemont's house by the English sculptor Simon Vierpyl. Work commenced in 1762 and was completed 15 years later. It is particularly noteworthy for its elaborate stone carvings and compact structure, which make it appear to be a single story tall (it is actually two stories tall).

Malahide Rd., Marino, Dublin 3. ℂ **01/833-1618.** Admission €3 ($3.60) adults, €2 ($2.40) seniors and group members, €1.25 ($1.50) students and children, €7 ($8.45) families. Feb–Apr and Nov Sun and Thurs noon–4pm; May and Oct daily noon–5pm; June–Sept daily 10am–6pm. Closed Dec–Jan. Bus: 20A, 20B, 27, 27A, 27B, 42, 42B, or 42C.

The Fry Model Railway 🧒   On the grounds of Malahide Castle (see listing below), this is an exhibit of rare handmade models of more than 300 Irish trains, from the introduction of rail to the present. The trains were built in the 1920s and 1930s by Cyril Fry, a railway engineer and draftsman. The complex includes items of Irish railway history dating from 1834, and models of stations, bridges, trams, buses, barges, boats, the River Liffey, and the Hill of Howth.

Malahide, County Dublin. ℂ **01/846-3779.** Admission €6 ($7.20) adults, €5.25 ($6.30) seniors and students, €3.50 ($4.20) children, €18 ($21) families. Apr–Oct Mon–Sat 10am–5pm, Sun 2–6pm; Nov–Mar Sun 2–5pm. Closed for tours 1–2pm year-round. Suburban Rail to Malahide. Bus: 42.

Howth Castle Rhododendron Gardens   On a steep slope about 13km (8 miles) north of downtown, this 12-hectare (30-acre) garden was first planted in 1875 and is best known for its 2,000 varieties of rhododendrons. Peak bloom time is in May and June. *Note:* The castle and its private gardens are not open to the public.

Howth, County Dublin. ℭ **01/832-2624**. Free admission. Apr–June daily 8am–sunset. DART: Howth. Bus: 31.

Malahide Castle *Kids* About 13km (8 miles) north of Dublin, Malahide is one of Ireland's most historic castles. Founded in the 12th century by Richard Talbot, it was occupied by his descendants until 1973. The fully restored interior is the setting for a comprehensive collection of Irish furniture dating from the 17th to the 19th centuries. One-of-a-kind Irish historical portraits and tableaux on loan from the National Gallery line the walls. The furnishings and art reflect life in and near the house over the past 8 centuries. After touring the house, you can explore the 100-hectare (250-acre) estate, which includes 8 hectares (20 acres) of prized **gardens** with more than 5,000 species of plants and flowers, and a children's playground. The Malahide grounds also contain the **Fry Model Railway** museum (see above) and **Tara's Palace,** an antique dollhouse and toy collection.

Malahide, County Dublin. ℭ **01/846-2184**. malahidecastle@dublintourism.ie. Admission €6 ($7.20) adults, €5 ($6) students and seniors, €3.50 ($4.20) children under 12, €17 ($21) families; gardens free. AE, MC, V. Combination tickets with Fry Model Railway and Newbridge House available. Apr–Oct Mon–Sat 10am–5pm, Sun 11am–6pm; Nov–Mar Mon–Fri 10am–5pm, Sat–Sun 2–5pm; gardens May–Sept daily 2–5pm. Closed for tours 12:45–2pm (restaurant remains open). DART: Malahide. Bus: 42.

National Botanic Gardens Established by the Royal Dublin Society in 1795 on a rolling 20-hectare (50-acre) expanse of land north of the city center, this is Dublin's horticultural showcase. The attractions include more than 20,000 different plants and cultivars, a Great Yew Walk, a bog garden, a water garden, a rose garden, and an herb garden. A variety of Victorian-style glass houses are filled with tropical plants and exotic species. Remember this spot when you suddenly crave refuge from the bustle of the city. It's a quiet, lovely haven, within a short walk of Glasnevin Cemetery. All but the rose garden is wheelchair accessible. There's free roadside parking outside the garden gates.

Botanic Rd., Glasnevin, Dublin 9. ℭ **01/837-7596**. Free admission. Guided tour €2 ($2.40). Apr–Oct Mon–Sat 9am–6pm, Sun 11am–6pm; Nov–Mar Mon–Sat 10am–4:30pm, Sun 11am–4:30pm. Bus: 13, 19, or 134.

Newbridge House and Park *Kids* This country mansion 19km (12 miles) north of Dublin dates from 1740 and was once the home of Dr. Charles Cobbe, an archbishop of Dublin. Occupied by the Cobbe family until 1984, the house is a showcase of family memorabilia such as hand-carved furniture, portraits, daybooks, and dolls, as well as a museum of objects collected on world travels. The Great Drawing Room, in its original state, is one of the finest Georgian interiors in Ireland. The house sits on 140 hectares (350 acres), laid out with picnic areas and walking trails. The grounds also include an 8-hectare (20-acre) working Victorian farm stocked with animals, as well as a craft shop and a coffee shop. There's also a ter-rific, up-to-the-minute playground for children to let off some energy. The coffee shop remains open during the lunch hour (1–2pm).

Donabate, County Dublin. (*) 01/843-6534. Admission €2.50 ($3) adults, €1.50 ($1.80) seniors and students, €1 ($1.20) children, €6 ($7.20) families. Apr–Sept Tues–Sat 10am–1pm and 2–5pm, Sun 2–6pm; Oct–Mar Sat–Sun 2–5pm. Suburban rail to Donabate. Bus: 33B.

Skerries Mills   This fascinating 18-hectare (45-acre) historical complex has been open for only a few years and is already a major attraction. Why? Well, bread, for one thing. This site has provided it on and off since the 12th century. Originally part of an Augus-tinian Priory, the mill has had many lives (and deaths). Last known as the Old Mill Bakery, providing loaves to the local north coast, it suffered a devastating fire in 1986 and lay in ruins until it was reborn as Skerries Mills in 1999. An ambitious restoration project brought two restored windmills and a water mill—complete with grinding, winnowing, and threshing wheels—back into operation. And there's even an adjoining field of grains—barley, oats, and wheat, all that's needed for the traditional brown loaf—sown, har-vested, and threshed using traditional implements and machinery. The result is not only the sweet smell of fresh bread but an intrigu-ing glimpse into the past, brought to life not only by guided tours but also by the opportunity to put your own hand to the stone and to grind your own flour on rotary or saddle querns. Then, if you've worked up an appetite, there's a lovely tearoom, often hosting live music, Irish dancing, and other events. Besides all this, there are rotating special exhibits and a fine gift shop of Irish crafts.

Skerries, County Dublin. (*) 01/849-5208. Admission €5.50 ($6.60) adults; €4 ($4.80) seniors, students, and children; €12 ($14) families. Apr–Sept daily 10:30am–6pm; Oct–Mar daily 10:30am–4:30pm. Closed Dec 20–Jan 1. Suburban Rail. Bus: 33. Skerries town and the Mills signposted north of Dublin off the N1.

WHERE TO STAY
VERY EXPENSIVE
Clontarf Castle Hotel ⚜ If you want to be within striking distance of Dublin airport (8km/5 miles away), you can't beat this

luxurious castle hotel in Clontarf, a pretty seaside suburb served by both the DART and several bus routes. But if you'll be spending most of your time in the city center, this hotel will probably feel too remote. The castle was built in 1172 by Normans and retains its impressive castellated exterior. Much later, in the 1600s, it was given to one of Oliver Cromwell's loyal servants, whose family retained ownership for the next 300 years. There's a regal quality about the magnificent entrance hall and the guest rooms, some of which boast four-poster beds. The place was completely refurbished in 1998, blending the medieval elements of the castle with bang-up-to-date facilities. Clontarf Castle is also a leading entertainment venue, welcoming a variety of musical and comedic guests throughout the year.

Castle Ave., Clontarf, Dublin 3. ✆ 01/833-2321. Fax 01/833-0418. www.clontarf castle.ie. 111 units. €285 ($343) double. Breakfast €19 ($23). AE, DC, MC, V. Free parking. Bus: 130. **Amenities:** Restaurant (international); 2 bars; gym; room service; babysitting; laundry service; nonsmoking rooms. *In room:* A/C, TV, dataport, tea/coffeemaker, hair dryer, garment press, radio, voice mail.

INEXPENSIVE

Egan's House　　This two-story redbrick Victorian guesthouse is in the center of a pleasant residential neighborhood that's within easy access of the city center. It's within walking distance of the Botanic Gardens and a variety of sports facilities, including tennis, swimming, and a gym. Operated by Pat and Monica Finn, it offers newly redecorated rooms in a variety of sizes and styles, including ground-floor rooms. The comfortable public rooms feature traditional dark woods, brass fixtures, and antiques.

7/9 Iona Park (between Botanic and Lower Drumcondra roads), Glasnevin, Dublin 9. ✆ 800/937-9767 in the U.S. or 01/830-3611. Fax 01/830-3312. 23 units. €90–€110 ($108–$133) double. Rates include full breakfast. MC, V. Limited free parking available. Bus: 3, 11, 13, 13A, 16, 19, 19A, 41, 41A, or 41B. **Amenities:** Dining room; lounge; nonsmoking rooms. *In room:* TV, tea/coffeemaker, hair dryer.

Forte Travelodge　　About 13km (8 miles) north of downtown and 2.4km (1½ miles) north of Dublin airport, this recently expanded two-story motel offers adequate, no-frills accommodations at reasonable prices. Each of the basic rooms, with a double bed and sofa bed, can sleep up to four people. The hotel is located alongside the N1 motorway, and the interior is clean and modern. Public areas are limited to a modest reception area, public pay phone, and adjacent budget-priced Little Chef Irish chain restaurant and lounge.

Dublin-Belfast rd. (N1), Swords, County Dublin. ✆ 800/CALL-THF in the U.S. or 1800/709-709 in Ireland. Fax 01/840-9235. 100 units. €75–€95 ($90–$114) double. Breakfast €5 ($6). AE, DC, MC, V. Bus: 41 or 43. *In room:* TV, hair dryer.

Iona House   A sitting room with a glowing open fireplace, chiming clocks, brass fixtures, and dark-wood furnishings sets a welcoming tone for guests at this two-story redbrick Victorian home. Built around the turn of the 20th century, it has been operated as a guesthouse by Jack Shouldice since 1963. Iona House is in a residential neighborhood 15 minutes from the city center, within walking distance of the Botanic Gardens. Guest rooms offer modern hotel-style appointments, orthopedic beds, and contemporary Irish-made furnishings.

5 Iona Park, Glasnevin, Dublin 9. ℗ 01/830-6217. Fax 01/830-6732. 10 units. €96 ($116) double. Rates include full breakfast. MC, V. Parking available on street. Closed Dec–Jan. Bus: 19 or 19A. **Amenities:** Lounge; nonsmoking rooms; patio. *In room:* TV, hair dryer.

Red Bank House 😺😺 *Value*   This comfortable nook in the heart of Skerries town is only 20 to 30 minutes by car from Dublin Airport, so it can provide a convenient first or last night's lodging for your Ireland holiday. Better yet, it virtually abuts the award-winning Red Bank restaurant (see "Where to Dine," below), so you are guaranteed a memorable introductory or farewell meal in the country. There's an invitingly simply country style to the guest rooms— cream walls, dark woods, crisp white bedspreads, and floral drapes. The power showers are just the ticket after or before a long journey.

7 Church St. and Convent Lane, Skerries, County Dublin. ℗ 01/849-1005 or 01/849-0439. Fax 01/849-1598. www.redbank.ie. 18 units (several with shower only). €140 ($168) double. Rates include service charge and full Irish breakfast. Half-board (B&B and dinner) for 2 €180 ($216). AE, DC, MC, V. Parking on street and lane. Suburban rail. Bus: 33. **Amenities:** Restaurant (seafood). *In room:* TV, dataport, tea/coffeemaker, hair dryer.

WHERE TO DINE
EXPENSIVE

Abbey Tavern   SEAFOOD/INTERNATIONAL   Well known for its nightly traditional-music ballad sessions, this 16th-century tavern also has a full-service restaurant upstairs. Although the menu changes by season, entrees often include scallops *Ty Ar Mor* (with mushrooms, prawns, and cream sauce), *crepes fruits de mer* (seafood crepes), poached salmon, duck with orange and Curaçao sauce, and veal a la crème. After a meal, you might want to join the audience downstairs for some lively Irish traditional music.

Abbey St., Howth, County Dublin. ℗ 01/839-0307. www.abbeytavern.ie. Reservations required. Fixed-price dinner €35 ($42). MC, V. Mon–Sat 7–11pm. DART: Howth. Bus: 31.

The Red Bank 🐟🐟 SEAFOOD   The hugely popular Red Bank restaurant has been winning friends, influencing people, and garnering awards for nearly 20 years. A bank in a former life, the restaurant uses the old vault as its wine cellar. The mood here is charmingly old-fashioned and classy. Your waiter takes your order in the cozy lounge, where you wait with a drink until your meal is ready and you're brought to your table. Chef Terry McCoy is an exuberant and inspired chef, who gets his exceptional fresh seafood from local waters. His Paddy Attley is a platter of three fish of the day landed in the Skerries Harbor, each served in a uniquely enhancing sauce. McCoy is at his best with timeless icons such as scallops in a sauce of butter, cream, and white wine, or a truly divine lobster thermidor. A dinner here is a both a spectacle and a feast. Service is correct and respectfully old-school, highlighted when the dessert trolley is wheeled in, laden with a mouthwatering selection of confections.

7 Church St., Skerries, County Dublin. ⓒ 01/849-1005. www.redbank.ie. Reservations required. Dinner main courses €16–€30 ($20–$36); fixed-price dinners €45–€48 ($54–$57). AF, DC, MC, V. Mon–Sat 7–9:30pm; Sun 12:30–4pm. Suburban rail. Bus: 33.

INEXPENSIVE

Dee Gee's Wine and Steak Bar INTERNATIONAL   Facing Howth Harbour and Dublin Bay, this informal seaside spot opposite the DART station is ideal for a cup of coffee, a snack, or a full meal. A self-service snackery by day and a more formal, table-service restaurant at night, it offers indoor and outdoor seating. Dinner entrees range from steaks and burgers to shrimp scampi and vegetable lasagna. At lunchtime, soups, salads, and sandwiches are featured. Sit, relax, and watch all the activities of Howth from a front-row seat.

Harbour Rd., Howth, County Dublin. ⓒ 01/839-2641. Dinner main courses €6–€10 ($7.20–$12). MC, V. Year-round daily 7am–6pm. DART: Howth. Bus: 31.

3 County Wicklow

County Wicklow extends from Bray, 19km (12 miles) S of Dublin, to Arklow, 64km (40 miles) S of Dublin

The borders of County Wicklow, nicknamed the "Garden of Ireland," start just a dozen or so miles south of downtown Dublin. Within this county, you'll find some of Ireland's best rural scenery. If you're based in Dublin, you can easily spend a day or afternoon in Wicklow and return to the city for dinner and the theater, but you'll probably want to linger overnight at one of the many fine country inns.

One accessible, charming gateway to County Wicklow is the small harbor town of **Greystones** 👁👁, which you may not want to tell your friends back home about for fear of spoiling the secret. It is hands-down one of the most unspoiled and attractive harbor towns on Ireland's east coast. It has no special attractions except itself, and that's enough.

In general, though, Wicklow's most stunning scenery and most interesting towns and attractions are inland, between Enniskerry and Glendalough. A raised granite ridge runs through the county, containing two of the highest mountain passes in the country—the **Sally Gap** and the **Wicklow Gap.** The best way to see the **Wicklow Mountains** is on foot, following the **Wicklow Way** past mountain tarns and secluded glens. In this region, don't miss the picturesque villages of **Roundwood, Laragh,** and **Aughrim.**

In the southernmost corner of Wicklow, the mountains become hills and share with the villages they shelter an unassuming beauty, a sleepy tranquillity that can be a welcome respite from the bustle of Wicklow's main tourist attractions. Near **Shillelagh** village are lovely forests and the curious edifice of **Huntington Castle.**

ESSENTIALS

GETTING THERE   Irish Rail (© 01/836-6222; www.irishrail.ie) provides daily train service between Dublin and Bray and Wicklow.

Bus Eireann (© 01/836-6111) operates daily express bus service to Arklow, Bray, and Wicklow towns. Both Bus Eireann and **Gray Line Tours** (© 01/605-7705) offer seasonal sightseeing tours to Glendalough, Wicklow, and Powerscourt Gardens.

But the best way to see Wicklow is by car, so that you can stop where you like and let serendipity guide your way. Take the N11 south from Dublin City and follow turnoff signs for major attractions. Or, you can try out the "Route Planning" facility offered by Ireland's **AA Roadwatch** (www.aaroadwatch.ie). Simply plug in your starting point and destination, with as many places in between that you'd like to visit. It lets you avoid the rush or save money with nifty options like "avoid motorways" and "avoid toll roads."

VISITOR INFORMATION   The **Wicklow Tourist Office,** Fitzwilliam Square, Wicklow Town, County Wicklow (© **0404/ 69117;** www.wicklow.ie), is open Monday through Friday year-round, Saturday during peak season.

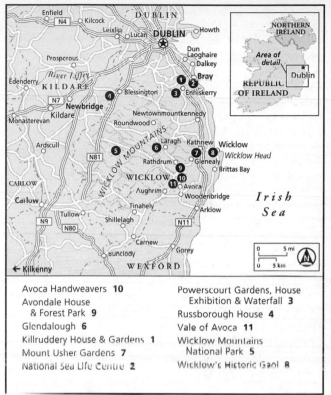

Avoca Handweavers **10**

Avondale House
& Forest Park **9**

Glendalough **6**

Killruddery House & Gardens **1**

Mount Usher Gardens **7**

National Sea Life Centre **2**

Powerscourt Gardens, House
Exhibition & Waterfall **3**

Russborough House **4**

Vale of Avoca **11**

Wicklow Mountains
National Park **5**

Wicklow's Historic Gaol **8**

SEEING THE SIGHTS

Avondale House & Forest Park *(Kids)* In a fertile valley between Glendalough and the Vale of Avoca, this is the former home of Charles Stewart Parnell (1846–91), one of Ireland's great political leaders. Built in 1779, the house is now a museum dedicated to his memory. Set in the surrounding 209-hectare (523-acre) estate and boasting signposted nature trails alongside the Avondale River, Avondale Forest Park is considered the cradle of modern Irish forestry. A new exhibition area commemorates the American side of the Parnell family, most notably Admiral Charles Stewart of the U.S.S. *Constitution*. The coffee shop serves teas and light lunches, featuring homemade breads and pastries. There's also a children's playground.

Off R752, Rathdrum, County Wicklow. © **0404/46111.** Admission €5 ($6) adults, €4.50 ($5.40) seniors and children under 12, €15 ($18) families. Mid-Mar to Oct 31 daily 11am–6pm. Parking €5 ($6).

Glendalough 創創創   This is Wicklow's top sight. In the 6th century, St. Kevin chose this idyllically secluded setting—whose name derived from the Irish phrase *Gleann Da Locha,* meaning "The Glen of the Two Lakes"—for a monastery. Over the centuries, it became a leading center of learning, with thousands of students from Ireland, Britain, and all over Europe, including St. Lawrence O'Toole, who visited in the 12th century. But like so many early Irish religious sites, Glendalough fell into the hands of plundering Anglo-Norman invaders, and its glories came to an end by the 15th century.

Today, visitors can stroll from the upper lake to the lower lake and walk through the remains of the monastery complex, long since converted to a burial place. Although much of the monastic city is in ruins, the remains do include a nearly perfect round tower, 31m (103 ft.) high and 16m (52 ft.) around the base, as well as hundreds of time-worn Celtic crosses and a variety of churches. One of these is St. Kevin's chapel, often called St. Kevin's Kitchen, a fine specimen of an early Irish barrel-vaulted oratory with a miniature round belfry rising from a stone roof. A striking visitor center at the entrance to the site provides helpful orientation, with exhibits on the archaeology, history, folklore, and wildlife of the area. Unfortunately, the main entrance to the monastic complex has been spoiled by a sprawling hotel and hawkers of various sorts, so you may want to cross the river at the visitor center and walk along the banks. You can cross back again at the monastic site, bypassing the trappings of commerce that St. Kevin once fled.

County Wicklow (11km/7 miles east of Wicklow on T7 via Rathdrum). © **0404/ 45325** or 0404/45352. Admission free; exhibits and audiovisual presentation €2.75 ($3.30) adults, €2 ($2.40) seniors, €1.25 ($1.50) students and children under 12, €7 ($8.45) families. Mid-Oct to mid-Mar daily 9:30am–5pm; mid-Mar to mid-Oct daily 9am–6pm.

Tips **Getting to Glendalough**

If you plan on driving a car from Dublin to Glendalough, consider taking R155. The trip may take a little longer, and the signage may not be the best, but the spectacular vistas and awe-inspiring scenery are well worth seeing. If you don't have a car, Gray Line offers a bus tour from Dublin to Glendalough. For information, contact Gray Line Desk, Dublin Tourism Centre, Suffolk Street, Dublin 2 (© **01/605-7705;** grayline@tlp.ie).

Kilruddery House & Gardens ☆☆   This estate has been the seat of the earl of Meath since 1618. The original part of its mansion, dating from 1820, features a Victorian conservatory modeled on the Crystal Palace in London. The gardens are a highlight, with a lime avenue, a sylvan theater, foreign trees, exotic shrubs, twin canals, and a fountain-filled, round pond edged with beech hedges. They are the only surviving 17th-century French-style gardens in Ireland.

Kilruddery, Bray, County Wicklow (off the N11). ☎ 01/286-3405. House and garden tour €8 ($9.65) adults, €6 ($7.50) seniors and students, €3 ($3.60) children; gardens only €5 ($6) adults, €4 ($4.80) seniors and students, €2 ($2.40) children. House May–June and Sept daily 1–5pm; gardens Apr weekends 1–5pm, May–Aug daily 1–5pm.

Mount Usher Gardens ☆   Encompassing 8 hectares (20 acres) along the River Vartry, this sylvan site was once home to an ancient lake and more recently laid out in the informal, free-range "Robin-sonian" style. It contains more than 5,000 tree and plant species from all parts of the world, including spindle trees from China, North American swamp cypresses, and Burmese juniper trees. Fiery rhododendrons, fragrant eucalyptus trees, giant Tibetan lilies, and snowy camellias also compete for your attention. Informal and responsive to their natural setting, these gardens have an almost untended feel—a floral woodland, without pretense yet with considerable charm. A spacious tearoom overlooks the river and gardens. The courtyard at the entrance to the gardens contains an interesting assortment of shops, which are open year-round.

Ashford, County Wicklow (off the N11). ☎ 0404/40116. http://homepage.eircom. net/~gardens. Admission €6 ($7.50) adults; €5 ($6) seniors, students, and children 5–12; €22 ($27) families. Guided tours €10 ($12); call for appointment. Mar 17–Oct 31 daily 10:30am–6pm.

National Sea Life Centre *Kids*   Admittedly, the national aquarium and sea park offers good family fun, but it's woefully overpriced considering its small size. Situated at water's edge, the center provides a child-focused introduction to the denizens of the deep. The labyrinthine path through the aquarium begins with a rock tunnel carved by a winding freshwater stream; from there, you follow the water's course toward the open sea, from freshwater river to tidal estuary to storm-pounded harbor and finally to the briny deep. Along the way, kids are quizzed on what they're learning, as they use "magic" glasses to read coded questions and find the answers on special scratchpads they've been given. One remarkable feature here is the close access visitors have to the sea life. When you bend over and eyeball the fish, they as often as not return the favor, surfacing and staring back only inches from your face. Once you reach "the Deep," the emphasis is on scary critters, like sharks (of course) and the blue-ringed octopus. Count on spending about an hour or so here—which works out to a pricey €.45 (55¢) a minute for a family.

Strand Rd., Bray, County Wicklow. © 01/286-6939. www.sealife.ie. Admission €8.50 ($10) adults, €6.50 ($7.85) seniors and students, €5.50 ($6.60) children, €27 ($33) families. Year-round Mon–Fri 11am–5pm, Sat–Sun 10am–6pm.

Powerscourt Gardens, House Exhibition, and Waterfall 𝕣𝕣𝕣

If you only have time to visit one of Wicklow's fabulous gardens, then let this be the one. On a 400-hectare (1,000-acre) estate less than 19km (12 miles) south of Dublin city, Powerscourt is one of the finest gardens in Europe, designed and laid out by Daniel Robertson between 1745 and 1767. This property is filled with splendid Greek- and Italian-inspired statuary, decorative ironwork, a petrified-moss grotto, lovely herbaceous borders, a Japanese garden, a circular pond and fountain with statues of winged horses, and the occasional herd of deer. Stories have it that Robertson, afflicted with gout, was pushed around the grounds in a wheelbarrow to oversee the work. An 18th-century manor house designed by Richard Cassels, the architect of Russborough House (see below) and the man credited with the design of Dublin's Parliament house, stood proudly on the site until it was gutted by fire in 1974. The real reason to come is for the gardens. Don't opt for the additional entrance fee to "the house," as the exhibition consists primarily of a mediocre video on the history of Powerscourt. The cafeteria serves up delicious, reasonably priced lunches and a view that's not to be believed. The adjacent garden center is staffed with highly knowledgeable green thumbs who can answer all your horticultural questions. If you've brought the kids, they can occupy themselves at a nearby playground. The waterfall is the highest in Ireland, at 121m (398 ft.), and is a favorite picnic spot.

Enniskerry, County Wicklow (off the N11). © 01/204-6000. Gardens and house exhibition €8 ($9.65) adults, €7 ($8.45) seniors and students, €4.50 ($5.40) children, free for kids under 5; gardens only €6 ($7.50) adults, €5.50 ($6.60) seniors and students, €3.50 ($4.20) children, free for kids under 5; waterfall €4 ($4.80) adults, €3.50 ($4.20) seniors and students, €3 ($3.60) children, free for kids under 5. AE, MC, V. Gardens and house exhibition Mar–Oct daily 9:30am–5:30pm; Nov–Feb daily 9:30am–dusk. Waterfall Mar–Oct daily 9:30am–7pm; Nov–Feb daily 10:30am–dusk.

Russborough House 𝕣𝕣

Ensconced in this 18th-century Palladian house is the world-famous Beit Art Collection, with paintings by Vernet, Guardi, Bellotto, Gainsborough, Rubens, and Reynolds. Art lovers adore the place. Trouble is, thieves love it, too. Since

1974, Russborough has suffered four art burglaries. In September 2002, thieves made away with masterpieces worth €10 million ($12 million). Most of the artworks were eventually recovered. The house is furnished with European pieces and decorated with bronzes, tapestries, and some fine Francini plasterwork. On the premises are a restaurant, shop, and playground.

Blessington, County Wicklow (off N81). ✆ 045/865239. Admission to main rooms €6 ($7.50) adults, €4.50 ($5.40) seniors and students, €3 ($3.60) children under 12. Apr–Sept daily 10am–5pm. Tours given on the hour. Closed Oct–Mar.

Vale of Avoca ✿ Basically a peaceful riverbank, the Vale of Avoca was immortalized in the writings of 19th-century poet Thomas Moore. It's here at the "Meeting of the Waters" that the Avonmore and Avonbeg rivers join to form the Avoca River. It's said that the poet sat under "Tom Moore's Tree" looking for inspiration and penned the lines, "There is not in the wide world a valley so sweet / as the vale in whose bosom the bright waters meet . . ." The tree itself is a sorry sight—it's been picked almost bare by souvenir hunters—but the place is still worth a visit.

Rte. 755, Avoca, County Wicklow.

Wicklow Mountains National Park ✿✿✿ Nearly 20,000 hectares (50,000 acres) of County Wicklow make up this new national park. The core area surrounds Glendalough, including the Glendalough Valley and Glendalough Wood Nature Reserves. *Hikers note:* The most mountainous stretch of the Wicklow Way cuts through this park (**www.irishwaymarkedways.ie**). You'll find an information station at the Upper Lake at Glendalough. Information is available here on hiking in the Glendalough Valley and surrounding hills, including maps and descriptions of routes. Free guided nature walks—mainly through rolling woodland—begin from the center on Tuesdays (departing 11am and returning 1:30pm) and Thursdays (departing 3pm and returning 4pm). The closest parking is at Upper Lake, where you'll pay €2 ($2.40) per car; instead, just walk up from the Glendalough Visitor Centre, where the parking's free.

Glendalough, County Wicklow. ✆ 0404/45425. Visitor center admission free. Park admission €2.75 ($3.30) adults, €2 ($2.40) seniors, €1.25 ($1.50) students and children, €7 ($8.45) families. May–Aug daily 10am–6pm; Apr and Sept weekends only 10am–6pm. Closed Oct–Mar.

Wicklow's Historic Gaol ✿ It's hard to believe that Wicklow Gaol ceased operation as a prison only as recently as 1924, after more than 2 centuries of terror. After passing under the hanging beam, visitors are lined up against the wall of the "day room" and confronted with some dark facts of prison life in 1799, when more than 400 prisoners, most of them rebels, occupied the jail's 42 cells. After being fed once every 4 days and allowed to walk in the prison yard for just 15 minutes a month, prisoners must have warmed to the idea of facing the hangman's noose. Within the main cellblock, you can roam the jail's individual cells and visit a series of exhibitions and audiovisual presentations. The impact of these stories is immediate and powerful for children as well as for adults, because this jail held both. Because many prisoners were sent off to penal colonies in Australia and Tasmania, that story, too, is told here, with the help of a stage-set wharf and prison ship. There's an in-house cafe, but your appetite might have been killed off by the time you've finished your tour. Overall, it's very informative and moving.

Kilmantin Hill, Wicklow Town, County Wicklow. ⓒ **0404/61599**. www.wicklows historicgaol.com. Tour €6.50 ($7.85) adults, €4.70 ($5.65) seniors and students, €3.75 ($4.50) children, €18 ($21) families with up to 3 children. Apr 17–Sept daily 10am–6pm (last admission at 5pm).

SHOPPING

Wicklow offers a wide array of wonderful craft centers and workshops. Here is a small sampling:

Avoca Handweavers   Dating from 1723, this cluster of whitewashed stone buildings and a mill houses the oldest surviving handweaving company in Ireland. It produces a wide range of tweed clothing, knitwear, and accessories. The dominant tones of mauve, aqua, teal, and heather reflect the local landscape. You're welcome to watch as craftspeople weave strands of yarn spun from the wool of local sheep. The weaving shed is open daily May to October from 9:30am to 5:30pm. The complex has a retail outlet and a tea shop (p. 169). There are other branches throughout Ireland, including one on the N11 at Kilmacanogue, Bray, County Wicklow (ⓒ **01/ 286-7466**), open daily 9am to 6pm. Avoca, County Wicklow. ⓒ **0402/ 35105**. www.avoca.ie.

Bergin Clarke Studio   In this little workshop, Brian Clarke hand-fashions silver jewelry and giftware, and Yvonne Bergin knits stylish, colorful apparel using yarns from County Wicklow. Open May to September daily 10am to 8pm, October to April Monday to Saturday 10am to 5:30pm. The Old Schoolhouse, Ballinaclash, Rathdrum, County Wicklow. ⓒ **0404/46385**.

Fisher's of Newtownmountkennedy   This shop, in a converted schoolhouse, stocks a wide array of men's and women's sporting clothes—quilted jackets, raincoats, footwear, blazers, and accessories. There's also a new tearoom. Open Monday to Saturday 9:30am to 5:30pm, Sunday 2 to 6pm. The Old Schoolhouse, Newtownmountkennedy, County Wicklow. (© 01/281-9404.

The Woolen Mills Glendalough   This long-established crafts shop in a converted farmhouse offers handcrafts from all over Ireland, such as Bantry Pottery and Penrose Glass from Waterford. Books, jewelry, and a large selection of hand-knits from the area are also sold. Open daily 9:30am to 6:30pm. Laragh, County Wicklow. (© 0404/45156.

WHERE TO STAY
EXPENSIVE

Rathsallagh House Hotel & Golf Club 🌸🌸   It's only an hour's drive from Dublin, but any trace of city tension or travel fatigue evaporates as soon as you cross the threshold of Rathsallagh House. A recent recipient of the American Express Best-Loved Hotels of the World award, this country-house hotel has a particularly warm, welcoming, unpretentious feel to it; it's a splendid place to relax and recharge. Converted from Queen Anne stables in 1798, the rambling, ivy-covered country house sits amid 212 hectares (530 acres) of parkland with its own walled garden and is surrounded by Rathsallagh Golf Course. Rooms are priced according to size, starting with standard rooms, which are rather cramped. A superior room costs €40 ($48) more but offers considerably more space. Most rooms have a sitting area, a huge walk-in closet, and window seats, and some have Jacuzzis. There are good reading lamps over the beds and antique furnishings throughout the hotel. Note that Rathsallagh does not cater to children under 12.

Dunlavin, County Wicklow. (© 800/323-5463 in the U.S. or 045/403112. Fax 045/403343. www.rathsallaghhousehotel.com. 29 units. €250 ($301) double. Rates include full breakfast. Fixed 5-course dinner €60 ($75). Greens fees: €50–€60 ($60–$75). AE, DC, MC, V. Closed Dec 23–31. No children under 12 accepted. **Amenities:** Restaurant (modern Continental); lounge/bar; small indoor pool; 18-hole championship golf course; tennis court; sauna; archery; billiards; croquet; steam room. *In room:* TV, tea/coffeemaker, hair dryer.

Tinakilly Country House & Restaurant 🌸🌸🌸   Tinakilly is one of Ireland's most relaxing, sought-after small hotels—the kind of place the Irish come to celebrate an anniversary or special event, and the kind of place that remains in your memory long after you've departed. Everything conspires to spoil you: luxurious accommodations, attentive service, and an award-winning restaurant. Dating from the 1870s, this was the home of Capt. Robert Charles Halpin,

---

Tips **Service Charges**

A reminder: Unless otherwise noted, room rates don't include service charges (usually 10%–15% of your bill).

---

commander of the *Great Eastern,* who laid the first successful cable connecting Europe with America. With a sweeping central staircase said to be the twin of the one on the ship, Tinakilly is full of seafaring memorabilia, paintings, and Victorian antiques. Every room is unique and in keeping with the Victorian style; most have either four-poster or half-tester canopy beds. The best have views of the Irish Sea. The Captain's Suites are quite grand (with enormous bathrooms), but even the standard doubles are cozy and charming in the true sense of the word. The restaurant, Brunel (p. 168), is duly famous for ennobling the "Irish country house" style of cooking.

On R750, off the Dublin-Wexford rd. (N11), Rathnew, County Wicklow. © 800/
525-4800 in the U.S. or 0404/69274. Fax 0404/67806. www.tinakilly.ie. 51 units.
€208–€256 ($251–$308) double; €258–€326 ($311–$393) junior suite;
€346–€436 ($417–$525) Captain's Suite with sea view. Rates include full breakfast and VAT. AE, DC, MC, V. **Amenities:** Restaurant (modern country house);
lounge. *In room:* TV, hair dryer, radio.

EXPENSIVE/MODERATE

Brook Lodge Hotel & Wells Spa ☆☆☆ *Value*   There may be no more luxurious place to stay in Ireland in this price range. Brook Lodge is a revolutionary idea in Ireland—not so much a hotel as a planned village built from scratch to include accommodations, fine dining, good pubs (nearby Acton's is a microbrewery), a chapel, a bakery, landscaped gardens, and a half dozen or so shops selling homemade wines, jams, crafts, and the like. The hotel itself is luxurious, modern, and comfortable, done up in warm, energized colors. Rooms have firm king-size four-poster beds, wood-paneled window seats, deep tubs, quality linens, and contemporary furnishings of natural elements. The chic mezzanine suites have king-size beds, plasma TV screens, and contemporary furnishings to rival any New York boutique hotel. Service is excellent and the personal touch extends to a decidedly Irish nightly turndown: chocolates on your pillow and a hot-water bottle between the sheets. The hotel's flagship is The Strawberry Tree restaurant (p. 168). From Rathdrum, follow signs for Aughrim and then 3km (2 miles) to Macreddin Village and the Brook Lodge Hotel. You can often get fantastic discounts by booking online.

Macreddin Village (between Aughrim and Aghavannagh), County Wicklow. ℂ **0402/ 36444.** Fax 0402/36580. www.brooklodge.com. 54 units. €170–€240 ($205–$289) double; €360 ($434) suite. Rates include service charge and full Irish breakfast. Fixed-price 4-course dinner €55 ($66); 3-course Sun lunch €35 ($42). AE, DC, MC, V. **Amenities:** 2 restaurants (organic, cafe); 2 pubs; full-service spa; laundry service. *In room:* TV, hair dryer.

MODERATE

Clone House 👁👁   Clone House was built in the 1600s, then burned down in the 1798 Revolution, and rebuilt in 1805. The house has changed hands several times since then, but today Jeff and Carla Watson run the place with panache. Carla was raised in Tuscany and has given the house a Mediterranean elegance. The guest rooms have a salubrious, Italianate feel, featuring king size beds, traditional wood floors, and richly colored fabrics on the curtains and bed canopies. Small luxuries like thick cotton towels, chocolates, and fresh fruit make you feel pampered. The best room, the Vale of Avoca, has a skylight above the bed and a working fireplace. As luck would have it, Carla is a superb cook, treating her guests to five-course gourmet meals that may include stuffed quails wrapped in pancetta, *osso buco,* and an irresistible focaccia bread.

Aughrim, County Wicklow. ℂ **0402/36121.** Fax 0402/36029. www.clonehouse.com. 7 units, all with private bathroom. €130–€180 ($157–$217) double. Rates include full breakfast. Dinner €45–€55 ($54–$66). MC, V. **Amenities:** Bar; small gym; sauna. *In room:* Tea/coffeemaker, hair dryer.

Glendalough Hotel   Without spending the night in a round tower, you can't get any closer to St. Kevin's digs than this seasoned, veteran inn situated in a wooded glen at the very entrance to Glendalough, beside the Glendasan River and within the Wicklow Mountains National Park. Dating from the 1800s, it was refurbished and updated in the mid-1990s with traditional Irish furnishings and standard modern comforts. This was once a sleepy and idyllic spot, but it is now rather overrun with tourists, their buses, and all that caters to them.

Tips Phoning around in Wicklow

Many phone numbers in Wicklow have changed in the past year and more changes are in the pipeline. If you have trouble getting through to one of the numbers listed, call directory assistance at ℂ **11811.**

Glendalough, County Wicklow. ✆ 800/365-3346 in the U.S. or 0404/45135. Fax 0404/45142. 44 units. €130–€170 ($157–$205) double. Rates include full breakfast. AE, DC, MC, V. Closed Jan. **Amenities:** Restaurant (Irish/Continental); pub. *In room:* TV, hair dryer.

INEXPENSIVE
Derrybawn Mountain Lodge   This elegant, comfortable field-stone manor house in an idyllic parkland setting looks out over the surrounding hills. The rooms are spacious, bright, tastefully furnished, and outfitted with orthopedic beds. Located just outside Laragh village, the place is convenient to fishing streams and hiking trails (including the Wicklow Way), and a great place from which to explore Wicklow's natural wonders.

Laragh, County Wicklow. ✆ 0404/45644. Fax 0404/45645. 8 units. €80–€90 ($96–$108) double. Rates include full breakfast. MC, V. **Amenities:** Recreation/billiards room; nonsmoking rooms; sitting room. *In room:* TV.

Slievemore   This mid-19th-century harbor house offers white-glove cleanliness, spacious comfort, and (if you book early and request a seafront room) a commanding view of Greystones Harbor, Bray Head, and the Irish Sea. Proprietor Pippins Parkinson says that "people stumble on Greystones, find it by accident." But forget relying on serendipity.

The Harbour, Greystones (signposted on N11), County Wicklow. ✆ 01/287-4724. www.slievemorehouse.com. 8 units (all with shower only). €65–€70 ($78–$84) double. Rates include full Irish breakfast. No credit cards. Bus: 84. **Amenities:** Sitting room. *In room:* TV.

Tudor Lodge ✿   This B&B, set on the slopes of the Wicklow Mountains, makes an especially attractive base from which to see the area. The whitewashed walls are fresh and inviting, with wooden ceiling beams recalling the rusticity of a country cottage. Bedrooms are spacious, and each has a small desk as well as both a double and a single bed. The dining room and living room are equally hospitable, with large windows opening onto views of green meadows and mountains. A brick fireplace and beamed ceilings make the living room a cozy retreat. In the summer, you can relax on the generous stone terrace or riverside patio overlooking the Avonmore River. There is an appetizing array of breakfast choices, and they will also prepare dinner for larger groups. Otherwise, the restaurants and pubs of Laragh are a short and scenic walk away.

Laragh, County Wicklow. ✆/fax 0404/45554. www.tudorlodgeireland.com. 6 units, all with private bathroom (shower only). €70–€75 ($84–$90) double. MC, V. **Amenities:** Nonsmoking rooms; living room; sunroom. *In room:* TV, tea/coffeemaker, hair dryer.

SELF-CATERING

Tynte House ⟨ (Kids) Dunlavin is a sleepy three-pub town in western Wicklow, 48km (30 miles) southwest of Dublin. It's as convenient as it is peaceful. Tynte House, a lovingly preserved 19th-century family farm complex with new apartment units and holiday cottages, offers an attractive array of options for overnight and longer-term guests. The driving force is Mrs. Caroline Lawler, "brought up in the business" of divining visitors' needs and surpassing their expectations. In 2000 she was named one of the top 20 "landladies" in the United Kingdom and Ireland.

The self-catering mews (renovated stables) houses have one to three bedrooms; the apartments hold one or two bedrooms; and the four new cottages range from two to four bedrooms and have working fireplaces. All are brilliantly designed and furnished with one eye on casual efficiency and the other on good taste. They have bold, bright color schemes, light pine furniture, and spacious tiled bathrooms. The no. 3 mews house and the open-plan apartment are favorites, but none will disappoint. This makes a great home base for families, with a grassy play area and treehouse, an outdoor barbecue and picnic tables, a tennis court, and a game room with Ping-Pong and pool tables. Exact prices depend on the season and the size of the unit. Shorter stays and weekend discounts are available in the off season.

Dunlavin center, County Wicklow. (ⓒ) 045/401561. Fax 045/401586. www.tynte house.com. / units, 4 homes, 4 apts, 4 cottages. Self-catering units €230–€520 ($277–$627) per week. Dinner €25 ($30). AE, MC, V. In room: TV, kitchen, dishwasher, microwave, washer/dryer.

Wicklow Head Lighthouse ⟨⟨ (Finds) This 18th-century octagonal lighthouse, situated on Wicklow Head just 3.2km (2 miles) from Wicklow Town, makes for a very unique getaway. The lighthouse was established in 1781, then struck by lightning and subsequently gutted by fire in 1836. It remained a neglected shell until the Irish Landmark Trust (ILT), whose mission is to rescue neglected historic buildings, transformed it into a wonderful place to get away from it all. The interior is chic rustic with whitewashed walls, pine furnishings, brass beds, and nautical memorabilia. There are five floors, each of which is an octagonal room: two double bedrooms, one bathroom, one sitting room, and the kitchen. The ground floor also has a sitting area and a small bathroom. Every window has a view to make even the most cynical jaw drop, and the sitting room is equipped with a telescope (great for watching seals frolicking below, or fishing trawlers returning home in the evening).

Like all ILT properties, there is no TV. *One caveat:* The spiral stair-case that corkscrews up the tower is not suitable for folks with hampered mobility or children under age 5.

Wicklow, County Wicklow. Contact the Irish Landmark Trust Ⓒ **01/670-4733.** Fax 01/670-4887. www.irishlandmark.com. €440 ($530) for 4 nights in low season, sliding up to €1,175 ($1,416) per week in high season. **Amenities:** Kitchen.

WHERE TO DINE
EXPENSIVE

Brunel Restaurant 𝒦𝒦 MODERN COUNTRY   This excellent restaurant, which *Bon Appétit* magazine once called "a beacon to restore hope to the traveller's heart," has won as many accolades as the Tinakilly Country House hotel, to which it belongs (see above). The table d'hôte menu changes daily and is confidently balanced—sophisticated without being fussy, elegant without acrobatics. The service, too, is precise and intuitive, letting the ritual follow its own course. All this makes for a meal you remember, like the chargrilled tiger prawns and lemon grass with fennel oil, the cream of roast chestnut and celery soup, the caramelized scallops on saffron potato mash, and the loin of Wicklow lamb. The wine list is vast and, while international, focuses on France. If dinner here is out of your budget, consider coming for a light lunch (1–3pm) or afternoon tea (3–5pm).

In Tinakilly Country House. Rathnew, County Wicklow (on R750, off the N11). Ⓒ **0404/69274.** Dinner main courses €24–€29 ($29–$35). AE, DC, MC, V. Tues–Sat 7:30–9pm; Sun 1–8pm.

The Strawberry Tree 𝒦𝒦𝒦 GOURMET ORGANIC   Winner of the Irish *Food & Wine*'s Best Restaurant award in 2003, this place has gone from innovative to iconic in a few short years. Only wild and organic foods are used to prepare memorable meals and then served up in a swish, dramatic dining room. Starters make for interesting reading—and eating—and might include grilled asparagus, confit tomato, and blue cheese cream or the unlikely sounding but delectable combination of goat's cheese, focaccia, roast pears, and red wine. Then try the beef filet with buttered beetroot, served in a balsamic *jus,* or the wild guinea fowl served alongside dried fruit compote. From Rathdrum, follow signs for Aughrim and then 3km (2 miles) to Macreddin Village and the Brook Lodge Hotel.

Macreddin Village (between Aughrim and Aghavannagh), County Wicklow. Ⓒ **0402/36444.** Fax 0402/36580. www.brooklodge.com. Reservations required. Fixed-price dinner €55 ($66); Sun lunch €35 ($42). MC, V. Wed–Sat 7–9:30pm; Sun 1–2:30pm.

The Tree of Idleness 𝒦 GREEK/CYPRIOT   Chef Susan Courtellas comes from a Greek Cypriot background—a fact she gleefully celebrates with ingredients you don't run across often on Irish menus. All the noble peasant classics are here—moussaka, taramasalata, roast suckling pig—each executed perfectly and with flair. This is a fun dining room, and it fills with a buzzy, energized clientele each evening. Leave room for one of the meltaway desserts.

Seafront, Bray, County Wicklow. ℃ 01/286-3498. Dinner main courses €19–€24 ($23–$29). AE, MC, V. Tues–Sun 7:30–11pm.

MODERATE

Hungry Monk Wine Bar ℱ INTERNATIONAL   This place has been around for a long time, but it continues to pull new fans because of its no-nonsense approach to good food and wine. If you're in the mood for a nice, three-course meal, then head upstairs to the upscale restaurant. Downstairs, at the wine bar, is where you come for a one-plate dinner and a bottle of nice wine. No wildly complicated or sophisticated dishes here, just good, honest, middle-of-the-road food at middle-of-the-road prices—something that is, sadly, becoming harder to find in Ireland. Think seafood chowder, vegetarian spring rolls, Bombay chicken curry, goujons of plaice, and scampi. Everything is good, but the Monk Burger, served with onion rings and extra cheese, is especially recommendable. The wines are well chosen and affordable, the service unobtrusive and correct, the crowd cheerful and enthusiastic.

Church Rd., Greystones, County Wicklow. ℃ 01/287-5759. Main courses €13–€18 ($16–$22). MC, V. Wed–Sat 7–11pm; Sun 12:30–8pm.

Roundwood Inn ℱ IRISH/CONTINENTAL   Dating from 1750, this old coaching inn is the one of the best reasons to head to Roundwood, a place of unspoiled mountain beauty. It has an old-world atmosphere, with open log fireplaces and antique furnishings. Nearly everything is home-baked or locally grown or raised—from steaks and sandwiches to traditional Irish stew, fresh lobster and salmon from Greystones, and seafood pancakes. In good weather there's a lovely, secluded garden to sit in, and in the bar between meal times, there's outstanding pub grub.

Main St. (R755), Roundwood, County Wicklow. ℃ 01/281-8107. Reservations recommended for dinner. Main courses €20–€30 ($24–$36). MC, V. Wed–Fri 7–9:30pm; Sat–Sun 1–2:30pm.

INEXPENSIVE

Avoca Handweavers Tea Shop ℱ BISTRO/VEGETARIAN   Forget for a moment that this is an informal cafeteria—at a tourist magnet, no less. It is a great place to eat, virtually guaranteed to deliver one of the better meals on your trip. The menu changes frequently, but starters might include a delicate pea-and-mint soup or the terrific Caesar salad. Main courses might offer sesame-glazed chicken, honey-roasted ham, Mediterranean sweet frittata, or smoked Wicklow trout. The tea shop attracts a loyal local clientele, in addition to the busloads of visitors who come to shop.

Avoca, County Wicklow. © 0402/35105. Lunch €4–€10 ($4.80–$12). AE, DC, MC, V. Daily 9am–5pm.

Poppies Country Cooking IRISH HOME-STYLE   This 12-table self-service eatery opposite the main square is justifiably popular for light meals and snacks all day. With the warm, familiar feel of a neighbor's kitchen—that is, a neighbor who can really cook—this is a local hangout. From fist-size whole-grain scones to vegetarian nut roast, the portions are generous. The menu ranges from homemade soups and salads to hominy pie, nut roast, baked salmon, vegetarian quiche, and lasagna. A new management team has recently brought in a good range of coffees and herbal teas. You'll find a second branch of Poppies on Trafalgar Road, in Greystones (© 01/287-4228).

Enniskerry, County Wicklow. © 01/282-8869. Lunch €4–€9 ($4.80–$11). MC, V. Daily 8:30am–6pm.

PUBS

Cartoon Inn   With walls displaying the work of many famous cartoonists, this cottagelike pub claims to be the country's only cartoon-themed pub. It's the headquarters for Ireland's Cartoon Festival, held in late May or early June each year. Pub grub is available at lunchtime. Main St., Rathdrum, County Wicklow. © 0404/46774.

The Coach House   Adorned with lots of colorful hanging flowerpots, this Tudor-style inn sits in the mountains, in the heart of Ireland's highest village. Dating from 1790, it is full of local memorabilia, from old photos and agricultural posters to antique jugs and plates. It's well worth a visit, whether to learn about the area or to get some light refreshment. Main St., Roundwood, County Wicklow. © 01/281-8157. www.thecoachhouse.ie.

The Meetings   This Tudor-style country-cottage pub stands idyllically at the "Meeting of the Waters" associated with poet Thomas Moore. An 1889 edition of Moore's book of poems is on display. Good pub grub is served daily, with traditional Irish music April to October every Sunday afternoon (4–6pm), and weekend nights all year. Avoca, County Wicklow. © 0402/35557.

Index

See also Accommodations and Restaurant indexes below.

MIT COOP @ KENDALL SQ. (617) 499-3200

177567 CASH-1   4475 0304 404

978184537327 TRADE
Ireland Travel Pac   MDS 1   14.95
978076457788 TRADE
Frommer's Portable   MDC 1   10.99
              SUBTOTAL   25.94
        5% SALES TAX   1.30
              TOTAL   27.24

ACCOUNT NUMBER   XXXXXXXXXXXX8157
    Visa/Mastercard   27.24
Expiration Date   XX/XX
    Authorization   03113A

TEXTBOOKS MUST BE RETURNED W/IN 3 DAYS

                       5/15/07 12:46 PM

ACCOMMODATIONS

RESTAURANTS

FROMMER'S® COMPLETE TRAVEL GUIDES

Alaska
Alaska Cruises & Ports of Call
American Southwest
Amsterdam
Argentina & Chile
Arizona
Atlanta
Australia
Austria
Bahamas
Barcelona, Madrid & Seville
Beijing
Belgium, Holland & Luxembourg
Bermuda
Boston
Brazil
British Columbia & the Canadian Rockies
Brussels & Bruges
Budapest & the Best of Hungary
Calgary
California
Canada
Cancún, Cozumel & the Yucatán
Cape Cod, Nantucket & Martha's Vineyard
Caribbean
Caribbean Ports of Call
Carolinas & Georgia
Chicago
China
Colorado
Costa Rica
Cruises & Ports of Call
Cuba
Denmark
Denver, Boulder & Colorado Springs
England
Europe
Europe by Rail
European Cruises & Ports of Call

Florence, Tuscany & Umbria
Florida
France
Germany
Great Britain
Greece
Greek Islands
Halifax
Hawaii
Hong Kong
Honolulu, Waikiki & Oahu
India
Ireland
Italy
Jamaica
Japan
Kauai
Las Vegas
London
Los Angeles
Maryland & Delaware
Maui
Mexico
Montana & Wyoming
Montréal & Québec City
Munich & the Bavarian Alps
Nashville & Memphis
New England
Newfoundland & Labrador
New Mexico
New Orleans
New York City
New York State
New Zealand
Northern Italy
Norway
Nova Scotia, New Brunswick & Prince Edward Island
Oregon
Ottawa
Paris
Peru

Philadelphia & the Amish Country
Portugal
Prague & the Best of the Czech Republic
Provence & the Riviera
Puerto Rico
Rome
San Antonio & Austin
San Diego
San Francisco
Santa Fe, Taos & Albuquerque
Scandinavia
Scotland
Seattle
Shanghai
Sicily
Singapore & Malaysia
South Africa
South America
South Florida
South Pacific
Southeast Asia
Spain
Sweden
Switzerland
Texas
Thailand
Tokyo
Toronto
Turkey
USA
Utah
Vancouver & Victoria
Vermont, New Hampshire & Maine
Vienna & the Danube Valley
Virgin Islands
Virginia
Walt Disney World® & Orlando
Washington, D.C.
Washington State

FROMMER'S® DOLLAR-A-DAY GUIDES

Australia from $50 a Day
California from $70 a Day
England from $75 a Day
Europe from $85 a Day
Florida from $70 a Day
Hawaii from $80 a Day

Ireland from $00 a Day
Italy from $70 a Day
London from $90 a Day
New York City from $90 a Day
Paris from $90 a Day
San Francisco from $70 a Day

Washington, D.C. from $80 a Day
Portable London from $90 a Day
Portable New York City from $90 a Day
Portable Paris from $90 a Day

FROMMER'S® PORTABLE GUIDES

Acapulco, Ixtapa & Zihuatanejo
Amsterdam
Aruba
Australia's Great Barrier Reef
Bahamas
Berlin
Big Island of Hawaii
Boston
California Wine Country
Cancún
Cayman Islands
Charleston
Chicago
Disneyland®
Dominican Republic
Dublin

Florence
Frankfurt
Hong Kong
Las Vegas
Las Vegas for Non-Gamblers
London
Los Angeles
Los Cabos & Baja
Maine Coast
Maui
Miami
Nantucket & Martha's Vineyard
New Orleans
New York City
Paris

Phoenix & Scottsdale
Portland
Puerto Rico
Puerto Vallarta, Manzanillo & Guadalajara
Rio de Janeiro
San Diego
San Francisco
Savannah
Vancouver
Vancouver Island
Venice
Virgin Islands
Washington, D.C.
Whistler

FROMMER'S® NATIONAL PARK GUIDES

Algonquin Provincial Park
Banff & Jasper
Family Vacations in the National
  Parks

Grand Canyon
National Parks of the American
  West
Rocky Mountain

Yellowstone & Grand Teton
Yosemite & Sequoia/Kings
  Canyon
Zion & Bryce Canyon

FROMMER'S® MEMORABLE WALKS

Chicago
London

New York
Paris

San Francisco

FROMMER'S® WITH KIDS GUIDES

Chicago
Las Vegas
New York City

Ottawa
San Francisco
Toronto

Vancouver
Walt Disney World® & Orlando
Washington, D.C.

SUZY GERSHMAN'S BORN TO SHOP GUIDES

Born to Shop: France
Born to Shop: Hong Kong,
  Shanghai & Beijing

Born to Shop: Italy
Born to Shop: London

Born to Shop: New York
Born to Shop: Paris

FROMMER'S® IRREVERENT GUIDES

Amsterdam
Boston
Chicago
Las Vegas
London

Los Angeles
Manhattan
New Orleans
Paris
Rome

San Francisco
Seattle & Portland
Vancouver
Walt Disney World®
Washington, D.C.

FROMMER'S® BEST-LOVED DRIVING TOURS

Austria
Britain
California
France

Germany
Ireland
Italy
New England

Northern Italy
Scotland
Spain
Tuscany & Umbria

THE UNOFFICIAL GUIDES®

Beyond Disney
California with Kids
Central Italy
Chicago
Cruises
Disneyland®
England
Florida
Florida with Kids
Inside Disney

Hawaii
Las Vegas
London
Maui
Mexico's Best Beach Resorts
Mini Las Vegas
Mini Mickey
New Orleans
New York City
Paris

San Francisco
Skiing & Snowboarding in the
  West
South Florida including Miami &
  the Keys
Walt Disney World®
Walt Disney World® for
  Grown-ups
Walt Disney World® with Kids
Washington, D.C.

SPECIAL-INTEREST TITLES

Athens Past & Present
Cities Ranked & Rated
Frommer's Best Day Trips from London
Frommer's Best RV & Tent Campgrounds
  in the U.S.A.
Frommer's Caribbean Hideaways
Frommer's China: The 50 Most Memorable Trips
Frommer's Exploring America by RV
Frommer's Gay & Lesbian Europe
Frommer's NYC Free & Dirt Cheap

Frommer's Road Atlas Europe
Frommer's Road Atlas France
Frommer's Road Atlas Ireland
Frommer's Wonderful Weekends from
  New York City
The New York Times' Guide to Unforgettable
  Weekends
Retirement Places Rated
Rome Past & Present

Travel Tip: He who finds the best hotel deal has more to spend on facials involving knobbly vegetables.

Hello, the Roaming Gnome here. I've been nabbed from the garden and taken round the world. The people who took me are so terribly clever. They find the best offerings on Travelocity. For very little cha-ching. And that means I get to be pampered and exfoliated till I'm pink as a bunny's doodah.

travelocity®

1-888-TRAVELOCITY / travelocity.com / America Online Keyword: Travel

Travel Tip: Make sure there's customer service for any change of plans — involving friendly natives, for example.

One can plan and plan, but if you don't book with the right people you can't seize le moment and canoodle with the poodle named Pansy. I, for one, am all for fraternizing with the locals. Better yet, if I need to extend my stay and my gnome nappers are willing, it can all be arranged through the 800 number at, oh look, how convenient, the lovely company coat of arms.

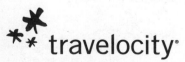

travelocity®

1-888-TRAVELOCITY / travelocity.com / America Online Keyword: Travel